World Wide Web Searching For Dummies®

Cheat Sheet

Ten Tips for Fast Web Searching

- ❒ Turn your graphics off.
- ❒ Use the images!
- ❒ Use your Back button.
- ❒ Use the Go or History list to leapfrog.
- ❒ Make fast search decisions.
- ❒ Use your hotlist (or bookmark list).
- ❒ Knock twice (try again).
- ❒ Build a bookmark list.
- ❒ Ask directions in newsgroups.
- ❒ Avoid Web prime time.

Web password cheat sheet

Name of Web Site	Your Password
_____	_____
_____	_____
_____	_____
_____	_____
_____	_____
_____	_____

Ten Fun and Useful Web Directories

Directory	Address
Achoo	http://www.achoo.com/
The Huge List	http://thehugelist.com/
The Internet Sleuth	http://www.isleuth.com/
Starting Point	http://www.stpt.com/
WWWomen	http://www.wwwomen.com/
World Wide Web Pavilion	http://www.catalog.com/tsw/Pavilion/pavilion.htm
WebWise Library	http://webwise.walcoff.com/library/index.html
Yehaa!	http://www.yehaa.com
Culture	http://www.december.com/cmc/info/culture-people-lists.html
Yecch!	http://www.yeeeoww.com/yecch/yecchhome.html

World Wide Web Searching For Dummies®

Cheat Sheet

Bookmark These Search Sites!

Search Site	Address
Yahoo!	http://www.yahoo.com/
Lycos	http://www.lycos.com/
Excite	http://www.excite.com/
AltaVista	http://www.altavista.digital.com/
Open Text	http://www.opentext.com/
Deja News	http://www.dejanews.com/

Essential Search Operators

Using This Search Operator	Gives This Result
AND	Includes both (or all) keywords in search results
	Example: cleveland AND indians
OR	Includes either keyword in search results
	Example: cleveland OR indians
NOT	Excludes a keyword from search results
	Example: indians NOT baseball
( )	Groups keywords together using other operators
	Example: cleveland AND (indians OR tribe)
*	Wildcard
	Example: legislat* (returns "legislature" and "legislation")

...For Dummies: #1 Computer Book Series for Beginners

WORLD WIDE WEB SEARCHING FOR DUMMIES®

by Brad Hill

IDG BOOKS WORLDWIDE

IDG Books Worldwide, Inc.
An International Data Group Company

Foster City, CA ♦ Chicago, IL ♦ Indianapolis, IN ♦ Southlake, TX

World Wide Web Searching For Dummies®

Published by
IDG Books Worldwide, Inc.
An International Data Group Company
919 E. Hillsdale Blvd.
Suite 400
Foster City, CA 94404
http://www.idgbooks.com (IDG Books Worldwide Web site)
http://www.dummies.com (Dummies Press Web site)

Library of Congress Catalog Card No.: 96-77075

ISBN: 0-7645-0022-8

Printed in the United States of America

10 9 8 7 6 5 4 3 2

1A/QW/QZ/ZW/IN

Distributed in the United States by IDG Books Worldwide, Inc.

Distributed by Macmillan Canada for Canada; by Transworld Publishers Limited in the United Kingdom and Europe; by WoodsLane Pty. Ltd. for Australia; by WoodsLane Enterprises Ltd. for New Zealand; by Longman Singapore Publishers Ltd. for Singapore, Malaysia, Thailand, and Indonesia; by Simron Pty. Ltd. for South Africa; by Toppan Company Ltd. for Japan; by Distribuidora Cuspide for Argentina; by Livraria Cultura for Brazil; by Ediciencia S.A. for Ecuador; by Addison-Wesley Publishing Company for Korea; by Ediciones ZETA S.C.R. Ltda. for Peru; by WS Computer Publishing Company, Inc., for the Philippines; by Unalis Corporation for Taiwan; by Contemporanea de Ediciones for Venezuela. Authorized Sales Agent: Anthony Rudkin Associates for the Middle East and North Africa.

For general information on IDG Books Worldwide's books in the U.S., please call our Consumer Customer Service department at 800-762-2974. For reseller information, including discounts and premium sales, please call our Reseller Customer Service department at 800-434-3422.

For information on where to purchase IDG Books Worldwide's books outside the U.S., please contact our International Sales department at 415-655-3172 or fax 415-655-3295.

For information on foreign language translations, please contact our Foreign & Subsidiary Rights department at 415-655-3021 or fax 415-655-3281.

For sales inquiries and special prices for bulk quantities, please contact our Sales department at 415-655-3200 or write to the address above.

For information on using IDG Books Worldwide's books in the classroom or for ordering examination copies, please contact our Educational Sales department at 800-434-2086 or fax 817-251-8174.

For press review copies, author interviews, or other publicity information, please contact our Public Relations department at 415-655-3000 or fax 415-655-3299.

For authorization to photocopy items for corporate, personal, or educational use, please contact Copyright Clearance Center, 222 Rosewood Drive, Danvers, MA 01923, or fax 508-750-4470.

About the Author

Brad Hill spends most of his time with computers and considers them living creatures with personalities. For this reason alone, he should be treated with caution. Nevertheless, this affinity with digital life forms has led him to the far corners of cyberspace.

Brad turned to computers with abandon when MIDI, the digital music standard, arrived in the 1980s. As a soundtrack specialist, Brad composed music for many audio theater projects (including "The Fall of the House of Usher" and " 'Twas the Night Before Christmas" for National Public Radio); industrial and feature films; and television shows. His soundtrack productions have garnered five-star reviews in national publications.

Buying his first modem, Brad joined every online service available and quickly became addicted to the whole online experience. He didn't resort to taking his meals intravenously in front of the computer, but he spent many sleepless nights roaming the alleys and avenues of the budding information highway. Soon he was a Sysop (System Operator) for CompuServe, and his friends have seen very little of him since.

For a while, Brad pursued music production and writing as parallel occupations. Words eventually prevailed over notes, and he glimpsed sunlight for the first time in years. He now writes books for beginners about the Internet, online services, multimedia, and music technology. He has never written a cookbook and never intends to. He did, however, recently review more than 600 CD-ROMs, and somehow survived the experience. Brad continues to manage virtual communities on the CompuServe and WOW! networks, including the eDrive Entertainment Community on WOW! and the New Age, Electronic Word, and B-Movies forums on CompuServe.

Brad enjoys hearing from people and can be reached electronically at his Internet e-mail address: brad@njcc.com.

ABOUT IDG BOOKS WORLDWIDE

Welcome to the world of IDG Books Worldwide.

IDG Books Worldwide, Inc., is a subsidiary of International Data Group, the world's largest publisher of computer-related information and the leading global provider of information services on information technology. IDG was founded more than 25 years ago and now employs more than 8,500 people worldwide. IDG publishes more than 275 computer publications in over 75 countries (see listing below). More than 60 million people read one or more IDG publications each month.

Launched in 1990, IDG Books Worldwide is today the #1 publisher of best-selling computer books in the United States. We are proud to have received eight awards from the Computer Press Association in recognition of editorial excellence and three from *Computer Currents'* First Annual Readers' Choice Awards. Our best-selling *...For Dummies®* series has more than 30 million copies in print with translations in 30 languages. IDG Books Worldwide, through a joint venture with IDG's Hi-Tech Beijing, became the first U.S. publisher to publish a computer book in the People's Republic of China. In record time, IDG Books Worldwide has become the first choice for millions of readers around the world who want to learn how to better manage their businesses.

Our mission is simple: Every one of our books is designed to bring extra value and skill-building instructions to the reader. Our books are written by experts who understand and care about our readers. The knowledge base of our editorial staff comes from years of experience in publishing, education, and journalism — experience we use to produce books for the '90s. In short, we care about books, so we attract the best people. We devote special attention to details such as audience, interior design, use of icons, and illustrations. And because we use an efficient process of authoring, editing, and desktop publishing our books electronically, we can spend more time ensuring superior content and spend less time on the technicalities of making books.

You can count on our commitment to deliver high-quality books at competitive prices on topics you want to read about. At IDG Books Worldwide, we continue in the IDG tradition of delivering quality for more than 25 years. You'll find no better book on a subject than one from IDG Books Worldwide.

John J. Kilcullen

John Kilcullen
President and CEO
IDG Books Worldwide, Inc.

**Eighth Annual
Computer Press
Awards ≥1992**

**Ninth Annual
Computer Press
Awards ≥1993**

**Tenth Annual
Computer Press
Awards ≥1994**

**Eleventh Annual
Computer Press
Awards ≥1995**

IDG Books Worldwide, Inc., is a subsidiary of International Data Group, the world's largest publisher of computer-related information and the leading global provider of information services on information technology. International Data Group publishes over 275 computer publications in over 75 countries. Sixty million people read one or more International Data Group publications each month. International Data Group's publications include: **ARGENTINA:** Buyer's Guide, Computerworld Argentina, PC World Argentina; **AUSTRALIA:** Australian Macworld, Australian PC World, Australian Reseller News, Computerworld, IT Casebook, Network World, Publish, Webmaster; **AUSTRIA:** Computerwelt Osterreich, Networks Austria, PC Tip Austria; **BANGLADESH:** PC World Bangladesh; **BELARUS:** PC World Belarus; **BELGIUM:** Data News; **BRAZIL:** Annuário de Informática, Computerworld, Connections, Macworld, PC Player, PC World, Publish, Reseller News, Supergamepower; **BULGARIA:** Computerworld Bulgaria, Network World Bulgaria, PC & MacWorld Bulgaria; **CANADA:** CIO Canada, Client/Server World, ComputerWorld Canada, InfoWorld Canada, NetworkWorld Canada, WebWorld; **CHILE:** Computerworld Chile, PC World Chile; **COLOMBIA:** Computerworld Colombia, PC World Colombia; **COSTA RICA:** PC World Centro America; **THE CZECH AND SLOVAK REPUBLICS:** Computerworld Czechoslovakia, Macworld Czech Republic, PC World Czechoslovakia; **DENMARK:** Communications World Danmark, Computerworld Danmark, Macworld Danmark, PC World Danmark, Techworld Denmark; **DOMINICAN REPUBLIC:** PC World Republica Dominicana; **ECUADOR:** PC World Ecuador; **EGYPT:** Computerworld Middle East, PC World Middle East; **EL SALVADOR:** PC World Centro America; **FINLAND:** MikroPC, Tietoverkko, Tietoviikko; **FRANCE:** Distributique, Hebdo, Info PC, Le Monde Informatique, Macworld, Reseaux & Telecoms, WebMaster France; **GERMANY:** Computer Partner, Computerwoche, Computerwoche Extra, Computerwoche FOCUS, Global Online, Macwelt, PC Welt; **GREECE:** Amiga Computing, GamePro Greece, Multimedia World; **GUATEMALA:** PC World Centro America; **HONDURAS:** PC World Centro America; **HONG KONG:** Computerworld Hong Kong, PC World Hong Kong, Publish in Asia; **HUNGARY:** ABCD CD-ROM, Computerworld Szamitastechnika, Internetto online Magazine, PC World Hungary, PC-X Magazin Hungary; **ICELAND:** Tolvuheimur PC World Island; **INDIA:** Information Communications World, Information Systems Computerworld, PC World India, Publish in Asia; **INDONESIA:** InfoKomputer PC World, Komputek Computerworld, Publish in Asia; **IRELAND:** ComputerScope, PC Live!; **ISRAEL:** Macworld Israel, People & Computers/Computerworld; **ITALY:** Computerworld Italia, Macworld Italia, Networking Italia, PC World Italia; **JAPAN:** DTP World, Macworld Japan, Nikkei Personal Computing, OS/2 World Japan, SunWorld Japan, Windows NT World, Windows World Japan; **KENYA:** PC World East African; **KOREA:** Hi-Tech Information, Macworld Korea, PC World Korea; **MACEDONIA:** PC World Macedonia; **MALAYSIA:** Computerworld Malaysia, PC World Malaysia, Publish in Asia; **MALTA:** PC World Malta; **MEXICO:** Computerworld Mexico, PC World Mexico; **MYANMAR:** PC World Myanmar; **NETHERLANDS:** Computer! Totaal, LAN Internetworking Magazine, LAN World Buyers Guide, Macworld Netherlands, Net, WebWereld; **NEW ZEALAND:** Absolute Beginners Guide and Plain & Simple Series, Computer Buyer, Computer Industry Directory, Computerworld New Zealand, MTB, Network World, PC World New Zealand; **NICARAGUA:** PC World Centro America; **NORWAY:** Computerworld Norge, CW Rapport, Datamagasinet, Financial Rapport, Kursguide Norge, Macworld Norge, Multimediaworld Norge, PC World Ekspress Norge, PC World Nettverk, PC World Norge, PC World ProduktGuide Norge; **PAKISTAN:** Computerworld Pakistan; **PANAMA:** PC World Panama; **PEOPLE'S REPUBLIC OF CHINA:** China Computer Users, China Computerworld, China InfoWorld, China Telecom World Weekly, Computer & Communication, Electronic Design China, Electronics Today, Electronics Weekly, Game Software, PC World China, Popular Computer Week, Software Weekly, Software World, Telecom World; **PERU:** Computerworld Peru, PC World Profesional Peru, PC World SoHo Peru; **PHILIPPINES:** Click!, Computerworld Philippines, PC World Philippines, Publish in Asia; **POLAND:** Computerworld Poland, Computerworld Special Report Poland, Cyber, Macworld Poland, Networld Poland, PC World Komputer; **PORTUGAL:** Cerebro/PC World, Computerworld/Correio Informático, Dealer World Portugal, Mac*In/PC*In Portugal, Multimedia World; **PUERTO RICO:** PC World Puerto Rico; **ROMANIA:** Computerworld Romania, PC World Romania, Telecom Romania; **RUSSIA:** Computerworld Russia, Mir PK, Publish, Seti; **SINGAPORE:** Computerworld Singapore, PC World Singapore, Publish in Asia; **SLOVENIA:** Monitor; **SOUTH AFRICA:** Computerworld SA, Network World SA, Software World SA; **SPAIN:** Communicaciones World España, Computerworld España, Dealer World España, Macworld España, PC World España; **SRI LANKA:** Infolink PC World; **SWEDEN:** CAP&Design, Computer Sweden, Corporate Computing Sweden, Internetworld Sweden, it.branschen, Macworld Sweden, MaxiData Sweden, MikroDatorn, Nätverk & Kommunikation, PC World Sweden, PCaktiv, Windows World Sweden; **SWITZERLAND:** Computerworld Schweiz, Macworld Schweiz, PCtip; **TAIWAN:** Computerworld Taiwan, Macworld Taiwan, NEW ViSiON/Publish, PC World Taiwan, Windows World Taiwan; **THAILAND:** Publish in Asia, Thai Computerworld; **TURKEY:** Computerworld Turkiye, Macworld Turkiye, Network World Turkiye, PC World Turkiye; **UKRAINE:** Computerworld Kiev, Multimedia World Ukraine, PC World Ukraine; **UNITED KINGDOM:** Acorn User UK, Amiga Action UK, Amiga Computing UK, Apple Talk UK, Computing, Macworld, Parents and Computers UK, PC Advisor, PC Home, PSX Pro, The WEB; **UNITED STATES:** Cable in the Classroom, CIO Magazine, Computerworld, DOS World, Federal Computer Week, GamePro Magazine, InfoWorld, I-Way, Macworld, Network World, PC Games, PC World, Publish, Video Event, THE WEB Magazine, and WebMaster; online webzines: JavaWorld, NetscapeWorld, and SunWorld Online; **URUGUAY:** InfoWorld Uruguay; **VENEZUELA:** Computerworld Venezuela, PC World Venezuela; and **VIETNAM:** PC World Vietnam.   10/22/96

Dedication

This book is for my parents, Betty and Russ, with love and admiration. From my mother I've learned persistence; from my father, self-reliance. They continue to be my greatest influences.

Author's Acknowledgments

I wouldn't have been involved in this project if it hadn't been for Mary Corder, who encouraged me from our very first conversation. My earnest thanks go to Mary, and I wish her trouble-free hard drives forever.

Pat Seiler dealt with a harrowing deadline with no apparent panic. She scrutinized every word of this book, and her editorial suggestions were invaluable. Thanks a million, Pat, for your patience and dedication. (And don't you dare edit this paragraph!)

I also want to thank Tammy Goldfeld, in IDG's Foster City office. I haven't forgotten her patience in the face of endless detailed queries that to me were of highest import, but which to her must have seemed like the petulant ruminations of yet another cranky author. Of course, she was right.

Thanks also to Mary Bednarek and Seta Frantz, and to Kristin Cocks, who was always willing to share her e-mail box when the chips were down.

Burgess got me through the days of uncertainty, which are always the hardest days. Words of thanks don't do her justice.

Finally, I acknowledge the entire, vast community of souls who inhabit, even sporadically, the global Web that is under construction. They are the pioneers of a new frontier.

Publisher's Acknowledgments

We're proud of this book; please send us your comments about it by using the Reader Response Card at the back of the book or by e-mailing us at feedback/dummies@idgbooks.com. Some of the people who helped bring this book to market include the following:

Acquisitions, Development, & Editorial

Project Editor: Pat Seiler

Acquisitions Editor: Tammy Goldfeld

Product Development Manager: Mary Bednarek

Permissions Editor: Joyce Pepple

Technical Editor: Dennis Teague

Editorial Manager: Mary C. Corder

Editorial Assistant: Chris Collins

Production

Project Coordinator: Sherry Gomoll

Layout and Graphics:
Brett Black, Cameron Booker, Elizabeth Cárdenas-Nelson, J. Tyler Connor, Todd Klemme, Jane Martin, Michael Sullivan

Proofreaders: Jenny Overmyer, Michael Bolinger, Rachel Garvey, Nancy Price, Rob Springer, Ethel Winslow, Karen York, Carrie Voorhis

Indexer: Richard Shrout

Special Help: Gwenette Gaddis, Reprint Editor; Stephanie Koutek, Proof Editor; Suzanne Packer, Lead Copy Editor

General and Administrative

IDG Books Worldwide, Inc.: John Kilcullen, CEO; Steven Berkowitz, President and Publisher

Dummies, Inc.: Milissa Koloski, Executive Vice President and Publisher

Dummies Technology Press and Dummies Editorial: Diane Graves Steele, Vice President and Associate Publisher; Judith A. Taylor, Brand Manager

Dummies Trade Press: Kathleen A. Welton, Vice President and Publisher; Stacy S. Collins, Brand Manager

IDG Books Production for Dummies Press: Beth Jenkins, Production Director; Cindy L. Phipps, Supervisor of Project Coordination; Kathie S. Schutte, Supervisor of Page Layout; Shelley Lea, Supervisor of Graphics and Design; Debbie J. Gates, Production Systems Specialist; Tony Augsburger, Reprint Coordinator; Leslie Popplewell, Media Archive Coordinator

Dummies Packaging and Book Design: Patti Sandez, Packaging Assistant; Kavish+Kavish, Cover Design

◆

The publisher would like to give special thanks to Patrick J. McGovern, without whom this book would not have been possible.

◆

Contents at a Glance

Cartoons at a Glance

By Rich Tennant • Fax: 508-546-7747 • E-mail: the5wave@tiac.net

page 7

page 261

page 53

page 167

page 309

page 349

Table of Contents

Welcome to Information Overload

● ●

*T*he Web.

It sometimes seems that the entire digital revolution boils down to those two words. (It used to be four words — *the World Wide Web* — but if you say that too many times, you begin to pwonounce evewything with *W's*.) The whole online universe and the burgeoning information superhighway are implied and referred to in that simple, spidery phrase: *the Web*.

Actually, the World Wide Web is just a portion of the Internet, and the Internet is just a portion of the total online scene. But the Web has gotten most of the hype for three main reasons:

- ✔ It's easy to use (after you get hooked up, which isn't always so easy).
- ✔ It's brilliantly colorful.
- ✔ Anybody can contribute to it.

It's a winning combination: simple, attractive, and inviting. Add to this the dazzling variety, the awesome exponential growth, and the Web's planet-shrinking capacity for making connections around the globe in a flash, and it's no wonder that you've given up the rest of your life to surf the Web. (I'm not the only one, am I?)

What effect has wild popularity had on the Web? Utter chaos! You heard me — it's a mess. It's as if the whole planet discovered gardening at once. Things are sprouting all over; there are a thousand turnip beds, each a little different; tomatoes are here, there, and everywhere; and nobody knows who's going to do the weeding. The Web can get away with being chaotic because going from one of its garden plots (sites) to another is as easy as a mouse click, whether the site is located down the street or on another continent. This has led to an entire culture of browsing — people sitting at home into the night, clicking their way around the world and back again, gleaning information, meeting people, looking at pictures, listening to music, networking on message boards. Getting lost on the Web is such a delightful adventure that the disorganization is almost an advantage.

Until, that is, you really want to find something fast. Or until you get sick of surfing and are ready for the Web to become practical and useful. The World Wide Web is an astounding resource of information, software, and people. But you need tools to search it effectively. Two kinds of tools are available:

- ✔ Online tools, such as directories and search engines
- ✔ Tools of understanding

This book gives you tools of understanding.

Isn't Web Searching Easy?

Yes and no. At the simplest level, using a Web directory or entering a keyword in a Web search engine is easy if you've been on the Web before, but you may not get satisfactory results by taking only the simplest steps. If the Web remains an unwieldy, impenetrable resource, people will get discouraged about using it at all. This book gives you searching alternatives and tells you how to use them in detail. In these pages you can learn which of the online searching services are currently the best, where they are located, and how their advanced features work. My goal is to guide you step by step through every search process, from the easy ones to more complicated (and rewarding) operations, giving you sound searching principles in the process.

Furthermore, I want this book to be practical in a different way. Not only does it show you different directories and search engines, but the chapters in Part III, called "Search Expeditions," show you how to attain typical search goals by using *all* the online tools that you're reading about. You discover, on two levels, how Web searching works: First you look at the online tools individually, and then you conduct actual searches using all those tools.

As you explore Web searching, you discover some online help when you have a question. Each directory and search engine (at least, the ones covered in this book) offers some explanations about its features and requirements. But, like much "help" (also called *documentation*) in the computer world, these explanations assume a certain amount of experience, or even expertise, on the user's part. This book assumes nothing of the sort! My hope is that you will fall back on this book for rock-solid, start-at-the-beginning-please, take-it-slow-and-don't-rush-me explanations of how Web searching works.

To top it off, I've thrown in a lot of self-serving jokes (I'll do anything for a cheap laugh) to remind you that all this is supposed to be *fun!*

Who Are You?

You're no dummy, regardless of the cute title slapped on the cover of this book. You may *feel* like a dummy sometimes when trying to understand the intricacies of computers, but that's not your fault. It's because most computer stuff is badly explained, without regard for the questions that occur to a smart beginner. If you've bought this book, you have some interest in taming the World Wide Web, which is an ambitious and intelligent goal.

This book has a lot to offer beginners, of course, but it also has a thing or three to teach Web veterans. In fact, I learned quite a bit myself while writing it. If you don't yet have an online account and don't enjoy computer access to the World Wide Web, you won't be able to follow along with the instructions in this book. If you're planning to get on the Web soon, this book will prepare you with background to help cut through the online jungle. If you're already venturing onto the Web, you're set — you can start using these pages immediately. And if you are a confident Web searcher already, you're bound to find some advanced Web-searching features that you didn't know about and some great sites that you haven't bookmarked yet.

Do you know anyone who complains about how hard it is to find things on the Web? Giving this book to that person is a good way of saying, "You're *not* a dummy!"

How to Read This Book

The best way to read this book is with one copy in each hand and another on the shelf in case you spill coffee on the others. But if that seems extreme, just having one near the computer will do. This book is a reference companion, not a novel. Don't try to read it from cover to cover — it will only make you dizzy, and boring at parties. All the chapters are self-contained, and if you need to look up something in another chapter, I tell you then and there where to find it in the book. You can surf the book like surfing the Web, in fact, and still learn a lot. But the best advice is to look at the Table of Contents, pick a chapter that strikes your interest, and start your explorations there.

I've divided the book into big chunks called *parts*. Here's what's in them:

Part I: Searching with Directories

This is where you learn about online megadirectories that attempt to organize the entire World Wide Web. There are a few major, seriously ambitious directory systems that work daily to catalog the Web's growth, impossible though that may seem. I focus my descriptions and instructions on Yahoo!, Lycos, and

Excite, because they are the most popular and comprehensive directories. Each directory is different, but they are all similar, and the two chapters in this part tell you how to cope with their differences and similarities.

Part II: Searching with Keywords

Have you seen those keyword entry boxes on Web pages? Even if you've figured out how they work, have you wondered whether you're making the most of them? This part introduces you to several major keyword searching services on the Web and explains the features of each. The first two chapters explain how keywords work and provide a multitude of tips for using them well. The goal with keywords is to find the best sites as quickly as possible, and you can use all kinds of tricks to speed up your search and narrow it down to the good stuff.

Other chapters in this part detail the features and lurking complexities of individual search engines (as they are called), such as Lycos, Open Text, Excite, AltaVista, and others that you may have heard of and even visited. Finally, a roundup chapter brings you up to speed with a few other keyword sites that don't get as much publicity but are still pretty darn useful.

Part III: Search Expeditions

Go straight to this part if you know how to use keywords and directories and you're eager to find Web sites in certain subjects. This part contains chapters on finding pages on sports, money, health information, education, culture, software, and current events. These chapters show you how to put together a whole repertoire of searching techniques to zero in on a subject. Each chapter tells you how to use directories, keywords, and Usenet newsgroups to uncover good sites, and even points you toward the best Web locations in each field. The final chapter in Part III explains how to find people — perhaps the greatest resource the Web has to offer.

Part IV: Searching with Online Services

Why should online services be left out of the picture? If you belong to one of these services, I'm sure that you agree that they should be included. In the past, commercial services such as CompuServe, America Online, Prodigy, and The Microsoft Network were separate from the World Wide Web. Almost proudly so, as if they wanted nothing to do with it. But as the Web has become popular (to say the least), they have found ways to provide their members with access to it. These days, in fact, distinguishing between the Web and an online service is getting harder, because the services are making it easier to drift back and forth between the two.

The online services compete vigorously with each other, and just two of them have emerged as major networks with millions of members. They are America Online and CompuServe. Most subscribers to a commercial service belong to one or the other, so I've focused on them in this part. Here you can learn how to get to the Web *through* either service, and also how to search *within* both services.

Part V: The Part of Tens

Don't you love lists? I do. But don't confuse these lists with top-ten lists, because they are not rated in any way. These chapters just contain collections of tips and sites that I want you to know about. Browse through them when you are looking for ideas, or to glean new locations if you get bored during a Web session, or when you get tired of staring at your screen saver, or for no reason whatsoever.

I almost couldn't stop writing this book. After the main chapters were done, I was still itching to put in additional information that I think is useful.

The Appendix describes lots of little software programs — called *utilities* — that make Web searching more enjoyable and productive.

Conventions Used in This Book

Normally I don't like conventions. Thousands of people all stuffed into one giant room, noisy displays, bad food. . . . Oh, sorry, wrong type of convention. This book uses certain typefaces and other layout properties to indicate particular things that appear on your screen. To make it easy to follow along with the book online, I've been consistent with these conventions. Consistent conventions create continuous clarity. (That's an old Swahili proverb.)

URLs (Uniform Resource Locators) — the addresses of Web pages — are indicated with this kind of type:

```
http://www.webpage.com
```

Whenever I refer to hypertext, whether a single word or phrase, it appears like this: <u>This is a hypertext link</u> (just as it appears on your screen, except without the colors).

From time to time I refer to keywords that can be entered into search engines. Whenever I give an example of such a keyword, it appears like this: **keyword**. (How's that for an imaginative example? Thank you very much.)

When I introduce a new term for the first time, I *italicize* it to get your attention, and to reassure you that there's no reason you should know what it means.

Icons Used in This Book

Since I can't stand next to you waving my arms every time you use this book, these icons are meant to get your attention.

This icon appears whenever a paragraph is trying to awaken your inner nerd. It notifies you that I have flaunted the geekish side of my nature by degenerating into techno-babble. For your own protection, try to avoid all such paragraphs.

If you don't heed the information associated with this icon, I may have to send you e-mailed reprimands. The Web is not a dangerous place. But these warnings let you know that you might waste your time with something or complicate your session unnecessarily.

I've stuffed this book with tips that are worth their weight in gold. Of course, they don't weigh anything. Still, you might find them useful. If not, it's time to send *me* e-mailed reprimands.

This icon means . . . umm . . . well, I don't recall *what* it means. But it probably has something to do with reminding you of an important point.

Write Me!

I may live much of my life on the Web, but I'm a real person. (At least, my computer thinks so.) And I love getting mail of the electronic persuasion (e-mail). Fire up your modem, boot up your software, and send me some words at this address:

```
brad@njcc.com
```

In the meantime, happy searching, and may you always find the unexpected jewel.

Part I
Searching with Directories

In this part . . .

Mapping the vast terrain of the World Wide Web is a task best left to fearless explorers. Fortunately, brave cyber-cartographers have stepped forward to meet the challenge. These hardy individuals have created Web directory services that can chart your way through the tangled growth of the ever-expanding World Wide Web.

This part introduces you to the main Web directories — Yahoo!, Excite, and Lycos. Before the introductions, the first chapter gives you a general tutorial about what directories are, how they work, why they're useful, and what you should wear when using them. (Just kidding about that last part.)

You're about to discover the locations, differences, similarities, and quirks of some of the most useful destinations in cyberspace: Web directories.

Chapter 1

Getting the Big Picture

• •

In This Chapter

▶ Viewing a directory menu

▶ Following links through levels of a directory

▶ Finding your topics — tips and hints

• •

*I*magine that you're an archaeologist who is traveling to a foreign country for research. (If you really are an archaeologist, substitute an even more glamorous scenario.) To locate the site of your dig, you use a series of maps. First, a global atlas to situate the country of your destination in an international context. Then a map of the country to acquaint yourself with regions, geographical features, and main highways. To further narrow the perspective, you use a local map to familiarize yourself with the roadways and towns of the area. A town map might come into play, if it exists, to identify all the streets, shops, and local attributes.

Locating something on the Internet is as complex as locating something in any country. With either destination, maps are a great help in finding your way around. The *World Wide Web* (the Web, for short), which is the hyperlinked portion of the Internet, has attained popularity as an environment for browsing and surfing the Internet. The emphasis on the Web has been on unfocused wandering, following trails of information from one Web page to another. Serious (and even casual) research has traditionally been performed in other, less glitzy, Net interfaces that don't contain the Web's easy click-and-travel hyperlinks. But because the Web interface is so easy and friendly to use, why can't it suffice as an information tool? Why shouldn't the Web browser, everyone's favorite new software program, be an all-purpose vehicle for traveling the Internet, whether for recreation or research? The truth is, it can be.

So, what is it that you're searching?

You're searching the World Wide Web, of course, but what exactly is that? Is it the Internet? An online service? A gigantic experiment in computer hypnotism? (If so, the experiment is working in my case.) Okay, enough guessing. It's not exactly any of those things.

The Web is a software invention that enables people to explore the Internet very easily. (I cover the Internet a little later in this sidebar.) Basically, the *Web* is an enormous (and growing) collection of computer files (called *Web pages*) that link to each other when you use a program called a *Web browser* to view them on your screen. These Web pages live on computers all over the world and contain *hyperlinks*. A hyperlink can be a word, a group of words, a picture, or a part of a picture. When you click on a hyperlink, it tells your Web browser to display another Web page, gives the browser the location of that page (which is embedded in the hyperlink), and sends you off.

The World Wide Web is part of the Internet, but it is not the entire thing. The Internet is a whole bunch (millions, actually) of computers called *servers* that are connected by telephone lines. It's a planetary network of computer systems. This global network wasn't built according to any grand design — it just evolved over time, and it crosses over national boundaries as easily as a phone call does. The Internet also includes *Usenet newsgroups*, which are electronic bulletin boards for conducting discussions by means of typed and posted messages. (There are about 13,000 newsgroups!) The Internet also includes file libraries, where software and texts are stored.

You can enjoy all these different aspects of the Internet by using a single piece of software: the Web browser. The browser interprets the special codes that make up Web page files and displays those pages on your screen in an attractive way. It also knows exactly what to do when you click on a hyperlink — which is what you do to get around on the Web. The browser is like a magic carpet that takes you right to the Web location that's embedded in the hyperlink that you just clicked, whether the server for the destination file is across town or on the next continent. (If you want to experience true tedium, see Appendix A for a detailed discussion of Web browsers.)

If you're on the Web, you hear a lot about *Web sites*. You also hear the term *home page*. In the early days of the Web, some people were taking advantage of the unrestricted Internet by putting up a Web page describing personal interests, and linking to favorite locations on the brand new World Wide Web. These homegrown efforts were called *home pages,* because they represented the online home of their authors. Then people quickly learned how to create several related pages and link them together with the Web's hyperlink standard. Home pages were suddenly more than one page, and everyone began referring to multipage destinations on the Web as *sites*. (A site is really any location on the Web, even if it's only one page.) Then corporations got involved, and you can imagine what happened. *Big* isn't the word. Some corporate Web sites are humongous affairs with dozens — even hundreds — of pages. However, the term *home page* is still sometimes used to indicate the main, front page of such megasites. I use *home page* in this book to refer to the first, main page of Web search engines.

With a few well-directed clicks of the mouse, your Web browser delivers maps to virtually everything on the Internet. These Web maps are called *directories* (not to be confused with *indexes, crawlers, search engines, spiders, robots,* or other unsavory online creatures that you don't need to deal with at the beginning of the book). Like the maps used by the imaginary archaeologist, some directories cover broader areas than others. Some serve as global Web atlases, and others consolidate information about certain local areas on the Internet.

Directories work like a restaurant menu that divides dishes into soups, appetizers, salads, entrees, and (save room for it!) desserts. Within those meal categories, you can find selections of specific dishes. In the same way, Web directories start with broad topics and then enable you to click your way deeper into each topic, finding more specialized subjects. Then you can go deeper still until you are pointed toward exactly the type of information that you need. You can get an idea of how directories work by visiting Yahoo!, which not only is one of the most popular directories, but certainly has the happiest name. You can get there with this URL:

```
http://www.yahoo.com/
```

After you use a directory to reach a site of interest, you can use specialized tools to dig for more information. Web directories have more levels than restaurant menus — and you don't have to call ahead for a reservation. (Does that mean people are hungrier for information than for food?)

Web directories are the best place to begin searching the World Wide Web. Keep the following points in mind about Web directories:

- Many Web directories are available for searching the Net.
- Each Web directory is different.
- Each Web directory is accurate.

The Web is an enormous, constantly changing, ever-growing, continually evolving, deeply complex living landscape of information and resources which is virtually impossible to catalog exhaustively. Each Web directory takes its own approach to what is worth searching for — and each approach is legitimate, just as several newspapers might have different editorial perspectives on the news. After sampling many directories, you may settle on some favorites and return to them habitually to chart your searches. Despite their differences in content, all Web directories operate pretty much the same way.

Can a Web directory ever be a complete map of everything on the World Wide Web? Probably not, for a couple of reasons. First, the Web is growing and expanding every hour. Web directories find and add new Web pages to their databases pretty quickly, but accurately indexing a constantly shifting situation is difficult. (The task is similar to taking a picture of a moving object.) Also, no central clearinghouse exists for new Web pages. Anyone can put a page on the

What directories aren't

In my quest to eliminate all possible confusion from the Web searching process, I want to introduce you to a *V.I.D.* — a *Very Important Distinction*. The distinction is between a directory and a search engine. Directories and search engines are both Web searching features, and this book covers both of them at great length. Stands to reason, then, that you should know what they are, right?

Directories provide maps of the World Wide Web. Their multilevel structures enable you to investigate the Web sites available in both broad and finely-tuned categories, as I describe in this chapter. Web directories are meant to be browsed and are organized coherently to make browsing easy and productive.

Search engines work differently, allowing you to type in keywords that indicate what you're trying to find. The engine searches and displays the results as a list of hyperlinks to Web sites that match your search request. (The search request is usually in the form of keywords — one or more words that represent your search goal. Chapters 3 and 4 explain keywords at such length that you may be sorry that I brought them up.)

Now, here's the tricky part. Web directories may contain search engines. But not necessarily. By the same token, search engines do not necessarily come with directories. (Did you follow that?) The three largest directories of the World Wide Web — Yahoo!, Lycos, and Excite — have built-in search engines. They are convenient, all-in-one services in which you can choose whether to browse directory levels or type in a search engine request. (You know that a directory also has a search engine when you see a keyword entry form.) On the other side of the coin, some of the largest, most powerful, and popular search engines — such as AltaVista, Open Text, Inktomi, and the World Wide Web Worm — don't give you a directory, so you can't do any browsing.

A search engine without a directory is like a library without a card catalog. But imagine if such a library had workers who scurried around finding books related to what the library's users are interested in — that's what a search engine does. A directory without a search engine, on the other hand, is like a library with no librarians at all. The stacks are well-organized, but you're on your own.

Web, but no one has to register a page. If a directory doesn't find the new page because nobody manually entered it into the directory (which directories allow you to do), then the page will not come up in that directory.

Viewing a Directory Page

A Web directory consists of many levels. The top level gives you the broadest overview of the Internet; it is the global atlas. However, Web directories are not very maplike when it comes to graphics. Rather than relying on pictures of the cyberterrain, most Web pages offer what is basically a glorified list. Not very glitzy, but definitely useful. On the Web, where the local mode of transportation is a mouse riding on a hyperlink, these lists are charged and ready to take you places. To check out a typical top-level directory page, go to this URL:

```
http://a2z.lycos.com/
```

Web directories work like any other Web page. Words that are "live" (hyperlinked) are underlined, and they appear in a color that is different from the color that is used for the other text on the screen. When you position the mouse cursor over one of these words, the cursor changes shape (usually from an arrow to a pointing finger). Then when you click the left mouse button, the Web directory interacts with your Web browser to show you a new page of directory options.

Everybody seems hyper about "hyper" words: *hyperlink, hypertext, hyperspace* — well, *hyperspace* has nothing to do with the Web. But hyperlinks and hypertext have everything to do with the Web. Without them, the Web wouldn't be much of anything at all. Anytime your mouse cursor changes shape when resting on a screen object, whether a picture or a word, the object is a hyperlink. Hyperlinks that are words can be called *hypertext.* Hypertext is a kind of hyperlink. Several years ago, before there were many pictures (graphics) on computer screens, hypertext was the only kind of hyperlink. Now, with all the graphics in multimedia computing, *hyperlink* is a common term, and it includes text links as well as pictorial links. In this book, I refer to all Web links as either *hyperlinks* or simply *links.*

The top-level directory page is always divided into the widest, most general possible subject areas. Usually about 12 to 15 of these subject areas are shown — for example, entertainment, computers, government, and sports — each linked to a second directory level (on a separate page) that divides that topic into subtopics.

Many typical top-level categories appear in virtually all Web directories. The following topics are the global attractions of the big online map.

- **Business:** This top-page link, which is sometimes called Money or Finance, leads to online brokerages, stock market information, financial software download sites, and all kinds of other business-related Internet pages.

- **Computers:** A single common denominator that links every person who has ever logged into a Web directory is that they have all used a computer. Not surprisingly, a great deal of computer-related information is on the World Wide Web.

- **Current Events:** This category may also be called Politics, World, or News. Whatever it's called, it enables you to link your way to the kind of current news information that is in the front section of a newspaper.

- ✔ **Entertainment:** Because entertainment subjects, especially movies, music, and television, comprise many of the most popular sites in the online universe, this category is a certain top-menu find.

- ✔ **Sports:** Fan sites and sports news services are the two most common Web-site types in this category. Sports is almost always separated from general news in the top level of a Web directory.

Directories usually contain other main topics as well. The subjects for these topics depend on how the particular directory organizes its links to the Web.

Venturing Downward

After you make a top-level selection by clicking on a hyperlink, you begin a process known as *drilling down* through the directory levels. In other words, you trade in your global atlas for local maps.

The next page to appear on your screen looks similar to the top-level page, though perhaps much larger, with more choices. Differences in design between the various directory services become apparent at lower directory levels.

In some cases, the second page is laid out identically to the first, with a short list of subcategories. Other sites provide that short list, but in addition list many hyperlinks that jump to specific Web locations outside of the directory. Providing these outside links in the second directory level cuts to the chase in many situations. You may find a site of interest from the second level, or you may need to drill down to lower levels before leaving the directory to visit specific sites.

As you continue delving deeper into your chosen topic, the pages become more weighted to the list of outside Web sites, and the menu selections within the directory become fewer as your search becomes more specific. To see how this works, imagine a directory search that takes you four levels down before you leave the directory to explore some actual Web pages. Here's an overview of what the levels would offer. (Feel free to follow along with your Web browser.)

- ✔ **Top level:** You log into the Yahoo! directory (one of the most popular Web directories) to find some Web pages of movie actors. The Yahoo! top page contains a general menu of 14 subject categories (see Figure 1-1). You click on <u>Entertainment</u>, and are taken to the second level.

- ✔ **Second level:** Here, the broad Entertainment topic is split into more than 25 subtopic links (see Figure 1-2), including <u>Comics and Animation</u>, <u>Television</u>, <u>Magazines</u>, <u>Theater</u>, <u>Radio</u>, and the one you're interested in, <u>Movies and Films</u>. Pleased by your progress, you click on the <u>Movies and Films</u> hyperlink.

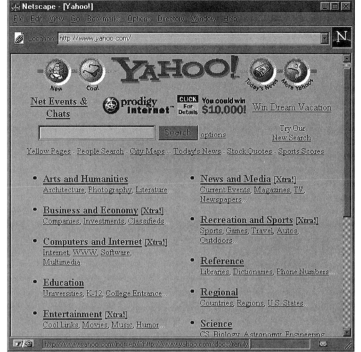

Figure 1-1:
The top
level of the
Yahoo!
directory,
showing
<u>Entertainment</u>
among the
list of links.

✔ **Third level:** At this level, the subject is splintered into topical links such as <u>Film Making</u>, <u>Home Video</u>, <u>Screenplays</u>, <u>Animation</u>, and <u>Producers</u>, and <u>Actors and Actresses</u>. Furthermore, the page has a second section below these divisions that lists hyperlinks to Web pages outside the directory that you're using (see Figure 1-3). These links include such intriguing names as <u>Movies.com</u>, <u>Mr. Showbiz</u>, <u>Flicker</u>, and <u>The Hollywood Network</u>. Still, they don't include the pages for the actors and actresses that you want to find. Undeterred, you go back up to the top of the third-level page and click on <u>Actors and Actresses</u>.

✔ **Fourth level:** Now you're deeply immersed in the directory, but this search path doesn't offer any further categories. You've come to the bottom level of this particular expedition. The entire page is devoted to links to Web pages about film actors (see Figure 1-4). The page is huge, and its alphabetical links will keep you happily surfing the celebrity sites for hours.

The <u>Movies and Films</u> link

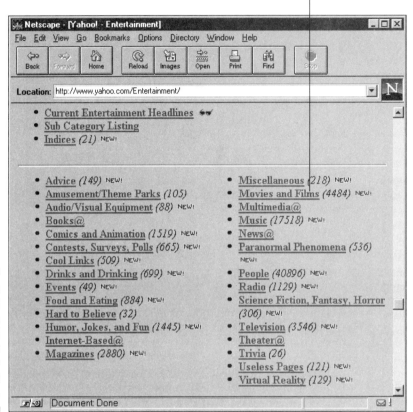

Figure 1-2:
The second
level of a
Yahoo!
directory
search for
movie
actors.

How many levels do directories have? The number depends on the individual directory that you're using. Some descend to as many as eight levels below the top page. The number also depends on the category that you started with. In some cases, depending on the specific service and the subject, only two or three levels will plumb a subject's depth. Some services give an indication of what's ahead by placing numbers next to their menu selections. For example, Yahoo! indicates that 3,474 listings are gathered under the <u>Movies and Films</u> category; on the same page, the <u>Audio/Visual Equipment</u> link promises only 63 items. So you know that you have a lot of browsing ahead of you in the first case, but you're near the end of the road in the second.

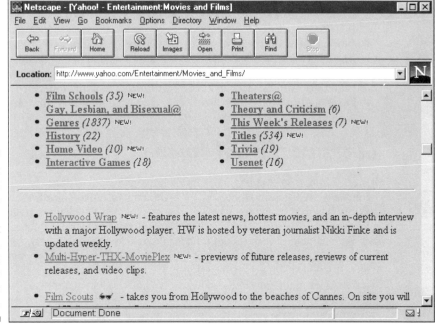

Figure 1-3:
A third-level
page of the
Yahoo!
Entertainment
directory,
showing
subtopics
and page
links.

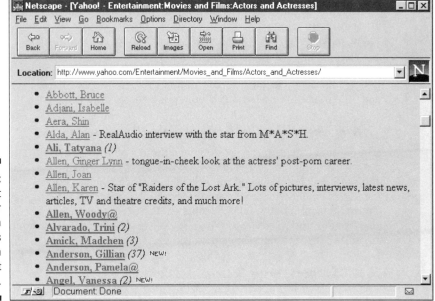

Figure 1-4:
Bingo! A list
of actor
links on
Yahoo!'s
fourth
Entertainment
level.

Basic Lessons in Using Directories

Directories seem simple to use, and in fact they are. That's one thing that makes them so appealing — anyone able to use a mouse can begin making sense of the World Wide Web through one of its directories. What's that? You want to be a power-user of Web directories? I can't promise unearthly directory skills, but the following tips will at least help you avoid potential directory tangles.

Choosing the right map

It stands to reason that if you're traveling to Spain, a map of Africa is of limited usefulness. By the same token, if you're looking for online information about your favorite baseball team, you won't get far by picking the Science category of your favorite Web directory. That much is obvious. But not all selections are so clear cut. For example, if you're searching for financial investment software, should you follow the <u>Business/Investments</u> or <u>Computers/Software</u> directory path? In many cases, the quickest method is to simply dive in and try all the possibilities. But here are a few guidelines for you to use so that you can avoid dealing with typical categorization confusion. Remember — each Web directory is different, and each one groups topics according to its own editorial viewpoint.

Entertainment versus Arts

Entertainment topics tend to be popular show-business subjects that are prone to daily change. Included are items about movies, television, actors, humor, radio, and theater. Arts subjects are usually more static and refined, such as photography, painting, sculpture, architecture, dance, museums, and drama. Intellectual and spiritual arts are sometimes represented by philosophy and religion links. Sometimes artistic spinoffs such as science fiction (literature) and pop music are on the Entertainment directory pages.

Government versus World Affairs versus Social Sciences

These three category types often have quite a bit of overlap, and their subtopics vary in each directory service. Government categories usually list political, international, law, military, and official U.S. Government pages, such as the page for the Internal Revenue Service. World Affairs generally refers to regional information, almanacs, cultural sites, and language resources. Social sciences choices link you to advocacy sites, social services locations, community organizations, and minority affairs issues.

Social Sciences versus Society and Culture

When these two social categories appear in the same Web directory, they are divided by whether their subtopics are more scientific or more cultural. Under Social Sciences you're likely to find humanities, economics, regional studies, political science, gender studies, and anthropology. Society and Culture links are more likely to include civil rights, environmental concerns, sexual issues, race relations, and abortion platforms.

Reference versus Regional

These two top-level categories can contain some topic overlap, thanks to the many statistical sites often found in the Regional area. In particular, almanac-style Web pages that are devoted to countries or states can include lists and numbers that are normally associated with the Reference category.

Elusive topics

Some subjects are like hinges between two general topics — they serve both equally well. When a directory cross-references these "hinge" subjects, all is well, because they will appear under two or more topics, and all their links will be available to you whichever place you look. In other cases, it can be a flummoxing experience to search in vain for a topic that you think should fit in the category you've chosen. Table 1-1 shows some of those annoyingly flexible topics, with suggestions as to where they may be lurking. Remember, the names of the broad categories that you see here are approximations of the actual words that appear in various Web directory menus.

Table 1-1   Tips for Searching Web Pages for Elusive Topics

If You're Looking for . . .	And It Isn't Here . . .	Try Here
Cyberculture	Society & Culture	Computers
History	Society	Science
Computer Science	Computers	Science
Information Technology	Science	Computers
Medicine (all kinds)	Science	Health
Fitness	Health	Society & Culture
Sexuality	Society & Culture	Health & Medicine
Law	Government	Social Sciences
Politics	Social Sciences	Government or News
Humor	Entertainment	Society & Culture
Multimedia	Computers	Entertainment
Online Courses	Education	Computers-Internet
Teaching	Education	Social Sciences
Economics	Business	Social Sciences
Humanities	Social Sciences	Art
Web Marketing	Business	Computers-Internet

Useful (maybe) comparisons

Web directories operate like telescopes: The more you extend a directory, the more magnified the detail. As you prowl more deeply into the directory levels of any particular search, you see the possibilities of your topic in greater detail. The Web is a great place for learning more than you expected. (It's equally good for wasting more time than you thought possible.)

You also can think of directories as a series of combs. Imagine raking smooth a sand trap on a golf course. If you start with a gardener's rake with widely-spaced prongs, you create a design of lines in the sand, and the result is a very general, unrefined smoothing effect. Switching to a hand rake with smaller spaces between its prongs smoothes the sand more finely, affecting more of the actual grains. Finally, using a hair comb (which is pretty far-fetched for this task, of course) creates a very finely groomed effect, aligning almost every grain of sand. In the same way, descending to the most specific directory level for any topic reveals, along the way, the thousands of sites that are available as links. Drilling deeply into a directory is a great way to comb through the Internet.

Bookmarking directory levels

Don't lose track of your landmarks! Almost all Web browsers include a bookmark (*hotlist*) feature with which you can add any page to a list with a single mouse click. Then you can return to that page during any session just by clicking on its place in the bookmark list. If you were exploring a new forest, you'd want to make note of the major trees, boulders, and other prominent landmarks around which your wanderings hinge. When drilling down through a directory, you might find the temptation to wander through some miscellaneous links irresistible. If, for example, you're searching for suitable and entertaining Web sites to share with your children, you may be distracted by a Magazines link that's on the same directory page as children's entertainment. You follow that link. Before you know it, your kids' bedtime is nearing and you're still browsing the cyberversion of your favorite newsmagazine. Not a problem, provided you bookmarked the page from which you went on your tangent. (And provided you have patient kids.)

Here's the rule of thumb: Every time you enter a Web directory page that has useful links, bookmark it immediately. Don't let yourself think, "I'll just follow one link and then come right back" — famous last words of every Net surfer. Bookmark it first and then play.

Retracing your steps

All Web browsers have a Back button that enables you to retrace your hypersteps one link at a time. Pressing it returns you to the previous Web page of your session.

There is a limit to how many steps backward the Back button will take you, and that limit is defined by the size of the memory buffer that your browser has set up in your computer. Use the Options or Preferences menu of your browser to increase or decrease the buffer size. The buffer size determines the number of Web pages stored for backtracking.

Experienced users of Web directories make good use of the Back button as part of their searching style. As you drill down through the directory levels, you are always leaving a trail, as if you were unrolling a long piece of string. Because many directory searches are experimental, you can use the Back button often to follow that string back to the page from which you started so you can try a different direction. This type of Web searching resembles a dog in the woods — dashing down each hyperlink path, sniffing out information, and then returning to the main path to try new links. Remembering to use the Back button gives you the freedom to experiment with new paths without worrying about getting lost or wasting time starting from scratch at each dead end.

And now we pause . . .

. . . for a commercial message? Yes, it's true. You will encounter advertising in Web directories. After all, some of these directories are commercial enterprises; yet the service is free to you. Advertising pays their bills, and these ads are more prevalent all the time. They take the form of graphic hyperlinks. Often the hyperlink is a button that, when clicked, takes you to the sponsor's Web site. Follow these links as your curiosity dictates, and use the Back button to return to your search.

Don't confuse advertising links with actual directory content. They are not part of the informational lists that you are browsing. Their top position on the page, plus distinctive graphic presentation (often a company logo and tagline), give them away.

Chapter 2
Using the Main Web Directories

*H*aving just one big, all-inclusive World Wide Web directory would make searching for things on the Web a lot easier. After all, you only need one phone book for your town, and one map. But the Web is different from a physical location in two important ways:

✔ It is growing and changing so rapidly that a single directory cannot keep up with it comprehensively.

✔ Users don't have to register descriptions of their Web sites with one central agency the way that they register their phone number and address, for example, with a local phone company. Anyone can have a page on the Web, but nobody needs to provide information about Web pages.

As a consequence, creating a directory of Web sites is a job that can be approached in various ways. Companies have formed to tackle this challenge, and the results differ from one directory to another. Confusing? When you are searching for information, the lack of a central authoritative directory may seem inconvenient, but, in fact, the situation presents you with more opportunities to find what you're looking for.

Choices, Choices

Multiple directory services make you work a little harder to find things, but the variety offers advantages.

- Each Web directory uses different methods for gathering its contents, so the sites that you can link to from each directory differ. One directory may consistently deliver the kind of links that you find useful, while another comes up empty repeatedly. Best of all are the times when an unexpected link reveals a location that you never would have thought to look for, but are glad that you stumbled across. The more directories you try, the better chance you have for serendipitous findings.

- Web directories categorize their content differently. If you drill down through the Entertainment topic of three Web directories, you will find not only links to different Web sites about entertainment subjects (no surprise, as there are many thousands), but also different subtopics in the lower levels. It amounts to an editorial choice, and topics are grouped in different ways in different services. These differences can freshen your outlook when you are searching, bringing to light new ways of looking at the information that you seek.

- Directories, though similar in appearance, have individual ways of displaying their menus and pages, just as different newspapers format the news in individual ways. You may just feel at home in one directory, simply because of its appearance and page design. Whether your search is simple and quick or complex and lengthy, it helps to use a directory interface that is naturally understandable and easy to navigate.

- As Web directories evolve into more complete services, they add features that their designers think will be useful. Some offer reviews of their linked sites. Others group new additions together for an easy overview of what's new. Directories may include editorial content in the form of articles and tutorials to give you a well-rounded searching experience.

In short, Web directories are in competition with each other, which is usually good news for the consumer. The result is a better online experience and the likelihood of finding things of interest with a minimum of hassle. The trick is to learn your way around the Web directories and become familiar with their individual characteristics. The following sections introduce you to the most popular directories.

Is bigger better?

Directories and search engines sometimes appear to be taking part in a World Wide Web bragging competition. They all rely on private indexes, created by robots, spiders, and worms, that scavenge the Web for new and updated pages. Every directory and search engine likes to assert that its index is the largest, most comprehensive, most totally exhaustive database of Web content. Can you trust these assertions? Even more important, does it make any difference whether you are using the biggest index?

The most important job that a Web index can do is help you find something, preferably without taking all night and without causing such frustration that you feed your modem to the neighbor's pit bull. To that end, big is good — but gigantic is not necessarily better. Several other factors besides sheer size come into play in determining which Web index serves you best.

By far, the biggest differences between all these indexes is how they are created and presented. Those differences are more important, practically speaking, than which index is the biggest, especially since the companies use different methods for counting the sites in their directories. Since any single Web site can consist of many pages, and any page can contain links to other items besides pages (such as downloadable files), any claim of 50 million sites in a directory is open to interpretation.

To top it all off, who in the world has time to search more than a bare fraction of the Web, anyway? If we're comparing zillions and gazillions, the upshot is simple: It doesn't really matter.

Yahoo!

I'm not just being jubilant. Yahoo! (complete with exclamation point) is the name of a Web directory. In fact, it is one of the most famous directories and was one of the first to gain a reputation as a good Web searching site. Venerability has hardly diminished its value; quite the contrary. Yahoo! is a dynamic, frequently updated, constantly evolving tool for helping you find stuff on the Web. Its URL is:

```
http://www.yahoo.com
```

The Yahoo! logo

The first thing that you see when you enter the Yahoo! site via its home page is the Yahoo! logo, which includes hyperlinked icons (see Figure 2-1). Run your cursor over it and notice how the arrow changes to a pointing finger, indicating a hyperlink. In fact, the logo has several different links embedded in it. Each of its icons links to a Yahoo! feature page.

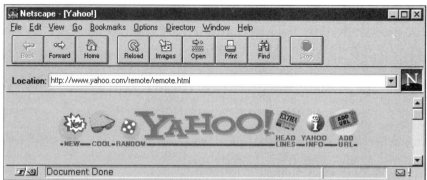

Figure 2-1:
The Yahoo!
logo. Each
of the
icons is a
hyperlink.

The what's new icon

```
http://www.yahoo.com/new/
```

Yahoo! changes so quickly that you need to check it almost weekly to keep up with the new features. Come to think of it, I guess that's the intention. Anyway, the What's New page gives you a rundown on recently added features. Perhaps more important than the new site features is its listing of all the new URLs (links to outside Web sites) that have been added to the directory. The URLs are listed by day of the week for the past week. They are further divided by category, which makes it especially easy to find new links to sites of interest.

The cool links icon

```
http://www.yahoo.com/Entertainment/Cool_Links/
```

"Cool Site" pages have been wildly popular ever since the "Cool Site of the Day" started the whole trend. Yahoo! carries on the tradition with elaborate thoroughness, using its directory style to divide the coolness into topics (see Figure 2-2). Some of the more entertaining topics are as follows:

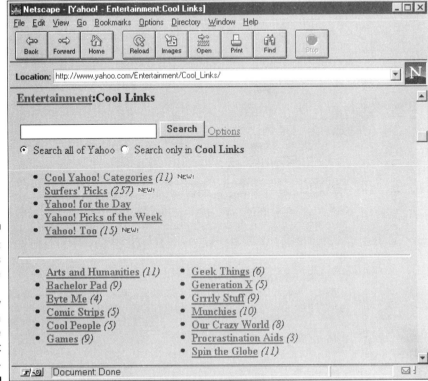

Figure 2-2:
Cool Links
brings the
Yahoo!
directory
style to a
bizarre
assortment
of links.

 ✔ **Bachelor Pad:** Following this path delivers links to virtual men's under-
wear stores, among other Web emporia of the masculine unwed condition.
Although the role that <u>Cockroach World</u> plays in bachelorhood is unclear,
<u>A Man's Life</u> seems more clear-cut. <u>Car and Driver</u> and a Bruce Lee page
round off the machismo mood of the directory.

 ✔ **Comic Strips:** Who doesn't like them? Not many links here, but the inclu-
sion of links to pages on Calvin and Hobbes, Doonesbury, Dilbert, and The
Far Side will make many strip-enthused surfers happy.

 ✔ **Cool People:** If anonymity is an aspect of coolness, then all the links here
qualify. You may not have heard of these obscure celebrities, so presumably their home pages will be an educational experience, as well as a brush
with cyber-hipness.

  ✔ **Geek Things:** To be hip used to be square, and in the digital age it's cool to be a geek. So don't be embarrassed to explore this directory path while someone is looking over your shoulder. The <u>Geek Site of the Day</u> promises "fascinatingly dull communication," while the <u>Cult of Macintosh</u> takes computer loyalties to the apex. But the best reason to check out this directory page is the link to the <u>Capt. James T. Kirk Sing-a-long Page</u>. Mankind's geekish future is revealed.

  ✔ **Grrrly Stuff:** With this antithesis of the <u>Bachelor Pad</u> directory, the fairer cybersex can link to milestones of feminism, as well as to a page devoted to odd wedding accessories. <u>The Lipstick Page</u> battles for political correctness with <u>NrrdGrrl!</u>.

  ✔ **Munchies:** One of the links in this directory offers information on how to grow enormous pumpkins. Whether giant squash qualifies as a munchie and whether the whole topic is imbued with enough coolness for this directory are both open questions. However, the <u>World Wide Sushi Restaurant Reference!</u> is cool beyond question, and the pie and beer pages don't hurt.

  ✔ **Procrastination Aids:** This directory is my personal favorite, at least in spirit. The <u>Centre for the Easily Amused</u> and the <u>Land O' Useless Facts</u> bring the mind-numbing potential of the World Wide Web into sharp focus.

The random links icon

At the top of the Yahoo! home page is an icon called Random. Use it only when you're experiencing an antisearch seizure. Clicking on the Random links icon plucks a URL from the vast Yahoo! directory database and takes you to that Web page. The selection has no rhyme or reason, and it is, therefore, browsing at its least intentional. But hey — it's fun.

The headlines icon

```
http://www.yahoo.com/headlines/
```

The Headlines icon offers a quick and easy way to check daily news. Clicking on it links to a directory page that's divided into subject categories, followed by links to either headlines or story summaries (see Figure 2-3). You also can get sports scores, weather, and financial quotes from this page. (If you want to know about all kinds of alternatives for getting news on the Web, flip over to Chapter 18.)

The Xtra! feature also links to topic-oriented news headlines, from the top level of the Yahoo! directory. Just look for the categories with the <u>Xtra!</u> link next to them. Clicking on that link takes you right to the headlines in that subject area, such as sports, business, or entertainment. I use the <u>Xtra</u> links as one of the quickest ways to catch up on the news (since I don't pull myself away from the computer long enough to read a newspaper).

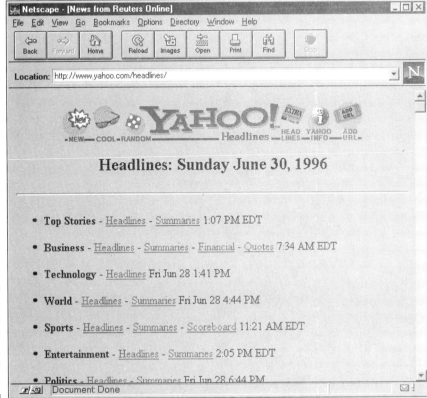

Figure 2-3:
Yahoo!
news
headlines,
directory
style.

The Yahoo! info icon

```
http://www.yahoo.com/docs/info/
```

Are you so impressed with Yahoo! that you'd like to work for the company? That topic is one of the ones covered in the comprehensive Info page. You also can buy a Yahoo! hat or T-shirt here or write to the people (via e-mail, of course) who make Yahoo! happen. Yahoo! Info is a clearinghouse of information about the service, and even if the merchandise doesn't excite you, you may like the general FAQ (Frequently Asked Questions) file, technical help, and company information.

Directory features

When you arrive at the main Yahoo! site, you see the top page of the directory, right below the logo. Here, as is typical, you can get in a broad overview of how Yahoo! categorizes sites on the Web (see Figure 2-4).

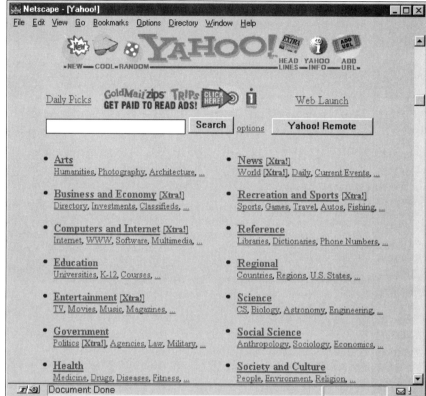

Figure 2-4:
The top-
level search
categories
of the
Yahoo!
directory.

Yahoo! shortcuts

Like all the major Web directories, Yahoo! is a multilevel index of topics, with each level of each subject contained on an individual Web page. You drill through the levels by clicking on hyperlinked menu items. Making your way through the levels is not hard or particularly time-consuming, but if you do it a lot, you can feel the tedium of constantly shuffling up and down the levels. Yahoo! offers a shortcut from the top level to the third level in the largest categories.

Each of the top-page main categories is immediately followed by a few subcategories that you would find if you clicked your way to the second level in that category. For example, the <u>News</u> category is followed by <u>World</u>, <u>Daily</u>, and <u>Current Events</u> links that would be found on the second level if you clicked the top-level <u>News</u> link. Clicking on a subcategory directly from the top page carries you immediately to the content of its page, which is located on the third level.

This shortcut is implemented only on the top Yahoo! page — but hey, we'll take what we can get.

The quickest shortcut of all is to search for Web sites by using keywords. Yahoo!, and the other directories discussed in this chapter, provide keyword entry forms so that you can do a keyword search. Using keywords and the entry forms is covered in excruciating detail in Part II of this book.

Yahoo! indices

Taking the high road to arcane grammatical usage, Yahoo! spells this word *indices* instead of the more common *indexes.* Nevertheless, *indices* refers to collections of indexes that the Yahoo! staff has gathered under various subject headings as a reference service.

You can usually find a link for the Yahoo! indexes for a subject (sorry to be grammatically gauche, but *indices* sounds like a medical condition) on the second level of the directory, near the top of the page. After you click on the Indices link, you see a page of reference links that lead to scads more links that are related to the category that you've chosen. All these links may sound confusing, but this is how it works:

1. **On the top Yahoo! page, click on the Government link.**

   A second-level page appears, listing subtopics for you to explore, plus the Indices link, which is just above the subtopics (see Figure 2-5).

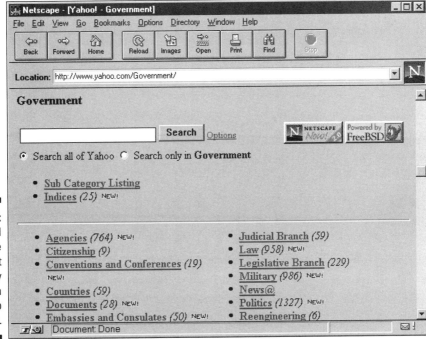

Figure 2-5: The second level of the Government directory contains a link to Indices.

2. **Click on <u>Indices</u>, in the upper-left part of the page.**

   A third-level page appears, listing links to indexes outside of the Yahoo! service (see Figure 2-6).

3. **Click on any one of the links, such as the <u>Comprehensive Government Resource Guide</u>, to visit a Web site that lists *other* Web sites related to Government.**

Sub Category Listing

A <u>Sub Category Listing</u> link is on every second-level page in the Yahoo! directory (see Figure 2-5) right above the <u>Indices</u> link, and it is a terrific time saver. When you first arrive at the Yahoo! site, you have no way of knowing how many levels you need to drill down before finding the links that you want. On some levels, numbers appear next to the menu items to indicate in a general way how much material you have to sift through. But you still don't know how many levels lie ahead in your search path. What you need is a map.

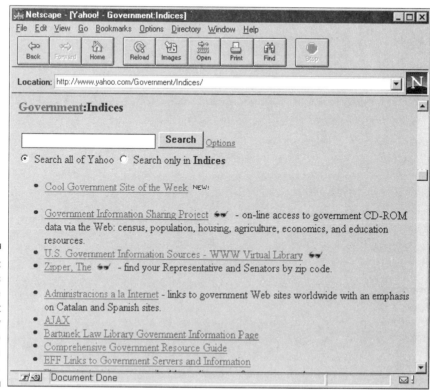

Figure 2-6:
The Indices page of the Government directory lists Web sites with more links.

The <u>Sub Category Listing</u> link comes to the rescue with such a map from each second level. When you click on this link, the Yahoo! system begins loading a large, tree-style directory menu of every possible search path under the current subject, down to the very last level. Figure 2-7 shows a small portion of the Sub Category Listing for the Recreation and Sports category. Each item on this extremely complex tree is a hyperlink, of course, so you can zip directly to the bottom level of any subcategory (which could be eight levels down).

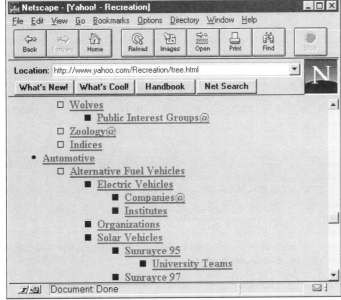

Figure 2-7: A small portion of a Yahoo! Sub Category Listing.

In the world of Web pages, *large* means *slow*. In other words, the *large* Sub Category Listing feature can take a couple of *slow* minutes to load into your browser. As a result, this feature saves time only when you are dealing with lengthy, possibly difficult searches. In those cases, having the entire directory structure for a single top-level topic on your screen in a single window is worth the initial wait. If you're not engaging in a thorough search, it may not be worth the finger-tapping wait.

Added attractions

In the endless quest for excellence, popularity, and utter Web coolness, many Web directories offer extra services in addition to raw search potential. Yahoo! is no exception. In fact, Yahoo! is a leader in offering a well-rounded site with its vast Web directory as the main structure. Here are the extras scattered around that main structure.

Yahoo! Xtra!

If all these exclamation points are making you giddy, the Xtra! feature will ground you in the here-and-now. Xtra! is a news service that is blended into the search directory structure. It is activated only in some of the top-level subjects, where you see its link, [Xtra!], next to the main topic listing. Click on the link to see a page of news wire headlines from which you can zip to complete stories. (Reuters New Media is the source of the news clips.)

This excellent feature is enhanced by a backlog of stories from the past week. You can access these older headlines by date, using links found at the bottom of the main Xtra! page.

Here is how to use the Xtra! feature to read a new story:

1. Click on Xtra! (on the top-level page).

2. Click on one of the headline links (on the second-level page).

3. Read the complete story (on the third-level page).

And here is the way to use the Xtra! feature to read a story from the past week:

1. Click on Xtra! (on the top-level page).

2. Click on a link for a date that is listed under Previous Days' Stories (on the second-level page).

3. Click on a link for a headline of a story for the date you have chosen (on the third-level page).

4. Read a past complete story (on the fourth-level page).

Yahooligans!

Yahooligans! is Yahoo! for kids. In an age when parents allow their children online with some trepidation, wondering what adult material they may stumble across, Yahoo! is attempting to provide safe searching for children. Yahooligans! is a risk-free kid zone in which every link has been reviewed and found acceptable for young surfers. Kids (and parents) can find their way there with this URL:

```
http://www.yahooligans.com/
```

The top level is obviously geared for kids (see Figure 2-8). It shows broad directory topics aimed at a young audience. The content is different, but the system works identically to the way the adult version works, featuring shortcut links to the largest third-level topics. There is no Xtra! feature in Yahooligans! because kids are presumably less inclined to read wire service stories.

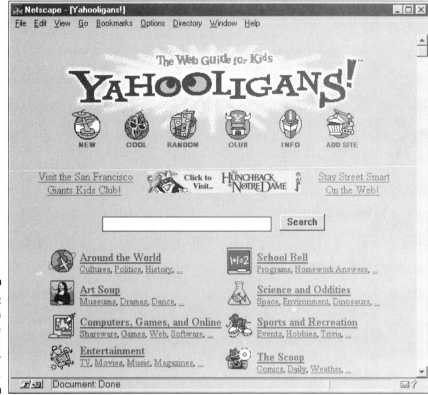

Figure 2-8:
The top
page of the
Yahooligans!
directory for
kids.

Yahooligans! sometimes uses games to turn directory searching into fun for kids, but the way that you find things differs little from what you do in the adult directory. The multilevel directory structure is in place here — just with different names and kid-appropriate links.

Yahooligans! and Yahoo! offer a text-only version (which you access by clicking a link at the bottom of either top-level directory page) for impatient kids of all ages who don't like waiting for graphics to appear.

Yahoo! San Francisco

```
http://www.yahoo.com/home/?http://sfbay.yahoo.com/
```

One of the more recent additions to the Yahoo! galaxy of services, Yahoo! San Francisco amounts to an interactive, resource-rich site for residents of the California city. The directory style remains the same as in the rest of Yahoo!, with a top-level selection of broad categories leading to lower levels of subtopics and specific sites. The difference is that everything relates to San Francisco. You can link to city maps, real estate information, local businesses, education resources, job listings, city sports and entertainment, and travel information.

San Francisco news headlines are an icon-click away from the home page, and the page even has a collection of message boards for connecting with other Yahoo! visitors. These boards are divided into the same topical groupings as the directory, so you can read (and post your own) messages on the city's best restaurants, the two major league baseball teams in the area, or gay and lesbian issues. You can use the boards to look for a carpool, discuss stocks, or set your kids loose on the children's message area.

You can link to Yahoo! San Francisco from the bottom of the Yahoo! top-level directory page. Just click on the Yahoo! SF Bay link. While you're down there at the bottom of the page, look around for other regional links. At the time of this writing, Yahoo! has plans to expand the feature to other countries and, perhaps, cities.

Yahoo! Japan

Ready to practice your Asian language reading skills? Oh. Well, don't bother following the Yahoo! Japan link, then. Or, if you do read Japanese, be sure that you have the necessary software to display the pages readably. You can see the software requirements (and link to sites for downloading that software) for your computer at the first stop in the Yahoo! Japan link. That link is found at the bottom of Yahoo! pages. Or you can enter the URL:

```
http://www.yahoo.co.jp
```

Yahoo! Net Events

```
http://www.yahoo.com/picks/events
```

Net Events are activities on the World Wide Web that happen live — that is, in realtime. A regular Web page is not an event, because it is static. A live event involves some kind of broadcast, conference, or chat experience in which many people can participate. Yahoo! Net Events is a schedule of live happenings for the current day, with summaries, plus links to the sites that are hosting the event (see Figure 2-9). It's a good place to check when you're in the mood for a more participatory Web experience.

Some live events require Web browser plug-ins (utility programs that plug in to your browser program), so you can hear a broadcast or chat with other attendees.

Yahoo! Internet Life

Internet Life is an electronic magazine that has links to fresh, new, original Web sites. The editorial focus is on "fun, profit, and personal growth," according to the home page banner. Internet Life offers zillions (that's an estimate) of links in those broadly defined categories. The sparse directory design is thrown out the window for Internet Life in favor of a lively, graphic approach complete with animated, moving icons.

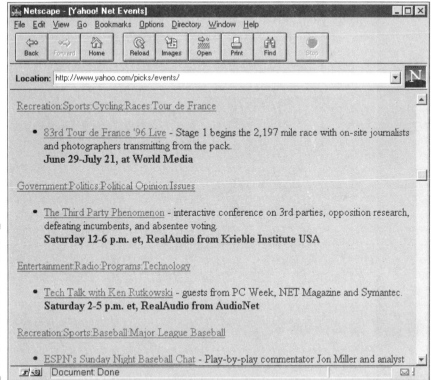

Figure 2-9:
The Yahoo!
Net Events
page points
you to live
conferences
and
broadcasts
on the Web.

The <u>Internet Life</u> link is at the bottom of the top-level Yahoo! page, as well as on many other pages throughout the directory. If you're navigating your Web browser with the graphics turned off for speed, you'll need to turn them back on for this part of Yahoo!. You can get to the magazine manually by using this URL:

```
http://www.zdnet.com/yil/
```

Lycos

Lycos is another of the prominent Web directories. It also provides keyword searching, which is described in Chapter 6. The directory part of Lycos is called a2z. You can start your directory prowl either from a separate a2z top-level page or from the Lycos main site. Here is the a2z directory URL:

```
http://a2z.lycos.com
```

The a2z directory is so called to give you the feeling that it covers the World Wide Web comprehensively, from A to Z. Although total Web comprehensiveness may to be too much to ask from *any* directory, a2z also lives up to its name by listing the sites on its pages alphabetically.

Directory features

The directory's top level (see Figure 2-10) is laid out in typical directory fashion, but it holds a couple of category surprises.

Figure 2-10: The main subject categories of the Lycos top-level directory.

✔ **Just For Kids:** Clicking on this link takes you to a second-level list of sites for young surfers. There are no subcategories or lower search levels beyond the second level.

✔ **The Road Less Traveled:** Subjects under this intriguing category touch on the paranormal and mystical realms, including Conspiracies & Hoaxes; The Mind; Crystal Ball; UFOs; and Spirituality & Mysticism. Lycos is the only major directory that prominently features such unusual and esoteric subjects.

✔ **Shopping the Net:** Materialists rejoice! This topic gathers tons of money-draining links under categories such as Apparel; Flowers; Virtual Malls; Autos; Books; Sporting Goods; Entertainment; Gifts; and Travel.

✔ **Internet:** Although other directories bundle Internet information under the broader topic of Computers, Lycos puts the Net into sharp focus. Second-level subjects include Access Providers; Ethics, Netiquette & Legislation; Web Publishing & HTML; Browsers & Interfaces; Internet News; and others.

Lycos descriptions

When you bore into the Lycos directory to the levels that list outside Web site links, you get more than just a bare list of hyperlinks. One of the Lycos strong points is that it includes a description of every listed site (see Figure 2-11) — not at great length, mind you, but even a short paragraph can persuade you to zip over to a site or dissuade you from wasting your time there. Determining the full nature of a site from a simple link name is, after all, impossible, and the descriptions make up for the space that they take by delivering good information.

Point reviews

More complete descriptions, called *point reviews,* are attached to selected Lycos links. You can tell which links have point reviews because they have a small point review icon next to them (see Figure 2-11). To read a point review, simply click on the icon.

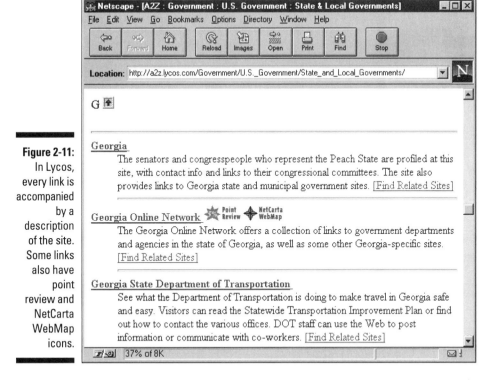

Figure 2-11: In Lycos, every link is accompanied by a description of the site. Some links also have point review and NetCarta WebMap icons.

In addition to providing a full paragraph critique of the site, the point review rates the site for content, presentation, and experience on a scale of 1 to 50 (see Figure 2-12).

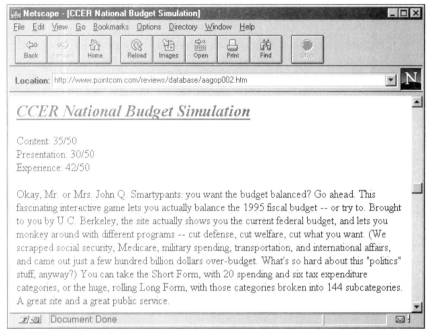

Figure 2-12:
A Point
review in
Lycos.

After perusing the review, click on its title to visit the site or use the Back button of your browser to return to the directory level you left. A link is also provided for returning to the previous directory, but using the Back button is quicker than reloading the page from scratch.

NetCarta WebMaps

In Lycos, some destination sites have NetCarta WebMaps, which are graphic representations of the sites. WebMaps enable you to navigate through sites more easily.

If a site has a WebMap, you see a small icon next to its link (refer to Figure 2-11). However, using a WebMap isn't simply a matter of clicking on the icon. For one thing, you need special software to read the WebMap, so clicking on a WebMap icon before getting the software is pointless. You would be offered a download of the WebMap but wouldn't be able to read it after you downloaded it.

Here is how to equip your computer to use NetCarta WebMaps:

1. **At the top of any second-level or lower directory page, click on the <u>NetCarta WebMap</u> link.**

2. **Click on the spelled-out link near the top of the page to go to a separate WebMap page.**

3. Click on the <u>Download the trial version</u> link.

This action initiates a software download and prompts you for a directory location on your hard drive. After the software is downloaded, the program will work in conjunction with either Netscape Navigator or Microsoft Explorer (but not other Web browsers). When you click on the WebMap icon that is next to a site in the directory, the NetCarta WebMap program pops open to interpret the WebMap.

NetCarta WebMap is currently available only for Windows 95 or Windows NT. Furthermore, you must be using one of the following three Web browsers: Netscape Navigator 1.2 or later, Spyglass Enhanced Mosaic 2.0, or Internet Explorer 2.0 or later.

Point

Lycos has its obligatory eZine (electronic magazine), which is similar to the Yahoo! Internet Life but not as extensive. (Don't misread that word as *expensive,* because both magazines are free.) The Lycos offering, which is called Point (see Figure 2-13), features highlighted sites, lists of links, and articles by cyber-columnists. You might find a collection of the best mystery sites (as I did in a recent edition), political pages, or sports news. Point is a nice diversion when you're burned out from the tedium of hardcore searching. You can get to Point by using the Point link at the bottom of the Lycos front page or go directly there with this URL:

```
http://point.lycos.com
```

To get to the following features of Point, either use the links at the top of the Point home page or the URLs that are given with the descriptions of the features.

Top 5%

```
http://point.lycos.com/categories/
```

The Top 5% is not a Point evaluation of site quality, but it does indicate the most popular sites on the Web according to the Point. Clicking on the Top 5% button from the Point front page displays a directory page that is deceptively similar to the main Lycos directory. The difference is that all the sites found in *this* directory fall into the Top 5% category and are presumably high-quality, high-traffic Web sites.

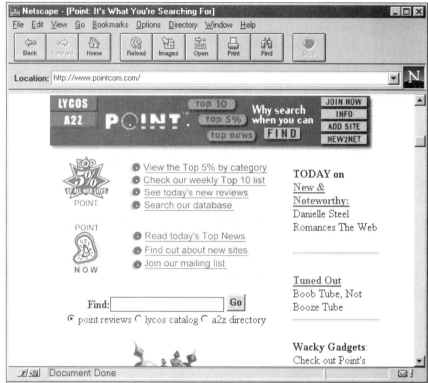

Figure 2-13:
Part of the
Point
electronic
magazine in
Lycos.

Top Ten

```
http://point.lycos.com/topsites/content.html
```

The Top Ten list changes weekly and is presented in a new category every time. One week it might be a list of the best shopping sites, and the next week the topic might be Community Affairs. Unlike the Top 5% feature, the Top Ten is an editorial evaluation by the Lycos staff. Based on the Point reviews of Web sites, each listing in the Top Ten is rated according to quality of the content, the presentation, and the overall experience (see Figure 2-14). The Top Ten links take you first to the full point review for that site, and from there you can link to the site itself.

New Reviews

```
http://point.lycos.com/columns/new/
```

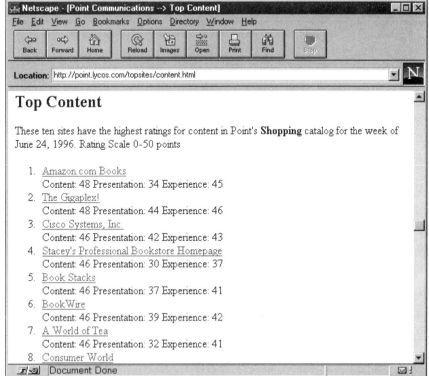

Figure 2-14:
The Top Ten
list rates
sites in
three
categories
and links to
full Point
reviews.

The Point reviews of Web sites are so useful that knowing which sites have been added to the review database is handy. Even handier is the fact that you can organize the list of newcomers in a few different ways (see Figure 2-15).

✔ **Date reviewed:** Click this option to get a chronological list (going backward from the current day) of new reviews. This choice is good if you visit Point frequently and just want to catch up on the past few days.

✔ **Content, Presentation, or Experience:** You use these choices to organize the list according to the highest scores in each of the Point review categories. If you're looking for newly reviewed informational sites, Content is your best bet. If your taste runs to glorious graphics and dazzling page design, clicking Presentation will group visually excellent sites near the top of the list. The Experience link weights the list toward sites whose overall impact is effective.

✔ **Alphabetic:** Listing newly reviewed sites alphabetically is a good way to find a particular Web page that you hope has been reviewed recently.

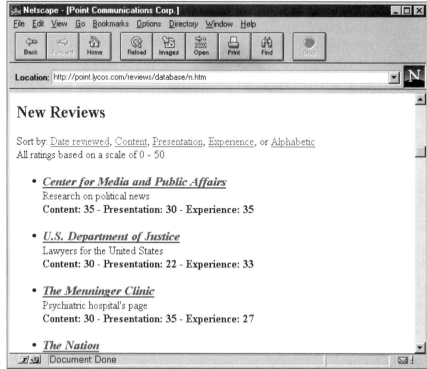

Figure 2-15:
When
checking
new reviews
in Point, you
can sort
them in five
different
ways.

Top News

http://point.lycos.com/now/

Point, like other directory eZines, provides a news service of sorts. Clicking on the Top News button from the Point home page takes you to a newspaper-like page that has links to the current day's news in several topical sections (see Figure 2-16). Now here's the catch. Lycos doesn't actually provide the news stories — it provides links to Web editions of newspapers and magazines where you can read up on news items. This arrangement has an advantage and a disadvantage:

✔ The advantage lies in variety and discovery. You end up reading news from several sources and getting a broader editorial perspective than if you got headlines from a single wire service. Furthermore, you end up discovering all kinds of Web news sites.

✔ The disadvantage is in the lack of speed. Instead of zipping through headlines archived within the site (as Yahoo! does), you have to ping-pong back and forth between the Top News page and the outside sites it represents.

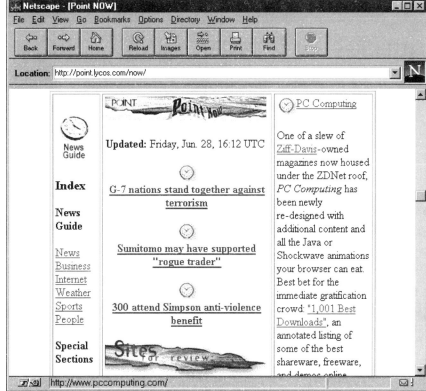

Figure 2-16:
The Lycos
Top News
page acts
like a
newspaper
but takes
you to other
sites to get
the stories.

New Sites

```
http://www.pointcom.com/now/updated.htm
```

The New Sites page tells you of freshly created or redesigned pages on the Web. The emphasis is usually on big-name corporate sites and high-profile Web publications, but an e-mail link is provided for reader suggestions. So check this page for new surfing locations, or if you've come across a terrific *new* Web site that you'd like Point to include in its list.

The Join Now button

```
http://point.lycos.com/subscribe/
```

Becoming a member of Lycos is free, and members have the advantage of receiving e-mail updates about the directory service and new Point features. If receiving additional e-mail is a disadvantage, then don't join. You can still use the service the same as any member, and no features are hidden. Lycos assures potential subscribers that their e-mail addresses won't be used for electronic junk mail.

a2z Op-heds

```
http://a2z.lycos.com/columns/contents/
```

Lycos saves its most striking page design for its collection of columnists. Linking to the Op-heds page from the a2z home page gives you the written musings of Net commentators Tin Lizzie, Glenn Davis, and the Grrl Zone. Yellow-on-black text interacts with deep blue swirling spirals to put you in the properly psychedelic frame of cybermind. It's political, it's cool, and it's even about the politics of cool. Great for when you need to take a break from searching.

Excite

The top level of the Excite directory is compactly laid out, which makes navigating through its uncluttered page easy (see Figure 2-17). A couple of surprises are lurking among the top-level subjects:

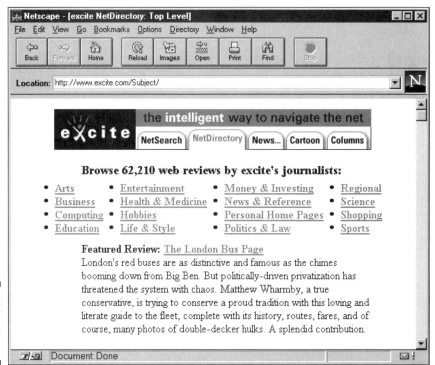

Figure 2-17: The top level of the Excite directory.

✔ **Personal Home Pages:** The World Wide Web first became famous as a repository of noncommercial, personal testimonials to cyberpersonality. Often created by college students, the early home pages featured collections of links to other home pages and descriptions of cultural tastes and personal revelations. As Web technology has evolved, personal home pages have grown in ambition and sophistication, but they still are fun and often quirky. This Excite directory category is the best way to browse personal home page links by topic.

✔ **Shopping:** For those who roam the Web with credit card in hand, this directory is like a guide to the planet's biggest mall. The directory spins off into a few dozen subtopics that represent all kinds of merchandise that is available on the Web, from clothes to tobacco.

Excite places a premium on selection and description. As a result, the directory is not the largest one on the Web, but every site linked to it is reviewed in a single-paragraph style that conveys the gist of the site before you spend time visiting it. This setup is handy, and it gives a sense of high class, like a brand of coffee that picks only the finest beans.

At the top of each directory page, the Excite logo has embedded links to other parts of the directory service (see Figure 2-18). The links look like tabs sticking up from a filing cabinet. Just click on the one you want, and your Web browser takes you to that page within the Excite service.

Figure 2-18:
The Excite logo provides hyperlinked tabs for other parts of the service.

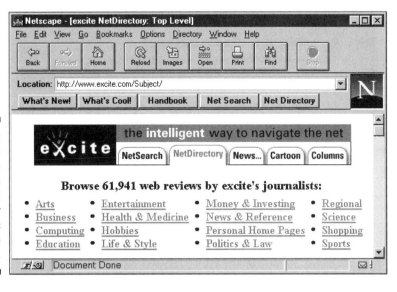

✔ **NetSearch:** Clicking on NetSearch takes you to the keyword searching part of Excite. That portion of the service is described in Chapter 7, using the kind of immortal prose that makes grown men weep.

✔ **News:** The Excite news service provides wire service reports in a very coherent fashion (see Figure 2-19). A one-line summary of the news item gives you the gist of the story, and clicking on the hyperlinked title sends you off to get the whole story. Meanwhile, a small link at the bottom of each story, <u>Related Web Documents</u>, displays links to related stories, slightly older reports, archives of gathered clippings, and Web sites that relate somehow to the new item. All in all, this news service is great whether you just want to get headlines or need to be well informed about a news topic.

Figure 2-19:
Headlines
from the
Excite news
service.

✔ **Cartoon:** Comic strips, right on your screen! And you can enjoy them without having anyone know that you read the funnies *before* the news.

✔ **Columns:** Just as you'd expect, this link takes you to a couple of opinion columns about Internet issues. The columns are not a full-fledged Web magazine by any means; they just provide a little light reading for when you can't decide where to go next.

GNN

GNN (Global Network Navigator) is a commercial online service, not just a directory. However, using the GNN directory service is free, and it is accessible to everyone. (Joining the larger service does cost money.) The URL for GNN is

```
http://www.gnn.com
```

Directory features

GNN is home to the Whole Internet Catalog (WIC), and the WIC takes the form of a Web directory that has the same basic style as Yahoo!, Lycos, and Excite (see Figure 2-20). However, this directory is different from the others in both intent and results. It is meant for the Web searcher who is more concerned with quality than quantity, and it emphasizes selection over comprehensiveness. The GNN editors hand pick the links that appear in the directory, bringing together a total of only about 2,500 sites.

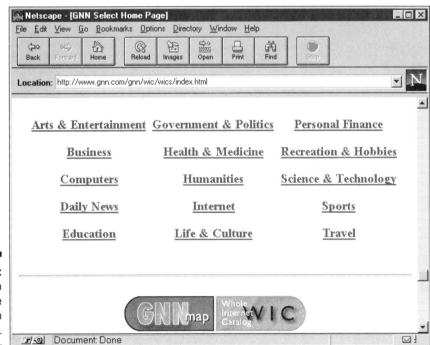

Figure 2-20:
The top level of the GNN Web directory.

What the GNN directory lacks in thoroughness, it makes up for in careful presentation. Every link in the entire menu structure is reviewed (not always favorably). When you click on a site, you are taken first to the GNN review; a further click then delivers you to the site itself. Using the WIC directory, you are assured of finding quality sites, but you should use it only if you don't care to rummage deeply in the Web's more hidden areas. The directory is superficial (only three levels deep), but well designed and well organized.

At the second level of the GNN directory, you get more than subdivided subject areas. GNN also provides a list of the most popular sites of that page's topic. Follow these steps for a good example of the list:

1. **From the GNN top-level directory, click on the <u>Daily News</u> link.**

2. **When the next page displays, scroll down until you see the list of most popular sites (see Figure 2-21).**

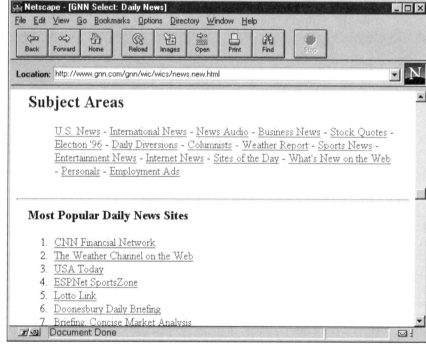

Figure 2-21:
GNN lists the most popular sites for each second-level directory topic.

This list helps you cut to the chase in certain searching situations. Rather than having to scrounge through a lower level of sites, you can link directly to specific high-traffic sites. If you're not searching for something in particular, or for an obscure site, this feature is useful. In the <u>Daily News</u>, you can zip directly from the second level to some of the biggest and best Web news sites.

Every site in the GNN directory is reviewed. Because of this feature, links within the directory don't take you to the site itself right away. Instead, they display a review page. (This setup is similar to the Excite system.) From that page, you can finally get to the site itself. The reviews are well written and can help you determine whether the site meets your search standards.

Business pages

GNN places a particular focus on Web sites where you can spend some of your plastic cash. (As if you didn't already have too many temptations in the real world.) It selects links for a directory of these sites and categorizes them in the usual multilevel fashion. A sort of support group for Web retail outlets, the directory includes sites where you can spend money on everything from books to contact lenses with which to read them, and from flowers to vases to hold them.

You can use the following URL to surf directly to the GNN Business Pages:

```
http://www.gnn.com/gnn/bus/index.htm
```

Or follow these steps:

1. **Go to the GNN home page at this address:**

```
http://www.gnn.com
```

2. **Click on the <u>GNN Select</u> link.**

3. **When the next page appears, click on the <u>Business Pages</u> link.**

Part II
Searching with
Keywords

The 5th Wave   By Rich Tennant

YOU'RE NOT A CYBERHOLIC... if you look for the Soup of the Day in the Format menu.

In this part . . .

The World Wide Web is a browser's paradise. You can easily get lost for hours among the Web's diverse and fascinating destinations, eagerly clicking your mouse to see what's around the next corner, and the next, and the next. . . .

But when you need to find something without spending half the night looking for it, keywords can save the day. For poor Web-addicted souls (like me), keywords can add years to life. They enable you to *have* a life, instead of whiling it away in front of the computer, browsing endlessly for the proverbial needle in a hyperstack.

This part introduces you to several *search engines,* the online services that take your keywords, do the dirty work of comparing them to the engine's immense knowledge of Web contents, and display links to matching destinations right on your screen. These services can get a little complicated, but that just adds to the fun. (Honest!) The trick is to start simple and gradually build up your expertise until you're a master (to whatever extent you want to be) of keyword searching. The chapters in this part start at the very beginning and walk you through all the possibilities at an easy pace. So decide what you want to search for and dive right in!

Chapter 3

The Flashlight Approach to Searching

. . . .

. . . .

Searching through menu-based Web directories can turn up some great finds. Plus, it's fun. And informative. And time-consuming! Furthermore, the tendency is to discover lots of information that you *weren't* looking for and not enough of what you really need. It's a way to search when you're also interested in browsing.

When you know exactly what you're trying to find, the Web's keyword search features can deliver what you need quickly and precisely. Web directories throw broad illumination on the Internet, lighting it in a wide context, but keywords take the flashlight approach, quickly revealing bits and pieces of the Internet that relate to your immediate information need.

Using Keywords to Narrow Your Search

Keywords are hints that you give the Web to make it find what you want. The Web (or any other gang of computers) is not very smart, and you can't count on having an intelligent discussion with it. You have to nurse it along by giving it clues. So, for example, if you're looking for information on the pitchers of the 1955 Cleveland Indians, some possible keywords would be **baseball**, **indians**, **cleveland**, **pitching**, and perhaps a few names of players. Being able to say, "Give me statistics on the pitching staff of the 1955 Cleveland Indians, including both starters and relievers," would be more convenient, but alas, Internet technology, although progressing nicely, isn't quite at the *Star Trek* stage yet.

The searching smorgasbord

The Web began as an experimental system of hyperlinking Internet documents, and before anyone knew it, it was the hottest thing since potato knishes. Soon everyone was putting up home pages. Then all kinds of companies and agencies began placing information on the Net in Web format. The Web quickly moved from being merely novel and entertaining to being downright useful, and even indispensable, for many people. The desire to surf and browse gave way to the need to search and find. And that's the pickle we find ourselves in today.

Online Web searching services were developed as a joint experiment in information retrieval and computer science. They caught on. They became competitive with each other. There are now many dozens of Web searching tools — some famous, powerful, and huge; others obscure, quirky, and specialized.

Yahoo! was the first search tool to achieve widespread recognition. Yahoo! became a household word in the homes of Internet users. Other tools, such as Lycos and Excite, have attracted prominence due to new approaches to searching. Relative newcomers, such as Inktomi, claim part of the stage for their unique indexes and the horsepower of their engines. There are even niche searchers that cover certain subjects or geographical areas. Most services, and all the ones covered in this book, are currently free of charge.

New developments and emerging services change the Web searching landscape almost daily. One way to keep up is by following the Internet magazines. Another way is to search the Web and Usenet for information on Web searching. And the best way to get a feel for the different search options is simply to use them. Start by placing the Web search sites used in this book in your browser's bookmark list, and go to them often. After you start searching, you'll see how easy it is, and the Internet will become a much more manageable place.

This chapter, and the others in this part, will help you learn how to make keyword clues as effective as possible, depending on which part of the Web you're giving them to.

Keyword sites

Some specific Web sites accept search keywords. They gobble them up, digest them for a few seconds, and then splash the results of their search on your screen. In Internet lingo, the following names are used for all of these specialized searching sites:

- ✓ **Web search sites:** Blindingly original, isn't it?

- ✓ **Web indexes:** They are called *indexes* because the sites search prebuilt indexes of the Web, not the Web itself.

- ✓ **Web crawlers, worms, or spiders:** These evocative names are used to help you imagine an industrious multilegged (or no-legged) creature that burrows deep into the Internet's resources on your behalf.

- ✓ **Search engines:** Sounds industrial, doesn't it? These sites are called *engines* because of the built-in software that drives the automated search routines. Each engine differs. You don't need to understand the technical differences, but you should know that the results of searches by different engines (sites) will vary, even if you use the same keywords — not unlike the different responses that different car models have to the same gasoline.

Whatever you call these sites, such indexes are distinguished by their ability to accept keywords and then search with them. That capability is the main difference between a Web directory and a Web search site — though, as you have seen, some directories include keyword search forms. And some crawlers (with their inevitable keyword search forms) include directories.

Entering keywords

So what are *keyword search forms,* anyway?

You type keywords into Web pages that contain *forms.* Forms on the Web look just like the paper forms that you've been filling out all of your life when you've applied for a job or a driver's license.

At their simplest, keyword search forms include a field for typing in one or more words and a Search button, as shown in Figure 3-1. Most forms are case-insensitive, so you don't have to worry about putting uppercase letters in the right place. To begin the search, you click on the Search button with your mouse, although in some cases pressing Enter will initiate the search. More complicated forms offer drop-down lists, additional slots for multiple keywords, and other helpful distractions (see Figure 3-2).

In the early days of the Web (way back in the archaic past — about two years ago), forms weren't visible in all Web browsers. Browsers that could read forms were called *forms-enabled browsers.* (Another inventive piece of terminology.) These days, virtually all modern browsers can view forms.

Keyword entry form   Search button

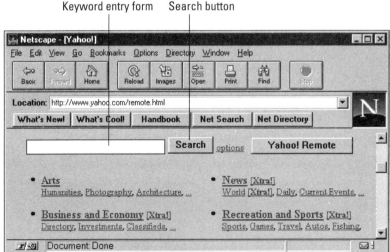

Figure 3-1:
A simple
keyword
form at the
Yahoo!
search site.

Figure 3-2:
Some
keyword
forms
include
options, but
you don't
have to use
them.

When you're ready to venture into the unknown by beginning a keyword search, just follow these steps for entering a keyword:

1. **Enter the URL for a keyword search site into your Web browser.**

   These URLs are sprinkled throughout this book, and the sites themselves are discussed extensively in separate chapters. But to get started with keywords, use any of these URLs:

   ```
   http://www.yahoo.com
   ```

   ```
   http://www.lycos.com
   ```

```
http://www.excite.com
```

```
http://www.altavista.digital.com
```

```
http://inktomi.berkeley.edu
```

```
http://webcrawler.com
```

The top page of the search engine appears. It includes a form that looks similar to what you see in Figure 2-1 for the keyword search. You can safely disregard any other slots and options that you see.

2. **Position the cursor in the form opening and click once to establish it there.**

3. **Type a word that relates to your search.**

   Almost any thing, place, or organization will do, even if you aren't looking for something specific right now. Try **potato**, **Ireland**, or **NASA**.

4. **Click once on the Search, Begin, or Enter button.**

   Some search engines let you begin the search process, after typing in the keywords, by pressing the Enter key on your keyboard. Others, though, require you to click an on-screen button.

The sparkplugs of the search engine

Entering a keyword is like starting a motor — Web search sites are called *search engines* for good reason. The search engine shows its horsepower by comparing your keywords to its entire index of Web material, and then it gives you the results of the comparison. In other words, it displays all the sites in its index that offer matches to your keywords. But not the whole site, you'll be glad to know; just a summary of it (the completeness and frequency of summaries vary among search engines), with hyperlinks that can take you to the actual site if you think that you've found something useful.

The largest, most famous search engines compare your keywords to indexes containing millions of sites and billions of words within those sites. (I'm not trying to sound like Carl Sagan, who seems to number everything exponentially; it's literally true.) So how long does displaying the results of such an awesome search require? Hours? No, not even minutes.

Assuming that your telephone line is in good working order and that you're not being stalled by prime-time Internet traffic, you'll get the results of any search you try within seconds. Isn't technology grand? Shouldn't you give up your social life to explore the Internet? Well, don't get carried away. But the impressive return times make it easy to conduct multiple searches through several engines when you are tracking down a difficult subject.

A mechanic's guide to search engines

The search engine is only one of the components that are required for the search process. The main component is the vast, hidden index of sites to which your keywords are compared. The search engine's job is to compare your keywords to the index. How is this immense index database formed?

Search indexes are usually created automatically, with the help of automated software programs that constantly scour the Internet for new material. These programs are sometimes called *robots*, or *bots*; and because of them, search sites are sometimes referred to as *worms* or *crawlers*. Like burrowing animals, these programs roam the Net continually and invisibly, following links, gathering new document and page titles, and in some cases, collecting every word of the sites that they visit. This raw data is collected and stored.

Next, the data is compressed and sorted according to the guiding search principles of the site. If word proximity is considered important, then such proximities are indexed and stored. If there is an attempt to gather concepts from word placements, then these concepts are extrapolated and saved. The index is a gigantic, evolving data organism.

You can thank the compressed index for the quickness of Web searches. All the time-consuming work has been done (and is still being done) by the ever-slithering bots. The search engine merely compares your keywords to the current, presumably up-to-the-minute, index, and returns the matches within seconds. The speed with which this is accomplished still is impressive.

Getting Specific with Keyword Qualifiers

As you can imagine, using single-word clues to find information in the vastness of the World Wide Web is akin to fumbling through the proverbial haystack with boxing gloves on. Surprisingly, it works; but you often have to sort through mountains of undesirable search results before you find something useful. You need to develop the skill of narrowing the search before you begin it by using the right keywords in the right combinations.

Assisting in this enterprise are special words that tell the search engines how to treat the terms you've entered. You can use these words to emphasize some keywords, de-emphasize others, link terms together by proximity, and exclude matches that coincide with certain terms. Don't panic; it's easier than it sounds! These special words are called *qualifiers* or *operators*.

  ✔ **AND:** Using *AND* between two keywords links them as a pair, so that matches must include both words. (Some search sites allow you to use the plus (+) sign instead of the word *AND*.) Documents and sites that contain only one of the words will be excluded from the result list. An example would be **cleveland AND indians**. This search, though simple, would greatly narrow the field by eliminating non-baseball information about the city of Cleveland, as well as information about Indians as an ethnic group (see Figure 3-3).

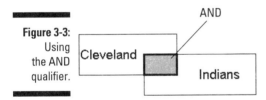

Figure 3-3:
Using
the AND
qualifier.

✔ **OR:** Using *OR* between two words opens wide the floodgates of information by allowing matches that correspond to either word. So to continue with the example, entering **cleveland OR indians** will deliver the whole gamut of responses relating to the city of Cleveland, Cleveland Amory, Grover Cleveland Alexander, Indian gurus, Native American sweat lodges, and who knows what else. The *OR* operator has its moments, especially for broadening a search that isn't yielding enough results (see Figure 3-4).

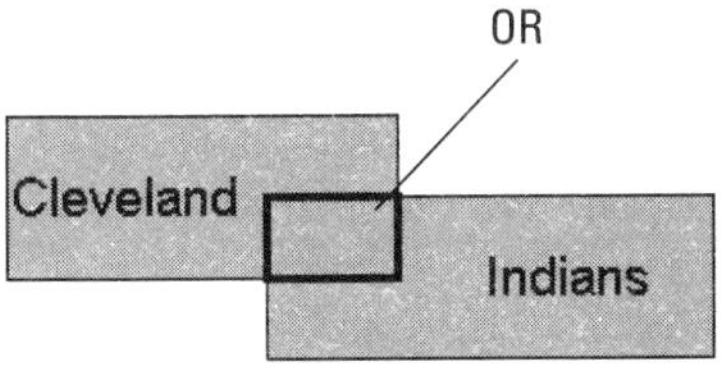

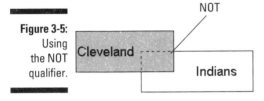

Figure 3-4:
Using the
OR qualifier.

✔ **NOT:** Using *NOT* between two keywords eliminates the second word from consideration as a match candidate. (Some search sites enable you to use the minus (–) sign as an abbreviation for *NOT.*) You can use *NOT* when you anticipate that the frequent presence of the second word will mess up your search. For example, if you were researching information on Cleveland but you didn't want to include anything on its baseball team, you could use the NOT qualifier and enter **cleveland NOT indians**. Using the NOT qualifier between **cleveland** and **indians** would eliminate the baseball aspect of the search (see Figure 3-5).

Figure 3-5:
Using
the NOT
qualifier.

✔ **( ):** You can use parentheses to surround words that you are grouping together with another operator. Using parentheses may bring back dreadful memories of high school math class, but it's not that complicated. Imagine saying to yourself, "I want information on the Cleveland Indians as they fought the Yankees for the 1955 pennant." (And if that's as interesting as your private mutterings get, I'm not going to bother eavesdropping.) If you entered this keyword string, **cleveland AND (indians OR yankees)**, you'd get references to sites that contain **cleveland AND indians**, as well as **cleveland AND yankees**.

✔ **The asterisk wild card:** As a search operator, the innocent asterisk (*) has a special meaning. As in a card game in which a specified card can have any value, placing an asterisk in a keyword string tells the search engine to match *anything* against the asterisk. What good is that? Doesn't it just open the floodgates to an infinite number of matches? Not really. The wild card asterisk is generally used as part of a single keyword, not between keywords. Here's an example:

```
indian*
```

Typing that keyword instructs the search engine to find sites containing all words that begin with **indian**. Such words would include **indians**, **indiana**, and **indianapolis**. Using the wild card asterisk saves the time of typing multiple, similar keywords. It also saves the day when you're not sure how a word is spelled. But you can't use it in the middle of a keyword — only at the beginning or end.

Combining Keyword Operators

You don't have to select just one keyword operator to use in your search strings. The operators can be used in combination with each other, in many configurations. Here are some typical combinations.

✔ **AND and NOT:** Combining the AND and NOT operators makes a search very specific. When used liberally, you're basically giving the search engine some very specific instructions: *Search for this AND this AND this, but NOT this.* Here's a simple example:

```
cleveland AND indians NOT american
```

This example results in matches with sites about the Cleveland Indians baseball team, but not American Indians. However, it also excludes sites about the American League, in which the baseball Indians compete. You could make things even more specific this way:

```
cleveland AND indians AND american NOT native
```

This example would help sift out the undesirable sites, but as the search string gets longer, it's increasingly evident that using only the AND and NOT operators is a bit clumsy.

✔ **AND, NOT and ():** Adding parentheses to the mix makes your keyword string a more flexible tool. Now you can group keywords together in a way the search engine recognizes. Here's an example of what you can do:

```
cleveland AND indians AND tribe NOT (native AND american)
```

The word **tribe** is included in the above example because it's the nickname of the Cleveland Indians baseball team. By excluding both **native** and **american** from the search results, the intent is to include sites that match the word **tribe** in a baseball context, but not in a Native American context. However, note that sites will be excluded only if they contain both **native** and **american**, not just one or the other. To be more precise, you need to add the OR operator.

✔ **AND, NOT, OR and ():** Things can get quite complex when using all the major operators at once. But actually, it's fun to play with them, and sometimes the results can be very encouraging! Since getting the results of a search takes only a few seconds, it's worth experimenting until you feel comfortable with using search operators fluently. Here's an example of the possibilities:

```
cleveland AND (indians OR tribe) NOT (native or american)
```

This example delivers results that match with the Cleveland Indians baseball team, including references to their **tribe** nickname, but not sites that match with either **native** or **american**.

What *Boolean* is, and why you don't need to know

The common keyword qualifiers *AND, NOT,* and *OR* are derived from a kind of search logic called *Boolean,* and you may run into that word in your searches. Don't be thrown. *Boolean strings* are a specific keyword order (sometimes called *Boolean syntax*) that is used for sifting information out of large databases.

Knowing this arcane syntax used to be very important, but now it is less so, thanks to the user-friendly features of most Web search pages.

Most of them default to a certain assumed syntax that is sufficient for quick searches. (Usually the *OR* operator is assumed between words.) For more advanced projects, the search tools furnish drop-down lists that spell out how to link keywords effectively. Nonetheless, I've provided details on how to use the *AND, NOT,* and *OR* Boolean operators for less hospitable Web situations.

Be careful not to confuse the search engine with conflicting instructions. These engines are smart, but not so smart that they can figure out a mistake on your part. So, for example, avoid keyword strings like this:

```
cleveland AND (american OR league) NOT (native OR american)
```

What's the problem with this string? Since the keyword **american** is used in both parentheses, one of them under the AND operator and the other under the NOT operator, the command conflicts with itself. The search engine doesn't know whether to give you matches including **american** or excluding it. Your computer won't explode or anything, but you'll get mixed results.

Remember that not all search forms understand these keyword operators. If you enter *ANDs, ORs,* and *NOTs* in a form that is not prepared for them, one of two things will happen. The form will consider them keywords, or it will deem them insignificant and ignore them.

Search pages will notify you when you can use keyword qualifiers. Some pages even offer a quick online tutorial on their use. (Needless to say, the tutorial is not nearly as lucid and invigorating as the explanation provided here.) Other pages build the qualifiers into drop-down menu choices between your key-words.

Good keyword strategy takes into consideration other factors besides the operators. Many times, a quick search with the right keywords can get you what you want without resorting to AND, OR, and NOT. Choosing effective keywords is part common sense and part practice. Chapter 4 covers all the keyword bases. Next, take a look at what happens after the keywords have done their job.

Making Sense of Keyword Results

After you click on the Search button, your keywords and the search engine work together to gather a list of results. During this time not much happens on your screen, though you may see an inconspicuous progress report at the bottom of the browser's window. You won't have long to wait. In less than a minute, if all goes well, you see a new Web page that is filled with matches to your query (see Figure 3-6).

Taming the numbers

The most common problem in Web searching is getting too much information (see Figure 3-7). Typical keyword results are overwhelmingly voluminous, sometimes returning many thousands of matches. Using crafty keyword

Link to Web page

Rating of match accuracy

Summary of Web page

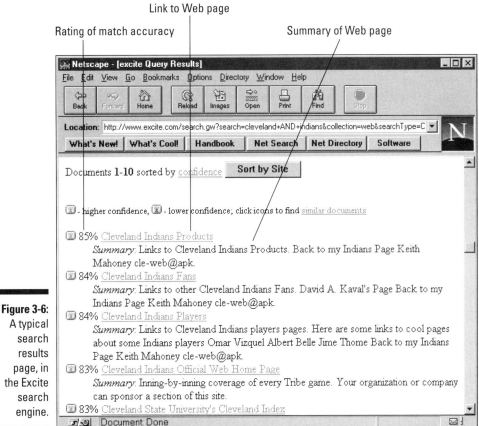

Figure 3-6:
A typical
search
results
page, in
the Excite
search
engine.

selections to narrow the search before beginning it is one way to cope. But
sometimes you want a truckload of matches for one reason or another. You may
need to narrow your focus by reading material on a broad topic before knowing
enough to search more specifically. Or you may just be in a browsing mood —
after all, searching doesn't always need to be serious business.

Most search sites will siphon large results to you in manageable amounts. There
may be a default limit of 20 or 30 matches per page, in which case there is a
hyperlink at the bottom of each page to bring up the next round of matches.
Often the results are sorted by grouping the best matches toward the top of the
list, making it unnecessary to look beyond the first page of matches. Such a size
limit per page prevents delays and is basically an advantage, but sometimes it is
undesirable. A few search engines enable you to choose the number of matches
per page from a drop-down list.

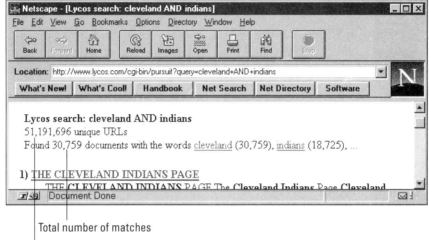

Figure 3-7:
Search
engines
sometimes
find
thousands
of matches.

Total number of matches

Number of pages in index

Hits and glancing blows

In search-speak, a match is called a *hit*. If you entered **cleveland AND indians**, a hit would be any result that contained both words. If you entered **cleveland OR indians**, a hit would be any result that contained either word. (The latter entry would generate many more hits.)

Not all hits are of equal significance or are equally useful to you. If, for example, you entered **cleveland OR indians**, some hits would contain one word or the other, and some results would have both words. Most likely, those containing both words would be more useful to you, and you'd want to see them first. Now if you entered **cleveland AND (indians OR yankees)**, all the results would contain either **indians** or **yankees**, along with **cleveland**, but only some would contain all three words. Again, the greatest number of word coincidences is likely to be of greater value. (Of course, you could always start a separate search on **cleveland AND indians AND yankees** to be sure of getting all three.)

Some Web search sites help you sift through the hits by grading their significance (see Figure 3-8). The sites do this with varying intelligence and according to differing criteria. Some simply count the number of keyword matches in each hit and grade the result. Others take into consideration the proximity of the keywords to each other. Another method notices where a matching keyword is located — in the document title or the body. Some engines determine whether the keyword is matched exactly or as a subword. (For example, entering **ski** would return matches of **skier** and **skiing** in some engines.) In all cases, the most highly scored hits are at the top of the list.

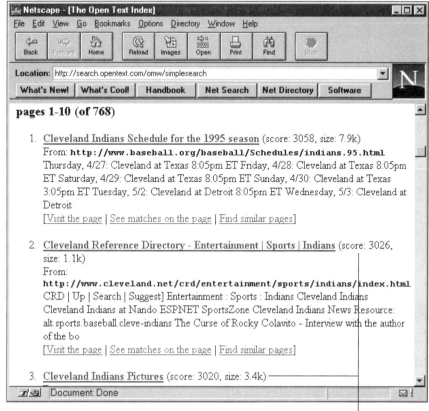

Figure 3-8:
Most search
engines
score their
hits, but you
can't always
tell how the
scoring
system
works.

Match score

You can sometimes decide how the results will be scored and sorted. That feature is nice, and it can free you to broaden your keywords because you know that you won't have to plunge through the lower-scoring matches toward the bottom of the list.

What's in those matches?

Figure 3-9 shows part of a result page from the Lycos search site. Though each service presents its results differently, they all have common elements.

✔ **Document title:** A *document* can be anything from a text file that's stored in an Internet library to a Web page. No matter what it is, the search result will just be a summary. The title sometimes corresponds to the document address (such as a Web URL), or it may carry a separate name.

✔ **Document summary:** The summary could be an abstract associated with the document, the first few lines of the document itself, or a short review stored in the search engine's index.

Document title and hyperlink   Site URL

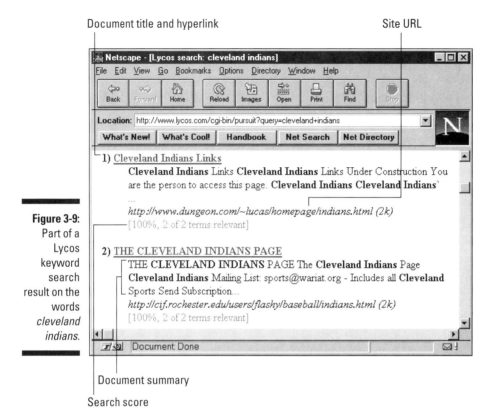

Figure 3-9:
Part of a
Lycos
keyword
search
result on the
words
*cleveland
indians.*

Document summary

Search score

- ✔ **Search score:** This score appears only in sites that grade their hits, of course.
- ✔ **Hyperlinks:** The hit would be worthless without some way of following up the lead. In the World Wide Web, that means one thing: a hyperlink that takes you directly to the site itself. The linked site could be a Web page, an FTP menu, or a newsgroup posting.
- ✔ **Address:** The Internet location, spelled out in case you want to make note of it without actually going there.

Following the result links

Most Web search engines are focused primarily on matches to World Wide Web pages. They build their indexes from those pages, and that's what you'll get in your matches. Some search engines, however, also take an interest in Usenet newsgroups and FTP file libraries. In those cases, you may get a mixed bag in your search results. Or, as a search feature, you may be able to limit the search to one portion of the Internet (such as Web pages) or another (such as Usenet).

Chapter 4

Keyword Tangles and Tips

Keywords are a terrific tool for searching the Web. Using them can save hours of fruitless searching through directories or spare you from seemingly endless unfulfilled surfing. They also can spawn confusion (occasionally), frustration (fairly often), and a distinct sense of being overwhelmed by the Web's hugeness (all too frequently). Three basic problems can emerge in a keyword search:

✔ No results

✔ Not the right results

✔ Too many results

Now, you may think that getting too many results is a happy problem, and indeed, it's better than coming up empty with a keyword search. But after spending an hour rummaging through screen after screen of search results, following links and returning to follow more, you'll want to find ways of narrowing the search right from the beginning. Of course, a blank result screen presents the opposite problem, and in that case you need to know how to broaden the search.

Ideally, the perfect keyword selection delivers a handful of results (25 or fewer is a manageable number), each of which is interesting, useful, or at least fun. You will rarely attain the ideal; but the closer you can get to it, the happier your trails will be.

Narrowing the Search

Most people begin searching casually, without putting a lot of thought into choosing keywords. Nothing is wrong with a hit-or-miss approach — a search based on a quick, general keyword entry usually provides a wealth of links to explore, as if a certain Web topic had been roped off for exploration. In most cases, the defined subject area is still too big for precise searching.

As an example, performing a quick search on the keyword **animals** provides results that would be either exhilarating or intimidating, depending on how much time you wanted to spend looking at animal sites. A recent test produced 42,009 links in the Lycos service, and Inktomi returned 95,815 hits (matched results). Those numbers would give even a dedicated Webaholic an overdose of surfing material. (By the way, a larger number of hits doesn't necessarily indicate a better service. Search results depend on how the service's index is organized and accessed. You may develop a preference for services that consistently deliver fewer hits, if they are also consistently more useful.)

At this point, having begun a casual search and having been most likely overwhelmed by the prospect of sorting through many thousands of results, the frazzled searcher would need to begin narrowing the field.

Picking a more specific keyword

This solution is the obvious one. Continuing with the present example and staying in the Lycos service that provided a generous return of 42,009 hits, the next step is to determine what kind of animal to use as the subject of the search. Entering **birds** in the keyword form begins the next round, and the results are narrower: only 20,134 hits. Anyone should be able to check out those links within a month, assuming no time out for meals. Getting still more specific, entering **cormorants** (a type of bird) brings 526 results. Definitely moving in the right direction. Sometimes, though, you need to use other ways to narrow the search.

Adding a keyword

Generally, adding a second keyword will reduce the number of hits in the search result. The second word is especially effective when the first keyword is ambiguous — that is, when it can have more than one meaning. If the first keyword is merely broad, as with an example such as **animals**, simply replacing the keyword with a more specific single keyword may work just as well.

If a searcher wanted to find Web information on state capitals in the U.S. and began casually by using the keyword **state**, that poor soul would probably be horrified to see 397,635 hits (in the Lycos service). However, by simply adding **capitals** to the search terms (the entire keyword phrase would be **state capitals**), the searcher would get a much shorter results list. Even more important, all the returned sites that match both **state** and **capitals** would be grouped at the top.

Using the AND operator

You often want to see only hits that contain *both* of your keywords. If sites containing only one keyword or the other are of no consequence to you, you may as well use the AND operator to eliminate them at the outset (see Figure 4-1).

Putting **AND** (or the symbol representing it, depending on the search service) between two words forces the results to match both words. All sites that match only one word will be excluded from the results. Using the state capitals example, forming a keyword phrase of **state AND capitals** in Lycos (**state + capitals** in some services) reduces the number of hits from 397,635 (for **state** alone) to 6. Not bad!

After experiencing the relief of seeing the results page shrink by thousands of hits, you may think that using even more keywords leads to cleaner, quicker searches. This outcome is true in some cases, but at some point, diminishing returns can reduce your search results to zero. Some search sites accept many

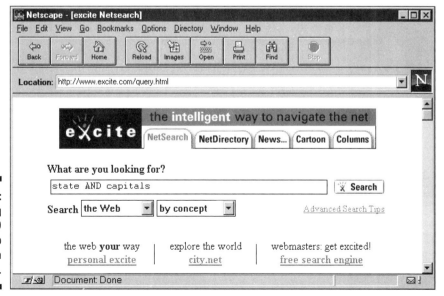

Figure 4-1:
Using
the AND
operator to
narrow a
search.

Finding where the AND lives

In order to use search operators such as AND, OR, and NOT, you must be at a site that accepts these search parameters on its keyword page. Fortunately, the major search engines do support search operators, but in different ways:

✔ Lycos offers a link underneath its main keyword form that is called <u>Enhance your search</u>. Click on the link to go to an enhanced keyword page that accepts operators. Or navigate directly to that page by using this URL:

```
http://www.lycos.com/lycos-form.html
```

✔ Yahoo! provides a link to an enhanced keyword form. The link is right next to the main keyword form on the Yahoo! home page and is called <u>enhanced</u>. The enhanced page, alas, supports only some of the keyword operators. Either link your way to the enhanced keyword form or use this direct URL:

```
http://www.yahoo.com/search.html
```

✔ Excite gives you a link called <u>Enhanced Search Tips</u>. This link takes you to a page of instructions that tell you how to use symbols for a few search operators. The direct URL is

```
http://www.excite.com/advanced.query.html
```

✔ Inktomi also provides a page of instructions and enables you to use symbols that represent the AND, OR, and NOT search operators. You need to scroll down the Inktomi home page a bit to find the link, which is called <u>Instructions for searching</u>. Or use this URL:

```
http://inktomi.berkeley.edu/query.html
```

keywords — Inktomi, for example, accepts up to ten keywords — but using more than three keywords rarely proves helpful, especially when you are using the search-narrowing AND operator. Forcing the service to find sites that contain three (or more) words doesn't produce many hits. Instead, having to match three keywords narrows your search into the ground.

Finding a new angle

In narrowing your search, you may reach a point at which the result list is satisfyingly short and reasonably relevant but not precisely what you need. If you use the **state AND capitals** search string, Lycos provides six hits, all of them seeming to be sites that provide broad information. All well and good, unless you're looking for information on the capital of California and you don't know what the capital of California is. In that case, if you tried adding **california** to the keyword list with the AND operator in place, the results would be imploded to absolute zero. (At least that's what happened to me, which just goes to show you that bad things happen to good searches.)

At this point, you need a new angle. Here's how to get it:

1. **Consider what you are really after.**

   Are you looking for the geographical location of the state capital? Are you looking for information on other cities in California? Do you want to learn about legislative processes and governmental files?

2. **Find a single keyword that embodies the new approach.**

   Examples are **government**, **geography**, **cities**, and **legislature**.

3. **Add the keyword, with the AND operator, to the main keyword that has gotten you this far.**

   California is the main keyword in this example. Using **state** as the main keyword and adding any of the examples in Step 2 would shift the focus away from **california** unnecessarily. The main keyword is not necessarily the broadest (**state**), but it is the one that is the most relevant (**california**).

Following this plan makes Lycos deliver a more targeted group of sites that is still in manageable numbers:

Keyword String	*Number of Hits*
california AND government	10
california AND geography	3
california AND cities	21
california AND legislature	8

NOT!

Using AND to require matches that include two keywords tightens a search field effectively, but in one situation the NOT operator is more to the point. You want to use NOT when you anticipate many matches that contain a word that is related to your keyword(s) and those matches are of no use to you. For example, if you were searching for travel sites in London, but didn't want to confuse the results with sites about the author Jack London, you could use the keyword string **london NOT jack** to solve the problem.

Don't be tempted to overuse the NOT feature. If you see it more than twice in a search string, chances are that you're overlooking a simpler way to get good results. If, for example, you want to see sites about the NASA space shuttle, Voyager, you might also remember that the spaceship in the popular space TV show, *Star Trek: Voyager,* has the same name. Trying to eliminate all overlapping sites, you might type **voyager NOT television NOT star NOT trek** . . . You probably won't nip all those sites in the bud, and furthermore, you can accomplish your goal with one elegant use of the AND operator: **voyager AND nasa**.

Widening the Search

At some point, you'll stump the system. Blithely, confidently, you'll enter a keyword or two, click on the Search button, wait a couple of seconds, and receive the following curt reply: "There are no matches to your search criteria." (Or rude words to that effect.) Nothing. Zilch. Or perhaps a straggling two or three sites when you expected dozens. At that point, it's time to widen your search keywords.

Using fewer terms

Just as you add keywords to narrow a search, you can shorten your string to broaden the search. (Unless, of course, you started with just one keyword.) Reducing the number of keywords usually is not a question of simple elimination; you need to rethink your search strategy. If you started with a specific person, location, product, news item, or other topic, you may have to think backward to figure out a good place to start. As an example, you may be looking for information on **Romanian folk dancing**, but **ethnic culture** may be a better starting point for a search. (In Lycos, the first string delivered no results, but the second search came back with 16 links.) From there, you can experiment with **ethnic romanian** and **romanian culture**.

Shorten your keywords

Many keyword services have certain default capabilities. Some of them can extrapolate longer words from short ones. A typical example is making a plural from a singular. Therefore, if the keyword is **cat**, the service will also return matches with **cats**. (Not to mention **cattle**.) However, the reverse is not true. You won't get **cat** from **cats**. (Or from a bunch of cows.) If you want to widen your search to get more results, try shortening all your words to their roots.

Returning to the search for Romanian folk dancing sites, if you change the search string from **romanian folk dancing** to **romania folk dance**, the search returns several right-on-target links. If you widen the search further by removing a keyword and entering **romania dance**, the list expands to a healthy, but not overwhelming, number of excellent and relevant site possibilities.

Getting flexible with OR

The great widening search operator is OR, which also happens to be the standard default operator for most keyword indexes. What does that mean? Simply that if you enter your keywords at the main home page without adding any operators, an OR will be assumed between every pair of words. The results will include any site that matches any *one* word, but not necessarily *all words*.

However, if you have set up a different default or have neutralized the assumed OR default and are punching in keywords with AND between them, you may be getting sparse results by forcing the service to match every word. Throwing in an OR or two can change all that in a hurry by enabling the system to return sites that match only one word.

The OR operator is also great for covering your bets when you don't know how to spell something or when a word has variant spellings. Simply type all your guesses separated by OR operators, and you'll get back all the links that match each of the words. If any of your spelling approximations are way off base, you won't get any matches for them (unless an equally bad speller put up a Web page). Not only will you find what you want, but you'll get a spelling lesson!

Hints for Better Hits

In all search situations, some basic guidelines can smooth your way. The ultimate goal of keyword searching is to get the perfect results page in the fewest possible attempts. Searching can be a kind of sport, and the more tips you have at your disposal, the better.

How insensitive!

Keyword searching services are generally, to use the standard technophrase, *case-insensitive,* which means that it doesn't matter whether you use uppercase or lowercase, even for proper nouns and names. You can use all uppercase, all lowercase, or mix the two crazily if you've really got time on your hands. The search index will not recognize the difference.

Taking your keywords elsewhere

Don't forget that whatever search index you're using, whether it be Yahoo!, Lycos, Inktomi, Excite, AltaVista, or one not featured in this book, there are other fish in the sea. Each service is different. They have differing indexes and use different methods of comparing your keywords to the index. If you're getting frustrated with the results at one place, try another! Sometimes, the quickest way to your destination is to get off the highway and take another road.

Getting fancy

If you're feeling adventurous and confident, you can really fine-tune your results by using the parenthesis operator (in the services that support it). Parentheses serve to group several words that you want treated in the same way by the search engine. There is usually another operator between those grouped words. An example is

```
food AND (bread OR wheat OR bakeries)
```

This string would return food sites that also contained a reference to *any, some, or all* of the words in parentheses. But it would eliminate all food sites that didn't focus on either baking or grain. You can reverse the results exactly with simple operator changes, like this:

```
food NOT (bread AND wheat AND bakeries)
```

Here, you would get all food matches *except* the sites returned in the first search.

You have to think carefully to use the parentheses operator. But then, what have you got to lose? Experimentation is a big part of searching — so give it a try.

Chapter 5

Yahoo! Keyword Searches

. . . .

. . . .

*W*hen Yahoo! burst upon the Web scene, this euphorically titled service lived up to its exciting name by providing the first popular way for Internet surfers to get a grip on the vast, sprawling terrain of the World Wide Web. Like a semi-intelligent weed-whacker, Yahoo! gave everyone a way to cut through the Web's tropical growth and find what they really wanted. Its directory provided a smarter browsing system, and its ability to accept keywords saved time for people who knew what they were looking for.

Other services have developed in the meantime, as Web searching evolves into a promising commercial venture. But Yahoo! has not gone the way of other innovative companies that make their mark, only to fall behind the field as others pick up the idea and run farther and faster with it. To the contrary, Yahoo! remains one of the most original, dynamic, and useful Web search tools. This chapter explores the ins and outs of using keywords for searches in the Yahoo! site.

Unlike some other search engines, Yahoo! doesn't search the full text of Web sites. Instead, it searches its own directory of the World Wide Web. The directory consists of Web page titles, sometimes with short descriptions provided by the page's designer. As such, Yahoo! is not a full text search engine. It matches keywords against all the words in its directory, but not against all the words in the Web sites that are represented by the directory. For full text searching, you need to use Open Text or another thorough search engine. (Open Text is described in Chapter 8.)

A Quick Search

You can begin searching with Yahoo! with just three simple steps:

1. **Go to the main Yahoo! Web page (see Figure 5-1) by entering this URL in your Web browser:**

   ```
   http://www.Yahoo.com/
   ```

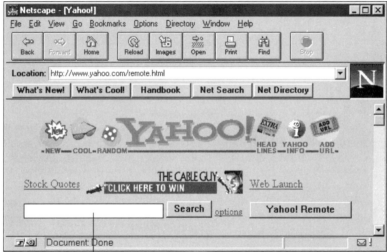

Figure 5-1: The Yahoo! home page.

Keyword entry form

2. **Type a keyword, or more than one, in the Search form.**

3. **Click on the Search button next to the keyword form.**

Within a second or two, a new page (called Search Results) appears on your screen, displaying (Surprise!) the search results (see Figure 5-2). If you used a general keyword, you'll get lots of matches. However, Yahoo! deluges you with only 25 results per page. At the bottom of the Search Results page is a link that, when clicked, displays the next 25 hits (keyword matches). And so on.

When you perform a quick search from the Yahoo! front page, the service tries to match *all* the keywords you enter if you enter more than one keyword. In other words, it assumes the AND search operator between each pair of keywords. Accordingly, the Search Results page does not display any links for sites that match only one keyword. Because you cannot overcome this default on the front page, the best thing to do is use only one keyword to perform a quick

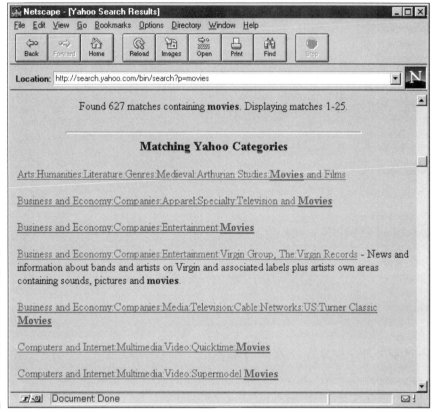

Figure 5-2:
The Yahoo!
Search
Results
page
displays
matched
keywords in
bold type.

search from the front page. This self-imposed restriction limits the precision with which you can search the Web, of course, and encourages serious searchers to proceed to the Yahoo! Search page by clicking on the <u>options</u> link on the front page. As you can see in Figure 5-1, this link is next to the Search button.

Yahoo! Search Options

Clicking on the <u>options</u> link takes you to the Yahoo! Search page (see Figure 5-3), where you can exercise more control over how your keywords are treated and conduct deeper searches within Yahoo!. The searches work the same way as a quick search from the main home page: You type in a keyword, or more than one, and click on the Search button. But the Yahoo! Search page offers four new ways to control your search. The four sections that follow describe how to use the four methods.

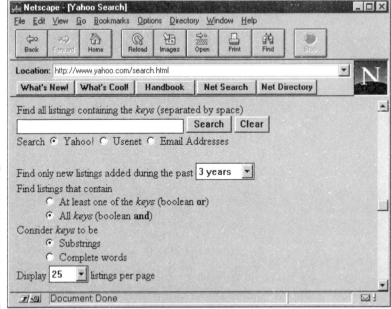

Figure 5-3:
The Yahoo!
Search
page, where
more
advanced
searches
begin.

Setting boundaries

Immediately below the keyword entry form are three search choices, representing areas of the Internet that Yahoo! can search for matches to your keywords:

✔ **Yahoo!:** This option includes the entire Yahoo! index of Web pages. Remember, Yahoo! searches only the titles of the Web pages, not the text content of the sites.

✔ **Usenet:** This area contains newsgroups — the bulletin boards of the Internet. Results of a Usenet search contain links to specific bulletin board messages that contain your keyword(s). This particular searching service is provided by Deja News; in Chapter 10, you learn how to use the entire Deja News service. Many of its features are missing in the Yahoo! version.

✔ **Email Addresses:** Entering a name (first or last) as the keyword when this selection is checked delivers a list of people with that name who have Internet e-mail addresses. Clicking on any name in the list will show you the exact e-mail address of that person. This service is provided for Yahoo! by Four11, an e-mail searching service that doesn't have Slurpees like 7-11, but which I nevertheless describe more completely in Chapter 19.

Choosing a keyword operator

Yahoo! is not as flexible with keyword operators as most of the other major services. Still, you do get two choices. When you enter more than one keyword and the system is comparing your words to its index, you can instruct it to find matches that contain the following:

- ✔ **At least one of the keys (boolean or):** When this selection is chosen, the Search Results page shows any match that corresponds with any one of your keywords or with more than one keyword. Only one keyword match is required to deliver a link to that site.

- ✔ **All keys (boolean and):** This selection requires the linked site to contain all your keywords. The Search Results page does not include any site that matches only one word.

To select either of these choices, position your mouse cursor over the small circle next to it and click once.

Don't be alarmed by the word *Boolean.* It's not a hideous reptilian sea creature. It is, however, a hideous system of organizing keywords by using a certain syntax. Keyword operators — or qualifiers — such as OR, AND, NOT, and others, are part of this syntax. Most keyword search services, such as Yahoo!, have saved you from the pain of learning Boolean syntax by using point-and-click systems that spell out your options. However, the word still crops up for the benefit of people who actually know how the Boolean language works.

A word is a word — or part of one

Yahoo! can use the keywords that you enter in one of the following ways:

- ✔ **Substrings:** When this choice is selected, all keywords are treated as potential word fragments, and Yahoo! matches each keyword with any site that contains the word's letters as part of a larger word. For example, it considers **auto** as a substring of **autos, automobile,** and **automobiles.** The Substrings option saves you the trouble of checking out each of those keywords individually, but it costs you time later because you have to sort through a much larger collection of matched sites on the Search Results page. Use the Substrings choice when you want to see a broad overview of sites on a particular topic.

✔ **Complete words:** This choice puts an unbreakable integrity into your keywords. Yahoo! reports only exact matches (including spelling mistakes, so watch out!). It does not assume that a pluralized version of your keyword is acceptable (**autos** for **auto,** for example). This option saves you time by delivering a shorter set of matches on the Search Results page than does the Substrings option, but it forces you to check several versions of a keyword in separate searches. Use this feature when you're pretty sure that you know exactly what you want.

Don't overwhelm me!

The last option on the Yahoo! Search page enables you to determine how many hits are displayed on each Search Results page. If you are in a bit of a hurry, nothing will slow down your browser more than receiving an enormous list of links in response to your keywords. The default number of hits displayed at one time is 25, but you can order Yahoo! to reduce that number to 10 or increase it to 50 or 100. If you are geared up for big search results, you may as well get them in big chunks and save the trouble of linking from one small page of results to the next. But if you're on the run, and want quick links to basically good Web sites, order up a small serving.

No matter how many links you command to appear on each search results page, Yahoo! will tell you how many total matches it has found. So you always know what lies ahead and whether you should be searching with more (or less) precise keywords — or perhaps forgetting the whole thing and getting a cup of cappuccino.

To use this feature, just click on the downward-pointing arrow next to the number in the box. A short list of options unfurls downward. Click on your choice and you're set. When you perform a search, the Search Results page shows only that number of matched links — a <u>next page</u> link will show you the next set.

Searching the Search Results

Whether you're on the Yahoo! front page or the Yahoo! Search page and anytime you enter keywords and click on the Search button, the next thing you see is the Search Results page. It is divided into two parts:

✔ **Matching Yahoo! Categories:** These categories are links to Yahoo! directory pages that are related to your keywords. Clicking on these links keeps
you within Yahoo! and takes you to a page of keyword-related Web links.

✔ **Matching Yahoo! Sites:** These links are to Web sites that are represented in
the Yahoo! index. Clicking on these links takes you outside of Yahoo! to a
keyword-related Web site.

Choosing Your Links

Yahoo! integrates its keyword service with its menu-based directory by connecting its search results to its directory pages. Every link that you get in return
for a keyword entry is associated with its Yahoo! location in the directory, as
shown in Figure 5-4. (The indented links lead to outside Web sites; the flush-left
links connect to internal Yahoo! directory pages.) You can click on a link that
takes you to a site outside of Yahoo! or on one that takes you to a Yahoo!
directory page, usually one that lists other related links.

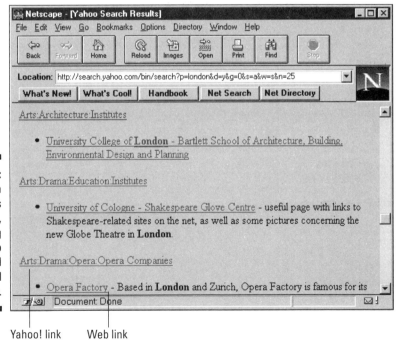

Figure 5-4:
The Search
Results
page,
showing
links to
internal and
external
Web sites.

Yahoo! link   Web link

A brief, one-sentence description heralds some sites returned in your search, giving you at least a slight indication of what to expect should you venture onto the hyperlink. Yahoo! doesn't spend its resources on elaborate reviews. Neither does it muster an evaluation of how good your matches are. Some services indicate how strong the keyword match is, how many repetitions of your keyword are found in the site, the degree to which all your words have been matched, or how closely (shown as a percentile) the site matches your search criteria. Because the Yahoo! index doesn't contain the full text of Web sites, all that evaluating is impossible. Hey, it's not fancy, but it is fast and useful.

Although Yahoo! lacks certain fine points that are becoming standard in other services, it has some strong features in its favor:

- ✔ It is highly accessible. I cannot remember a single time in my Web experience that I have encountered a stalled page in the Yahoo! site or been unable to get in, even during prime Internet time.

- ✔ The ability to restrict a search to only Usenet newsgroups or e-mail addresses is terrifically handy. Although Deja News enables you to search Usenet newsgroups and Four11 enables you to search for e-mail addresses, being able to access both of them from a common page is a convenient feature of Yahoo! However, to access all of the features of Deja News and Four11, you need to visit those sites.

- ✔ Altruistically, in a spirit of cooperation rather than competition, Yahoo! includes links for other search services at the bottom of its pages.

- ✔ The tight connection with its directory makes Yahoo! an integrated searching environment that enables you to browse and search from the same page. Because the Search Results page contains links back into the directory, as well as to pages outside of Yahoo!, you can easily explore the Web and the directory in the same session.

Chapter 6

Lycos Keyword Searches

. . . .

In This Chapter

▶ Using keywords in the Lycos search service

▶ Simple and enhanced Lycos searches

▶ Fine-tuning a Lycos search

. . . .

*T*he Lycos keyword searching service is a well-rounded, review-enhanced, speed-enabled, operator-capable site for finding stuff on the Web. And if that sounds like Greek to you (like the Lycos name itself), this chapter gives you the rundown on how it works and the steps that you take to use it. Everything begins at the Lycos home page. Surf there by typing this URL into your Web browser:

```
http://a2z.lycos.com/
```

A Quick Search

The best place to begin a keyword search in Lycos is at the Lycos directory, called a2z (see Figure 6-1). To begin using Lycos keyword searches right away, you need to follow a few basic steps:

1. **Direct your Web browser to the a2z page by using the URL shown previously.**

2. **Type a keyword, or more than one, in the Find box.**

3. **Click on the Go Get It button.**

After you click on the Go Get It button, Lycos searches the default database — the Lycos catalog database. In a few seconds, you see the results page, which displays links to all the sites that match your keywords (see Figure 6-2).

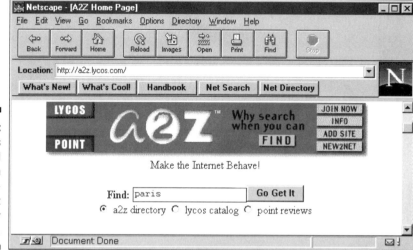

Figure 6-1:
The Lycos keyword search form at the top-level a2z directory page.

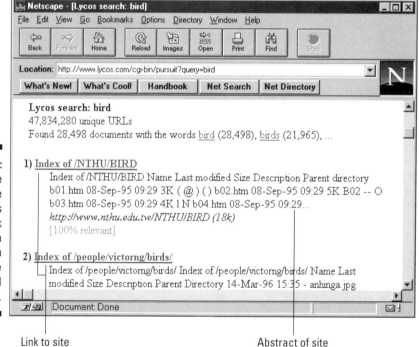

Figure 6-2:
Part of the result page from a Lycos quick search when you enter the keyword **bird**.

Link to site   Abstract of site

Each matched result has two parts:

- ✔ The link itself, which comes first. Click on it to go to the Web site it represents.

- ✔ An *Abstract,* which is a one-paragraph description of the site. The abstracts are not always terribly informative, as they are not written by the Lycos staff. Sometimes they're about as informative as a paragraph full of gibberish. But others are better — and the site itself is always just a mouse click away.

Choosing your source

Immediately below the keyword search form on the a2z home page, you can choose which of three Lycos databases the search engine will explore. When you first go to the Lycos site, the first of these databases is selected by default. But you can change the selection at any time, according to what kind of results you want. The following sections describe the three databases and explain what the advantages are to using each of them.

For some reason known only to the muse of Web design, the database choices are not available from the Lycos home page, but only from the a2z home page. Consider this aberration one reason to start your keyword searches from the a2z page, even though the Lycos home page has a keyword entry form.

a2z directory

The Lycos menu-based directory of Web sites is called *a2z.* This choice restricts your search to sites represented in the directory. The a2z directory does not necessarily contain all the sites found in the larger Lycos catalog for any particular topic or keyword. When you choose this selection for a keyword search, the results page contains links to both the outside Web site and the internal Lycos directory page that contains links to that site and to other related sites.

Why would you want to restrict your search? For one thing, linking to the Lycos a2z directory from the search results page is a cool feature that can open up your search by showing related sites (listed in the directory under the same general topic) that didn't exactly match your keywords. Also, the results page (see Figure 6-3) is cleaner, more compact, and easier to read than the one you see when searching the Lycos catalog.

Lycos catalog

The Lycos catalog is the basic and largest Lycos database. It contains the full text of many thousands of Web sites. It does not contain any text from the Usenet newsgroups (the Internet bulletin boards) or e-mail addresses.

Link to Web site

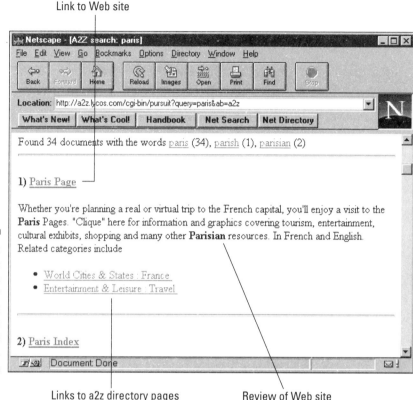

Figure 6-3:
Part of a
results page
after
searching
the Lycos
a2z
directory.

Links to a2z directory pages   Review of Web site

Using the Lycos catalog is the most complete way to do a quick search. However, searching the catalog is not a great advantage if you're overwhelmed with a huge number of results. Also, the Abstract paragraphs on the results page take up a great deal of room, they often aren't very helpful, and you can't eliminate them at this point. (You can eliminate them during an enhanced search, which is described later in this chapter in the section "Enhancing Your Lycos Search.")

Point reviews

Point is the Lycos magazine. It contains columns, entertaining information, and Web site reviews. You can integrate these reviews into a keyword search by choosing the third selection, point reviews. Lycos compares your keywords to every word in every Point review and displays the matches as a series of links. Click on any link to see the full review (one paragraph) for that site.

Lycos reviews only a fraction of the Web sites in the Lycos catalog, so this method of searching limits your results drastically. However, the advantage lies in seeing a review of any site you're considering visiting. The results page (see Figure 6-4) is clean, compact, and easy to use.

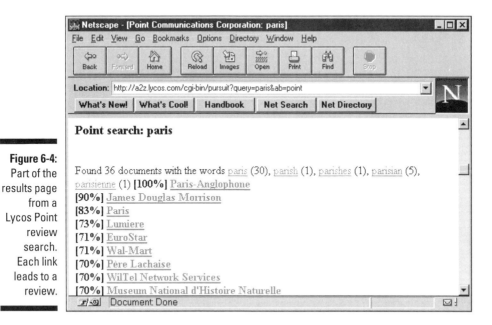

Figure 6-4:
Part of the
results page
from a
Lycos Point
review
search.
Each link
leads to a
review.

Try, try, and try

The best way to familiarize yourself with the three source choices is to simply give them each a try! Since a keyword search takes only a second or two, you can get a feel for each selection's pros and cons very quickly. Use the same keyword for all three searches so that comparing the results has more meaning. Here's what to do:

1. **On the a2z home page, make sure that the Lycos catalog selection is chosen by clicking once on the small circle next to it.**

2. **Enter a keyword.**

   Any keyword will do for this test, but make it broad enough to generate lots of results. Entering **paris** works well for comparative purposes.

3. **Click on the Go Get It button or press the Enter key of your keyboard.**

4. **Wait a couple of seconds for the results page to display. Tick . . . tick . . .**

5. **Check out the results page, noting what you like and dislike about having link information presented this way.**

   Are the abstracts useful? (See Figure 6-5.) Look at the top of the page to see how many results await you. Are you pleased to see so many possibilities, or do you want the system to narrow the list down for you?

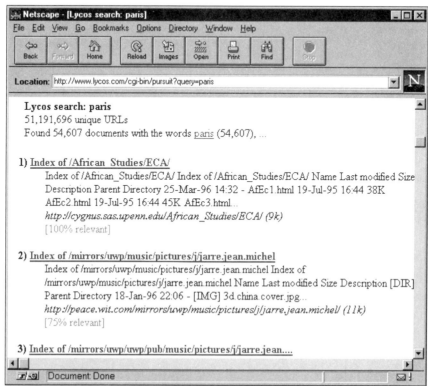

Figure 6-5:
In the Lycos catalog search results, the abstracts are not always useful.

6. **Click on the Back button of your Web browser.**

   You return to the a2z home page. Your keyword is still displayed in the keyword entry form.

7. **Select a2z directory and click on the Go Get It button.**

   (Because your first keyword is still displayed, Lycos will search with that word again.)

8. **When the search results page comes up, note the differences in layout and the type of link information you're given.**

   For one thing, the number of hits has been reduced by hundreds. For another, the descriptions are shorter, making the page more compactly informative. Try clicking on one of the directory links that's included with each site description. How useful will searching this database be in future searches?

9. **Click on the Back button to return to the home page.**

10. **Repeat the process by selecting the point reviews choice.**

11. **Scrutinize the results page.**

12. **Click on a link or two and read the reviews.**

    In some cases, some of the reviewed sites don't have much to do with your subject. Because the search compared your keyword with every single word in every Point review, some bad-context matches are bound to result.

Enhancing Your Lycos Search

Performing a quick search from the Lycos home page scratches only the surface of the options that are available to you. To dig deeper below the surface, you need to change your angle of approach into the Lycos service. Here's how:

1. **Go to the Lycos home page, which is different from the a2z directory page, at this URL:**

   ```
   http://www.lycos.com
   ```

2. **Click on the <u>Customize your search</u> hyperlink (see Figure 6-6).**

Link to customized searching

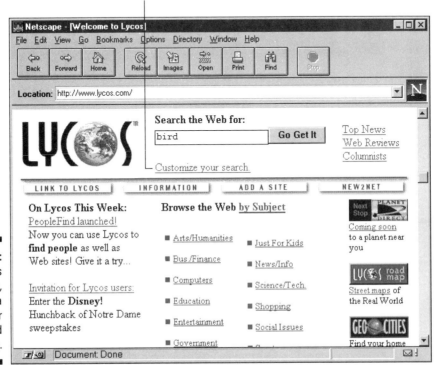

Figure 6-6:
The Lycos home page, which has a link for customized searching.

You also can scoot directly to the customized search page by using this URL:

```
http://www.lycos.com/lycos-form.html
```

When you get to the customized search page, you see yet another enhanced keyword search form that is bristling with options. These options enable you to tailor the results of your keyword searches.

From the customized search page, you are limited to searching the Lycos catalog, not the a2z database or the Point reviews. Don't feel deprived. The Lycos catalog is the largest of the three options, incorporating a2z and the Point reviews. Reviewed sites are mixed into your results, but you cannot restrict your search to them.

Getting a grip on your options

As you can see in Figure 6-7, the enhanced search page presents you with a form where you enter keywords and fields for two sets of options.

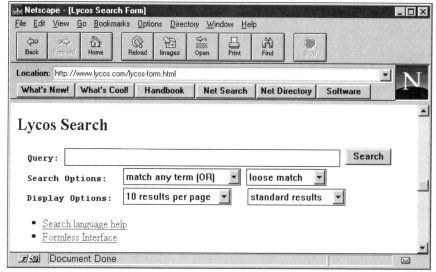

Figure 6-7:
The Lycos enhanced search options.

✔ **Query:** The *Query* form is where you enter the keyword or keyword string. It is called query, instead of simply keywords, because when you use the other options on the enhanced search page, you present Lycos with a more complicated search request than a mere keyword or two.

✔ **Search Options:** The Search Options enable you to select how the keywords will be interpreted by the Lycos system.

> ✔ **Display Options:** The Display Options enable you to tailor how the results page will look.

The first thing to do is become familiar with using the forms on the enhanced selection page. Fortunately, although you have several choices, making them is easy. Follow these steps to try out the forms:

1. **Click on any of the downward-pointing arrows in the forms for Search Options or Display Options.**

2. **Note how a list of options unfolds downward (see Figure 6-8).**

3. **Click on any item in the list to select it.**

Exploring the Search Options

The Search Options give you a handle on how Lycos will interpret your keyword string when you use more than one keyword and how exact it will be in forming matches.

Figure 6-8:
Clicking on an arrow causes a list to drop down with enhanced searching options.

Lycos interprets keyword strings using the standard keyword operators described in Chapter 4. These operators consist of words such as *and, not,* and *or.* When you place the operators between your keywords, these qualifiers tell the Lycos system how important the keywords are in relation to each other. Instead of forcing you to learn the actual words and the order in which they must be used, Lycos provides the first Search Options form. Click on the downward-pointing arrow next to the form to see these options:

- **Match any term (OR):** When you choose this option, Lycos provides matches to any one of your keywords, no matter how many you enter.

- **Match all terms (AND):** Choosing this option forces Lycos to find only Web sites that match every one of your keywords, no matter how many you enter. Generally, this option narrows the search results considerably.

- **Match any 2 terms:** Use this selection when you have entered three or more keywords. It forces Lycos to find at least two matches in a Web site before linking that site in the results page. In other words, any site on the results page will contain at least two of your words. This option narrows your search results somewhat, but not as drastically as does selecting match all terms (AND).

- **Match any X terms:** You can choose how many of your keywords need to match up. The list lets you choose to match 2 terms, match 3 terms, or more. Always choose to match *fewer* terms than the number of keywords you have entered, or you will confuse the system and make it whimper. Lycos will return only sites that contain at least the number of matches that you specify.

You can determine how exactly Lycos will match your keywords to the text of a Web site by using the second of the two Search Options. Click on the downward-pointing arrow next to the second Search Options form, and choose from among these self-explanatory selections:

- Loose match
- Fair match
- Good match
- Close match
- Strong match

Lycos does not divulge the exact formula by which it differentiates between these different levels of matching. However, you can see the results for yourself:

1. **Enter two keywords that are related —** seattle mariner **works well as a test.**

   The Seattle Mariners are a major league baseball team, but be sure to use the singular version of the second word in the test.

2. **Select loose match in the second Search Options form.**

3. **Click on the Search button or press the Enter key.**

4. **Notice the large number of search results.**

5. **Use the Back button to return to the enhanced search form, where your keywords are still displayed.**

6. **Change the second Search Options form to close match and click on the Search button or press the Enter key.**

7. **Note with satisfaction the reduced number of hits, presumably offering more precise links to your keywords.**

Why would anyone choose a Search Option other than close match? Primarily to broaden search results for very narrow topics. If you're having trouble finding matches to your keywords, selecting a looser match will relax the standards by which Lycos determines a match and result in more sites to visit.

Exploring the Display Options

The Display Options determine what the results page will look like and, as a result, the kind of information it will contain. Taking advantage of the Display Options can save loads of time and make the whole Lycos search process more comfortable because the results page is where you spend most of your time.

The first Display Option, results per page, is easy to comprehend. It simply defines how many links will appear on each results page. You have a choice of 10, 20, 30, or 40 hits per page. If the number of matches is greater than a page can hold, a link appears at the bottom of the search results page, taking you to the next page. Choosing a smaller number of results per page gives you quicker access to each page of results. But choosing a larger number is sensible when you know that the number of hits will be large and you want to see more links at a time.

The second Display Option makes a big difference in how the results page will look and in what it will convey. Here are your choices:

✔ **Standard results:** This is the default choice, which gives you a moderate amount of information about each link on the results page. Figure 6-9 shows part of a standard results page. Each site is represented by a one-line outline, a one-paragraph abstract, and a hyperlink to the site.

✔ **Detailed results:** Choose this option to get more detailed information about the matched sites (see Figure 6-10). In addition to the standard results information, you get a mysterious percentile ranking of how precisely the site matches your keywords, the number of links to outside resources contained in the target site, and a list of which keywords matched up with the site's text.

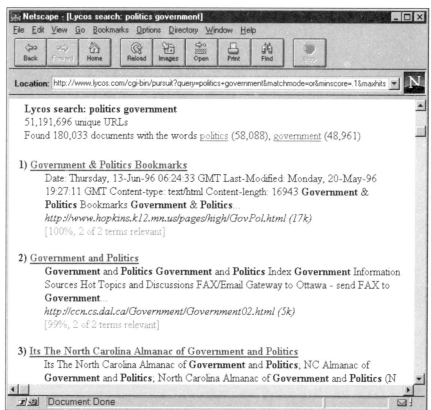

Netscape - [Lycos search: politics government]

File Edit View Go Bookmarks Options Directory Window Help

Back Forward Home Reload Images Open Print Find Stop

Location: http://www.lycos.com/cgi-bin/pursuit?query=politics+government&matchmode=or&minscore=.1&maxhits

Lycos search: politics government
51,191,696 unique URLs
Found 180,033 documents with the words politics (58,088), government (48,961)

1) Government & Politics Bookmarks
       Date: Thursday, 13-Jun-96 06:24:33 GMT Last-Modified: Monday, 20-May-96
       19:27:11 GMT Content-type: text/html Content-length: 16943 **Government &**
       Politics Bookmarks **Government & Politics**...
       http://www.hopkins.k12.mn.us/pages/high/GovPol.html (17k)
       [100%, 2 of 2 terms relevant]

2) Government and Politics
       Government and **Politics** **Government** and **Politics** Index **Government** Information
       Sources Hot Topics and Discussions FAX/Email Gateway to Ottawa - send FAX to
       Government...
       http://ccn.cs.dal.ca/Government/Government02.html (5k)
       [99%, 2 of 2 terms relevant]

3) Its The North Carolina Almanac of Government and Politics
       Its The North Carolina Almanac of **Government** and **Politics**; NC Almanac of
       Government and **Politics**; North Carolina Almanac of **Government** and **Politics** (N

Document: Done

Figure 6-9:
Part of a
standard
results page
from a Lycos
quick
search.

✔ **Summary results:** If you choose this option, you get a list of bare
hyperlinks with percentile rankings to indicate how precisely they match
your keywords (see Figure 6-11). Lycos doesn't divulge the formula by
which it ranks the accuracy of your matches, so you must take it on faith
that the search engine is grouping the best stuff near the top of the list. No
descriptions, abstracts, or statistics are presented. This option provides a
good way to see at a glance which sites match your keywords.

Hmmm . . .

With all these search and display options at your command, you need some
keyword strategies. Lots of experimenting, plus some basic tools, will put you
on easygoing terms with the Lycos enhanced search page in short order.

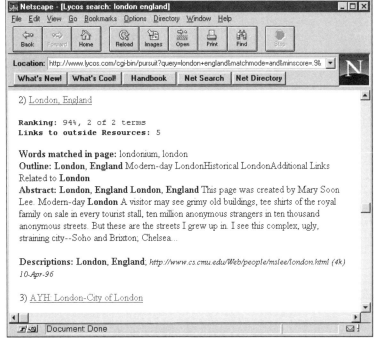

Figure 6-10:
A portion of the Lycos detailed results page.

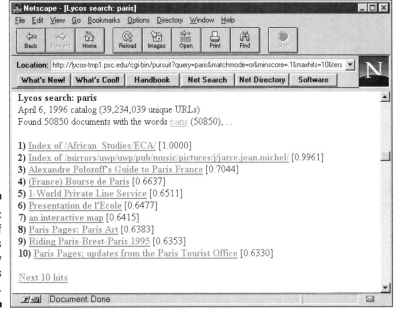

Figure 6-11:
A portion of the Lycos summary results page.

Starting big

One approach is find out how massive the Web is in the subject area that you want to search. It's sometimes better to start big and then narrow down. Here are some guidelines for the first stage of a wide search. (Figure 6-12 shows what these settings look like on your screen.)

✔ Use fewer keywords, rather than more. Don't try to narrow your search until you know what you're narrowing down from. Start with one or two keywords.

✔ Use the match any term (OR) Search Option. This option is the widest possible setting.

✔ In the Display Options line, select 40 results per page and summary results. This selection will give you the quickest overview of how overwhelmed you might be.

Narrowing down

Okay, you're overwhelmed! Unless you have a great deal of time for surfing huge lists of matches, you need to narrow your keyword commands. Figure 6-13 shows these settings:

Figure 6-12:
These Lycos settings cast the widest possible searching net.

Figure 6-13:
Set the
Lycos
search
options like
this to
narrow
down the
results.

✔ Use more keywords. If you're looking for sites about cars, add the names of actual automobile models, manufacturers, and years.

✔ Use the match all terms (AND) Search Option. Combined with more keywords, this option narrows the results drastically.

✔ Change the Display Options to read 10 results per page and standard results. You get more information about fewer sites per page — an appropriate selection now that you're honing in on better matches.

Fine-tuning

If you narrow down too much, you won't get any results at all. That's no fun. Widen cautiously back out using a combination of these tools (and check Figure 6-14):

✔ Take off a keyword or two from your string. Usually, three to five keywords will zero in on a good number of hits.

✔ Use the match *x* terms Search Option experimentally. Try selecting a number that is one or two keywords fewer than the number of keywords you have entered.

Figure 6-14:
These
moderate
Lycos
search
settings get
medium-
sized
results.

✔ Start using the summary results Display Option for fast results. This option enables you to slip back and forth between the enhanced search form and the results page with optimum speed, fine-tuning your search to get the right number of hits. Then you can change to detailed results to learn more about the matched sites.

Chapter 7
Excite Keyword Searches

. . . .

In This Chapter

▶ Searching by concept in Excite

▶ Doing quick keyword searches in Excite

▶ Using the Search Options forms

▶ Trying keyword operators with Excite

. . . .

*T*he Excite search service introduces a novel idea to the World Wide Web: searching by concept. Anyone who has spent some time entering keywords into a search engine and examining the results knows how literal the process is. It takes some effort to think of the best keywords — the ones that will lead the way to the best Web sites. Then, compounding the situation, are keyword operators, the AND, NOT, and OR words that fit between your keywords and help the search engine know exactly what you're looking for. (Keyword operators are described in Chapter 3.)

Enter the Excite search engine, offering a blissful promise: Just tell it in plain English what you want, and it will find it for you. No need to tangle yourself in keyword phraseology and operator syntax — a simple English phrase will do. Excite purports to deal in concepts every bit as fluently as it deals with literal keywords. Does it work? Yes. How well? That's up to you to decide because it depends on your needs. While you're finding out, Excite offers regular keyword functions, too, as well as a variety of surprising features that place it squarely in the forefront of Web searching.

The *concept* concept

How does the Excite search service, which after all is just a computer, understand concepts? Can computer software really stop being literal-minded long enough to be that smart?

The Excite search engine has a kind of learned intelligence that is based on how words work together. If certain words are often used in close proximity — such as *ice* and *cream* — they tend to imply a concept that differs from the meaning of either word separately. Furthermore, you can get the gist of that concept from the consistent proximity of words such as *eat, mouth, soft, dessert,* and *frozen.* Excite has been taught to recognize many different word groupings, and to recognize the concepts implied by those groupings.

In typical keyword searches, *synonyms* (words that mean the same thing) and *homonyms* (words that sound the same but have different meanings) can cause confusion. For example, the keyword **play** can have essentially the same meaning as **drama,** but the two words will not match when you are searching for drama sites. The keyword will match, however, with uses of the word *play* that mean *frolic,* which is an irrelevant match.

Excite gets around this problem by understanding words in context, according to a formula that takes word proximity into consideration. So if you enter the phrase, **plays by william shakespeare,** the Excite software may know enough to also link up pages that include the word *drama* close to the words *william shakespeare,* even if the word *play* isn't there. In this way, it strives to deliver search results that are based on concepts rather than on literal keyword meanings. Of course, in the competitive world of Web searching, each search engine's secrets are closely guarded, and this general explanation does not describe Excite's complex search formula.

Here's a concept for you: Try it! When searching by concept, the idea is not to think too hard. (Not thinking at all is my preference.) Type in what you're looking for as if you are telling a friend. Are you looking for pictures of the *Star Trek Voyager* crew? Type **pictures of the star trek voyager crew** into the keyword entry box. How about state senators in California? Just type the phrase in. You can be as conversational as you want, within the limits of a single phrase. If the results aren't satisfactory, you can always resort to more disciplined keyword searching.

Starting Quickly

The Excite home page is the starting point for concept-based Web searches. You get there by entering this URL into your Web browser:

```
http://www.excite.com/
```

The Excite home page (see Figure 7-1) presents its keyword form directly under the enticing and informal invitation, "What are you looking for?" You can test the waters in Excite immediately by following these steps:

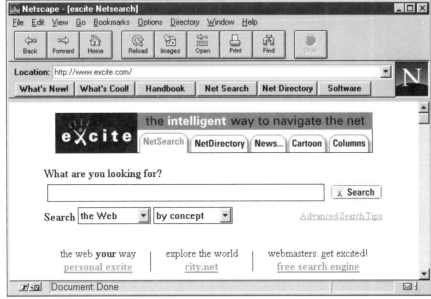

1. **Place your cursor in the keyword form and click once.**

2. **Type either a single keyword, more than one keyword, or a simple phrase describing what you want to find.**

   You can be informal and relaxed about keywords you use in Excite. When you first enter Excite, the search engine is set to respond to concept searches — you have to manually change it to accept literal keywords. So just type in any short phrase describing what you want, such as **low-fat cheesecake recipes**.

3. **Click on the Search button, which is next to the keyword form.**

A few seconds after you click on the Search button, you see the Query Results page, which lists your hits (see Figure 7-2). At this point, Excite has found Web sites that match any one (or more) or your keywords. Excite presents the sites that match your keywords in the order that the Excite search engine determines is most useful. Matches that correspond to more than one of your concept words are clustered at the top, as are those that match your words many times within the Web site. Each link is accompanied by a one-paragraph summary of the site and a percentage evaluation of the accuracy of the match. (Excite does not divulge the formula for determining hit accuracy, which it calls *confidence.* Just as well, since probably very few people would understand it.)

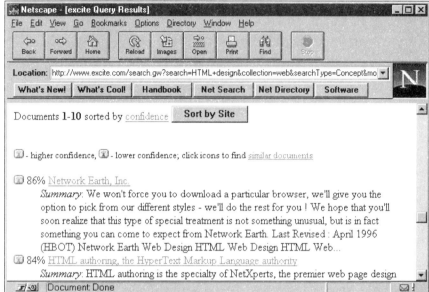

Figure 7-2:
The Query
Results
page
displayed
with the
Sort by
Confidence
option.

You can have Excite sort the Query Results page in two ways:

✔ **Sort by confidence:** This setting is the default. Your first search will sort the results this way, with the most confident links (presumably the most relevant and useful) at the top. What does *confidence* mean, exactly? Excite has a certain amount of confidence in the matches it gives you, based on how many of your keywords it matches, how many times each word is matched, and other criteria known only to Excite. During the course of several searches, you can decide for yourself whether Excite's confidence matches your own.

✔ **Sort by site:** When you choose this option, the confidence rating scheme is scrapped in favor of listing the matched Web sites in a directory style. Individual Web page links are grouped under the home page to which they belong (see Figure 7-3). In this fashion, you can see at a glance when multiple links all belong to a single, inclusive site.

You can switch between the two ways of sorting results by using the button near the top of the Query Results page. When *Sort by Confidence* is in effect, the button reads Sort by Site, and vice versa. Click on the button to switch from one setting to the other.

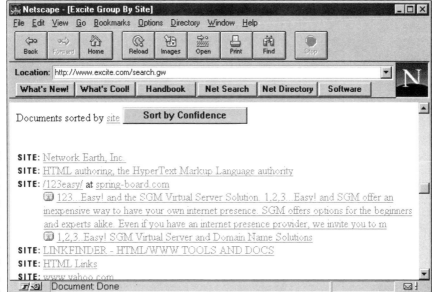

Figure 7-3:
The Query
Results
page
displayed
with the
Sort by Site
option.

Search Options

Simple, concept-based searching may get you where you're going by itself. If you need something more specific, or if you're a glutton for keyword punishment, Excite can give you a run for your money. (Not too hard, though, because Excite is a free service.)

The Excite search options are located below the keyword entry form on the home page. Two additional forms are located there, stocked with drop-down lists of selections (see Figure 7-4).

Where to search?

The first search option defines which part of the Internet you want Excite to search. You have four choices:

✔ **The Web:** This setting is the default when you first enter Excite. Your keywords are matched against Excite's index of Web sites.

✔ **Usenet:** Excite will search only the Usenet newsgroup postings if you want. (Usenet comprises the bulletin boards of the Internet.) If you choose this selection, the Query Results page displays links to Usenet message postings that contain your keyword(s). (Next time you're suffering from dreadful ennui, check out Chapter 10, which tells you how to search the Usenet more thoroughly.)

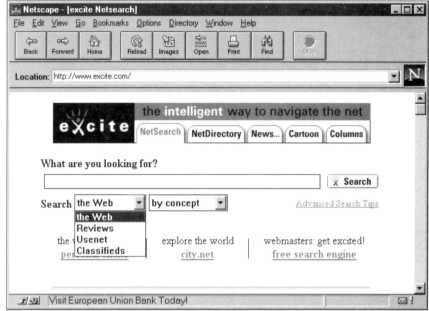

Figure 7-4:
The Excite
search
options are
drop-down
lists that are
below the
main
keyword
form.

✔ **Classifieds:** This selection is for a modified Usenet search. It compares
your keywords to the texts of Usenet postings in the many classified ad
newsgroups.

✔ **Reviews:** After you choose this setting, Excite limits the search to its
collected reviews of Web sites. The review database is smaller than the
total search index, but you get more critical information about any
matching sites.

Concept or keyword?

Even though Excite features its ability to understand phrase concepts and
search on them, it also accepts run-of-the-mill keywords. The default setting is
to search by concept. Change this setting by clicking on the small arrow next to
the second search option, and selecting the by keyword option. Excite will then
take a more literal approach to the words you enter. It will not extrapolate a
concept and try to match it.

After you select keyword searching, you can use the standard keyword operators. Here are your options and an explanation of how to apply them:

- **Using AND:** When you're entering more than one keyword, you can require the system to match all your words, not just one or some of them. Use the word AND in between the keywords, or substitute a plus (+) sign:

```
stephen AND king AND movies
```

```
stephen +king +movies
```

- **Using NOT:** Sometimes you may want to eliminate a word occurrence from your search, especially when you are using a keyword that might often bring up irrelevant results. When you anticipate such a word and want to eliminate results that contain it, place a NOT before the second keyword or use a minus (-) sign:

```
jazz NOT ragtime
```

```
jazz -ragtime
```

- **Using OR and parentheses:** You should use the OR operator when you want Excite to send back results on *any* of your keywords. Using OR gives you the most results of any of the operators. Using parentheses to group words — even when they are separated by other operators — narrows your search and gives you fewer results.

When you are using the plus and minus symbols (+ and -) in place of AND and NOT, don't leave a space between the symbol and the following word (which is the word the symbol refers to). The string may look a little weird, but what could be stranger than launching into cyberspace from your living room in the first place?

You can get very complex and technical with search operators. Sound like fun? I didn't think so. However, if you slip into an existential malaise, look in Chapter 3 for a complete tutorial on using search operators. It'll snap you right back to reality.

Chapter 8

Open Text Keyword Searches

*T*he Open Text Web searching site is aptly named, because it treats the entire World Wide Web like a gigantic cauldron of words. With the Open Text tools, you can search the Web for keywords as if it were a single immense text file. Open Text also shows that it has some smarts: It allows you to refine your search by narrowing it to certain portions of Web sites, such as the summaries, titles, or URLs. That feature may seem like Nobel-quality intelligence, but it sure comes in handy when you're trying to find the perfect *Star Trek* site (which is a big concern for most Nobel laureates).

Power and friendliness are nicely blended in Open Text. You can use keyword operators, but you don't have to know much about them — the system makes it all clear with drop-down lists that are built into its Web page. All in all, Open Text has emerged as a major searching service. Just keep reading along to find out how to use it.

Getting Started

The home page for Open Text is located at this URL:

```
http://www.opentext.com
```

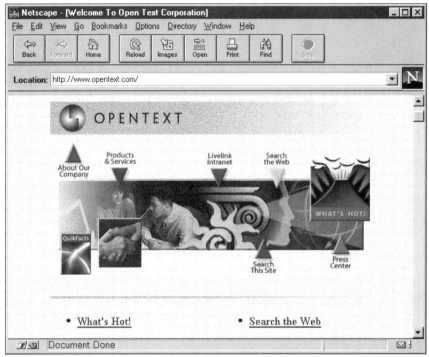

Figure 8-1:
The Open
Text home
page.

The page treats you to a lovely logo and links to the high points of the Open Text site (see Figure 8-1), but it's not a good place to begin searching. (Consider this a scenic stop.) To get to the first useful page, either click on the Simple Search link embedded in the Open Text logo or enter this URL into your Web browser:

```
http://www.opentext.com/omw/f-omw.html
```

Now you're in the right place. You can get a feel for the Open Text system by starting with a Simple Search.

You can try a search immediately by following these steps:

1. **Place your cursor over the keyword entry form immediately following the phrase "Search for these words" and click once.**

2. **Type one or more keywords.**

   For this test, the fewer keywords the better. Don't type a novel.

3. **Click on the Search button.**

In a few seconds, the search results page appears on your screen (see Figure 8-2).

Figure 8-2:
The search
results page
of Open
Text, after a
Simple
Search on
opera.

You also can perform a Simple Search by using a phrase instead of individual keywords. To use a phrase, return to the Simple Search page by clicking on the Back button of your browser and then follow these steps:

1. **Slide your mouse cursor over the small arrow next to the Search for these words box and click once (see Figure 8-3).**

2. **From the drop-down list that appears, click once on Search for this phrase.**

3. **Place the cursor on the keyword entry form and click once.**

   (It is now a phrase entry form, but it looks just the same.)

4. **Enter a phrase that you want to match.**

   As with individual keywords, keep it on the short side — like under five words. The more words you use, the harder it is to match them.

5. **Click on the Search button.**

   In a few seconds, you see a list of Web sites that contain your phrase.

Open Text is an extremely literal search engine. When you are using phrases, remember that the system treats every word in the phrase equally, even little

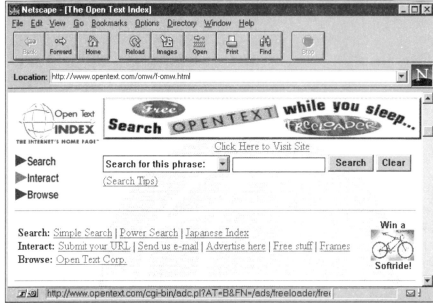

ones such as *the* or *and.* The results page may come up empty. As an example, this phrase recently produced no results whatsoever: **mission impossible reviews**. Open Text does not produce hits on sites containing only one of the words — it looks for the entire phrase. (The *Mission: Impossible* movie was one week old when this phrase was attempted.)

What's in a phrase?

You may have to play around a little to get the hang of phrases. The phrase **results of presidential primaries** turned up nothing in a recent session, but **presidential primary results** delivered 5 useful links. A broader variation, **primary election results**, made 12 matches. Table 8-1 shows some other phrase comparisons — they indicate that some experimenting is required to find just the right combination of words and that small changes make a big difference.

Table 8-1	Comparison of Search Phrases in Open Text
This Phrase Didn't Work Too Well . . .	*. . . But This One Got Good Results*
movies by woody allen	woody allen's movies
japanese tea ceremonies	japanese tea ceremony
airline disasters	airplane crashes
computers in the 21st century	computers of the future

These phrases all yield good matches:

- ✔ over the counter drugs
- ✔ hasta la vista
- ✔ trip down memory lane
- ✔ world series results

The trick to a successful phrase search is to think like a Web page designer. Imagine how you would write the phrase if you were creating a professional text document. If all this seems too cumbersome and you're not getting satisfactory results on your phrase searches, just switch back to keywords.

When you use the Clear button on the Simple Search page, your previous phrase disappears from the keyword entry form. In addition, the Search for this phrase selection reverts back to the default Search for these keywords choice. This sly change happens inconspicuously, and you may not notice it. Before starting your next phrase search, you have to reselect the phrase search option. Or, instead of using the Clear button, you can fool the page by just highlighting and deleting the phrase to clear the keyword entry form. Isn't it great that machines are so easily fooled?

Looking at Open Text search results

No matter what kind of search Open Text performs for you, it gives you one results page display. This is where you examine descriptions of the Web sites that match your keyword or phrase and decide whether to hyperlink your way to the site itself. The search results page presents only ten links at a time, and a notice near the top of the page tells you how many total hits await you. (There's an ominous phrase.) To see the next group of matches, click once on the More button at the bottom of any page.

You can always retrace your steps by using the Back button of your Web browser. You don't have to link to any Web site the first time it comes up on your screen. Instead, you can push deeply into the results of your search, clicking the More button to get a large overview of the search results, and then Back-button your way backwards to try out some links.

The results are laid out in a straightforward manner. You see the Web site title, hyperlinked to take you directly to the site; the HTTP address (URL) printed below the link; a one-paragraph description of the site, taken from the site's own text; and these three clever link options at the bottom of each item:

- ✔ **Visit the page:** This link works identically to the site title link. You can use either one to get to the Web site.

✔ **See matches on the page:** You can use this handy feature to see how your keywords match the text of the Web site.

✔ **Find similar pages:** Clicking on this link does just what you would expect. It brings up a list of Web sites that are relevant to your search but that do not necessarily match your keywords.

Opening Up Open Text

Simple Searches in Open Text are surprisingly productive, especially when you are searching on a phrase. But when you want to harness the power of the Open Text search engine and access its voluminous index in detail, you're ready for a Power Search. (The name alone gets your adrenaline flowing.) You launch Power Searches from a different page of the Open Text site. You can get there by clicking on the <u>Power Search</u> link on the Simple Search page or by entering this URL directly into your Web browser:

```
http://www.opentext.com/omw/xpowrsrch_c.html
```

You are now at the Power Search main page, and right away you can tell that it lives up to its billing (see Figure 8-4). It's bristling with boxes. Overflowing with options. Foaming with forms. But don't worry — all those choices actually make the index easier to search. Just read on to see how to do a Power Search.

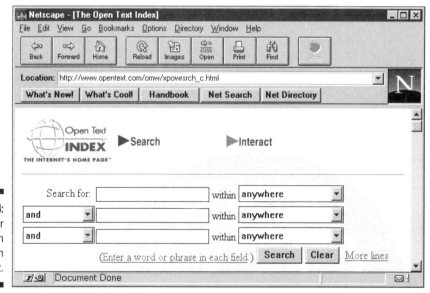

Figure 8-4:
The Power
Search
page in
Open Text.

The best way to approach the Power Search forms is as a single, continuous sentence. If you look at it that way, here's how it reads:

Search for: *[single keyword]* within *[portion of Web site]*

[and-or-near-but not] *[next keyword]* within *[portion of Web site]*

[and-or-near-but not] *[next keyword]* within *[portion of Web site]*

Everything within brackets in this example is changeable. Two sets of boxes already have something entered in them, as you can see in Figure 8-5. To make a different selection, click on the small arrow next to the box and then click on a new selection from the drop-down list.

Servers, domains, and other signs of feudal life

Open Text's ability to search only URLs in its index is pretty handy. Using this feature, you can bring up a list of every Web page at a certain multipage site. But to make sense of this feature, you need to know a few terms.

First of all, there are *servers*. Servers are not slaves. Well, they are in a way, but no human rights are being violated. A *server* is a computer that lives to service the requests of other computers (and the people operating those computers). Mainly, servers provide files upon request. The Internet (and the World Wide Web, which is a portion of the Internet) is really just a collection of servers that are sitting around waiting to be asked for something. When you visit a Web site with your browser, the server that contains the pages of that site receives a request from your computer to display the file for that page. It does so, and your browser displays the file in that Web-like way that browsers have. (Files for Web pages are called *HTML files* — for *HyperText Markup Language* — but you don't need to know that. Forget that I mentioned it.)

Second, there are domains. Domains are not empires. Well, actually, I'm wrong again — They are virtual empires. *Domains* are assigned designations that determine where in cyberspace a Web site is located. They are like cities in postal addresses. More than one domain can be on an Internet server, just as more than one city can be in a state. Not every Web site needs to have its own domain, just as not every street address gets its own city. A server holds several domains, each of which may have several Web sites — and each Web site may have several pages.

The *URL (Uniform Resource Locator)* links all this together. URLs point to individual pages within Web sites (which are contained within Web domains, which are housed on Internet servers). Just like a postal envelope, the URL spells out the entire address, so you can see the domain and site in which the Web page resides. The domain name is the part immediately following the `http://www.` that starts off most Web URLs. (Rarely, the three *Ws* are left off.) Here's an example of a URL:

`http://www.nytimes.com`

This URL is the address for *The New York Times* home page. The domain name is `nytimes.com`. An entire, vast site of pages is available by hyperlink from that home page, and each one has its own URL.

Deciding where to search

Locate the three boxes that have anywhere as the default option. Click on the top box and select from the following choices:

- ✔ **anywhere:** The default choice compares your keywords to every word of every Web site in the entire Open Text index. It is the widest possible search.

- ✔ **summary:** When you choose summary, your search is restricted to the summaries that Open Text has assigned to each Web site in the index. The summary texts are taken from the Web site itself; they are not newly created abstracts or reviews of the sites. In other words, they are not written by Open Text.

- ✔ **title:** This selection narrows your search even further by limiting it to the titles of Web sites. A Web page's title is chosen by the person or company responsible for designing the page. A few Web pages do not have titles.

- ✔ **first heading:** Choosing first heading results in some interesting searches! Open Text can compare your keywords to first-level headings in all the Web sites of its index. Choosing this option is a good way to eliminate matches that don't pertain to a main portion of a Web site.

- ✔ **web location (URL):** Choose this option when you only want to search the database of Web addresses. It's a good way to search for all the pages that are located on a certain server (Internet computer), if you know the server's domain name (such as usatoday.com).

Your selection in the top anywhere box affects only the first keyword that you enter (the one immediately to its left). You can set these fields any which way, without fear of confusing Open Text or tangling up the search engine with conflicting instructions. Of course, you may not get great results, either. The price you sometimes pay for complexity is a big, fat zero on the search results page. But a little experimenting, combined with a little foresight, can deliver compact, useful results when you use these selections to their fullest advantage.

Here's the rule of thumb for when you want to get fancy with an Open Text Power Search: Narrow down the big keywords and open up the little ones. To use this method, decide which of your words is likely to get the most results and then narrow it down by assigning it either a title or first heading area. Take your most specific keyword — the one likely to get the fewest results — and widen it by assigning it the anywhere selection. Figure 8-5 shows a successful search request using three keywords, each assigned to a different part of the Open Text database.

Operating with operators

Now locate the three boxes that show the word *and* as the default entry. These boxes help you use keyword operators (described fully in Chapter 3) with little or no pain — preferably none at all. You use these boxes only when you are entering more than one keyword. If you have typed (or will type) a second keyword, click on the first box that has the word *and* in it to select from these choices:

- ✔ **and:** This option is the default, and it forces Open Text to match *both* your keywords. Web sites that contain only one word or the other will not be included in the search results page.

- ✔ **or:** When you want to relax your requirements, this choice allows Open Text to match either keyword, but not necessarily both.

- ✔ **but not:** Here is a way to eliminate a keyword match-up. It's great when you want to search broadly, but also want to eliminate part of the anticipated results. As an example, you might enter **medical but not school**.

- ✔ **near:** This nifty operator includes both keywords if they are within 80 characters (letters of text) of each other. That's about 10 – 15 words.

- ✔ **followed by:** Similar to the previous choice, this one searches for the second keyword to fall within 80 characters *after* the first keyword.

Putting it all together

After you know how each of the boxes works, you can begin assembling some search strings. Start with just two keywords and experiment with the variables until you get good results. If you are extremely ambitious and brave and need to use more than the three keyword boxes provided, click on the More lines link (see Figure 8-5) to see a new page that has several more forms.

Here are some things to remember about using keywords in Open Text:

- ✔ The more keywords you use, the narrower your search will be. The exception to this rule is when you use the OR selection, which increases the number of search results.

- ✔ Enter only one keyword per box.

- ✔ Think literally! Open Text is more exact than some other search engines. It never treats words as portions of larger words, even when it comes to assuming plurals. Use the OR selection to cover your bases. For example: **sailing OR sailboat OR sailboats**.

- ✔ Experiment! Searching the Web should always be fun. Open Text gives you lots of tools to play with, so why not have a good time? Be prepared to find what you *didn't* expect.

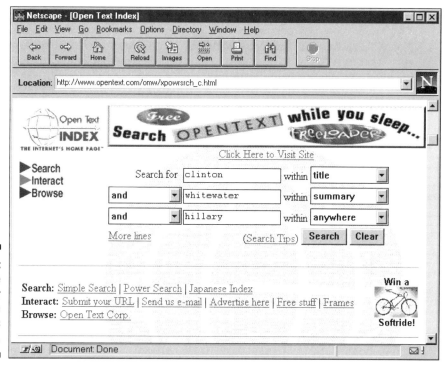

Figure 8-5:
Using the
Power
Search
fields
effectively.

Chapter 9

AltaVista Keyword Searches

AltaVista is a Web-searching service that is run by a company called Digital. It claims to use state-of-the-art hardware and software (with very impressive-sounding names, such as "scaleable indexing software" and "modular network hub"), and the service has certainly been scarfing up awards at a brisk pace. Divided into Simple and Advanced searching sections, AltaVista provides an exceptionally large number of search tools and options.

Simple Searches

Immediate gratification being a good thing, you can experiment with the AltaVista search engine right away by following these steps:

1. **Type this URL into your Web browser:**

   ```
   http://www.altavista.digital.com/
   ```

2. **When the AltaVista Main Page appears, type one or more keywords in the keyword entry form (see Figure 9-1).**

3. **Click on the Submit button to begin the search.**

Within a second or two, you see a results page that shows Web links that match your keywords. AltaVista searches entire Web sites, so the keyword match may occur in any part of the matched site's text. It could match in the page title or in a footnote way down at the bottom of the page. The search engine automatically places the "best matches" at the top of the list. How does it determine a best match, or even a mediocre one? Partly by counting how many times it

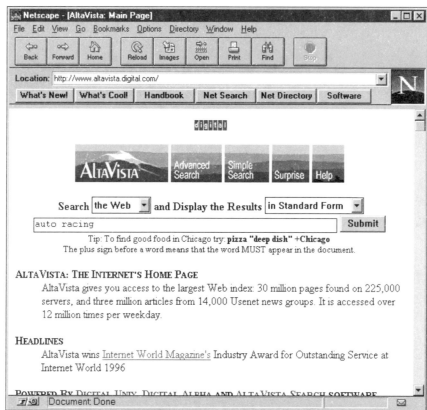

finds the keyword in the Web site and partly by looking to see where the keyword is located in the site. When the match is in the site's title or closer to the beginning of the site's text, the match gets a better score.

After a quick search, you see a results page that has links to matched Web sites (see Figure 9-2). Here are some things you should know about the results page:

✔ It contains only ten items, even if your search found more than ten matches. This limitation speeds the display process, and — just as important — prevents you from being overwhelmed by thousands of links all at once. You can link to other pages (each with only ten items) at the bottom of any results page.

✔ The keyword entry form appears at the top of every search results page. In effect, it "follows" you from the Main Page, where you began, to the results page. Sort of like a puppy. Having the form on the results page is handy: You can refine your search by entering new keywords without backtracking to the Main Page. Handier still, all the search options from the Main Page also followed along. So you can keep your keyword and switch

Figure 9-2:
Part of the
results page
in an
AltaVista
Simple
Search.

options without backtracking. And handiest of all, these options are paper-trained.

✔ Each matched item contains a site title, a brief summary paragraph, and a link address (URL). You can hyperlink to the site by clicking on either the link title or the URL, both of which are underlined in the traditional Web manner.

✔ Above the list of matched items, in very small print, is a breakdown of how your keywords matched. If you entered more than one word, here is where you look to see how many Web pages matched each word. Sites that matched *both* words are listed nearer the top of the results page.

Changing the results page

If you're happy with just a link, and can do without having a lot of information gumming up your results pages, you can view results in Compact Form. Follow these steps to choose compact results:

1. **Click on the small arrow next to the box where in Standard Form is selected.**

2. **From the list of selections, click on in Compact Form.**

3. **Enter one or more keywords and click once on the Submit button.**

Comparing the Standard and Compact results pages is easy. Just perform a search in either mode and then switch modes and submit the search again. You don't need to retype the keywords, but you *do* need to click on the Submit button. (AltaVista doesn't understand mental telepathy.) Using this method, you can switch back and forth a few times to see how the two modes differ.

The Usenet option

AltaVista can perform searches of Usenet newsgroup messages just as easily as it can search for Web pages. (Usenet is the bulletin board system of the Internet.) Here's how to switch into a simple Usenet search:

1. **Click on the small arrow next to the box where the Web is selected.**

2. **Select Usenet by clicking on it.**

3. **Enter one or more keywords (or leave your previous keywords) and click on the Submit button.**

Searching Usenet newsgroups brings up a different search results page (see Figure 9-3). From this nifty page, you can do the following:

✔ Clicking on the title of the Usenet message displays a copy of that message on your screen. Remember that seeing one message is different from reading a newsgroup from your news server: You see only the one message, so it is out of the context of the rest of the newsgroup.

✔ You can view of the message *in context* by clicking on the L column for the message. You then see a copy of the message from your local news server, instead of from the AltaVista archives. When you use this feature, the message is embedded with other messages from the newsgroup, some of which may be responses to the message.

✔ Clicking on the e-mail name of the person who wrote the message enables you to send e-mail directly to that person, right from your Web browser.

✔ You can view binary files (such as pictures) that are associated with the message by clicking on the B column for the message. Most newsgroups have no binary files to be seen. Usenet messages are mostly ASCII, not binary. Therefore, clicking on B usually just displays the message.

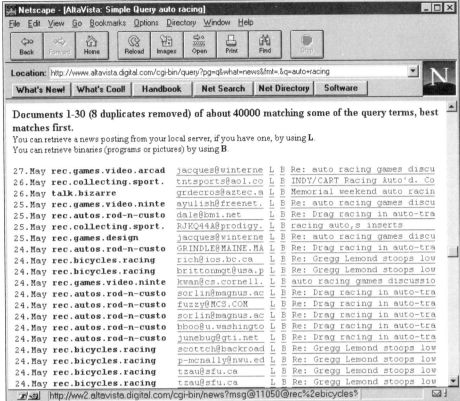

Figure 9-3:
The
AltaVista
results page
for a Usenet
search.

What details?

You may notice that in addition to Standard and Compact search results forms, there is a choice called *Detailed.* If you experiment, you may also notice that the Detailed search results page doesn't look any different from the Standard form when you are viewing Web site results. So what's it there for?, you ask with understandable irritation. Well, using the Detailed choice *does* make a difference when you are searching Usenet (see Figure 9-4). You can see the difference for yourself by following these steps:

1. **Perform a keyword search of Usenet.**

   Any keywords will do for this comparison.

2. **Click on the small arrow next to the box where in Standard Form is selected.**

3. **Click on in Detailed Form.**

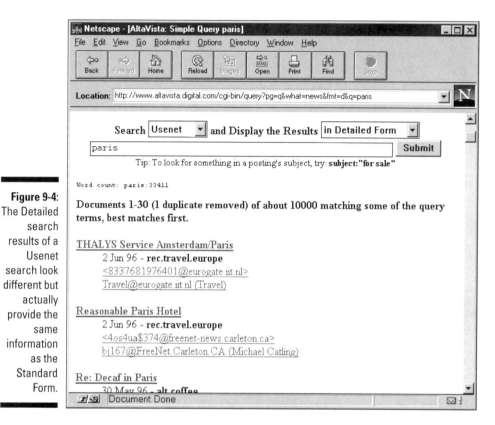

Figure 9-4:
The Detailed
search
results of a
Usenet
search look
different but
actually
provide the
same
information
as the
Standard
Form.

4. Leave your keywords in place and click on the Submit button.

You see the same search results as before, but in the new Detailed format.

Having choices is nice, even if they are purely cosmetic. The Detailed search results page, however, may be a complete waste of time. It expands the layout of Usenet search results but delivers the same information as the Standard search results page. It just looks less compact, which can hardly be considered an advantage since you have to scroll down the page more to see all the results. Still, a choice is a choice.

Advanced Searches

When the folks at AltaVista refer to an Advanced search, they're not kidding around. Even the keyword form is advanced (see Figure 9-5). To get a look at it on your own screen and begin learning about the options that are available, click on the Advanced Search button at the top of the AltaVista home page. You then see the Advanced Query page, which has an impressive array of multiple keyword forms. You can try out the Advanced Query page right away by following these steps:

1. **Click once in the large Selection Criteria box (that's just a fancy name for keywords).**

2. **Enter one or more keywords.**

3. **Click once on the Submit Advanced Query button a bit farther down the page.**

After you wait a couple of seconds, a search results page presents matched Web links to your keywords. Basically, you have just performed a Simple Search from the Advanced Query page. No problem. Now you can explore the additional options offered on this page.

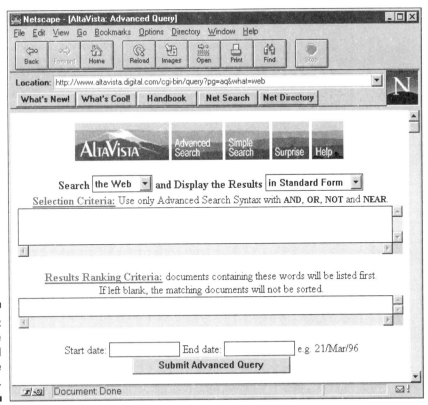

Figure 9-5:
The
Advanced
Query page
in AltaVista.

Advanced keyword options

Like other Web searching services, AltaVista enables you to incorporate keyword operators — the AND, OR, and NOT qualifiers that modify how the search engine interprets your keywords — into your search string. AltaVista also provides a couple of uncommon options that enable you to narrow your search in unusual and potentially useful ways. Chapter 3 sheds light on keyword operators in a general way. Here is how they work in AltaVista:

- **Using AND:** When you want to require the search engine to find matches to *all* your keywords, and not just one or two of a multiple-keyword string, place the AND operator between the words. The results page will list only links to Web sites that contain all your keywords. You also can use the & symbol.

  ```
  baseball AND cricket
  ```

  ```
  baseball & cricket
  ```

- **Using OR:** At other times, you may want to widen the search deliberately by allowing the results to match only one of your keywords. In that case, use the OR operator between your words. The results page will contain links to Web sites that match at least one keyword, and sites that match more than one keyword will be grouped nearer the top. You also can use the | symbol (the one that looks like a broken vertical slash on your keyboard and is often the uppercase choice of the backslash key).

  ```
  broadcasting OR radio OR television
  ```

  ```
  broadcasting | radio | television
  ```

- **Using AND NOT:** To use the NOT operator, you need to enter **AND NOT** when you are performing an AltaVista search. If you just use NOT, the system bounces back a blank results page, whimpers in confusion, and asks for "correct syntax." Use this operator when you want to exclude a word that would generate a match in irrelevant Web sites. You can substitute the ! symbol.

  ```
  magic AND NOT marker
  ```

  ```
  magic ! marker
  ```

- **Using NEAR:** This very useful operator ensures that two words or phrases are located within ten words of each other in the target Web site. If they are farther apart than ten words, a match will not result. Using NEAR provides a contextual aspect to your search. You also can use the ~ symbol.

  ```
  abbott NEAR costello
  ```

```
abbott ~ costello
```

✔ **Using parentheses:** AltaVista groups keywords together using parentheses so that you can use other operators within the parenthetical group. This way, you can create a subset of keywords that are interpreted differently from the way the other words are interpreted. AltaVista uses the parentheses search operator in a standard way, as described in Chapter 3.

```
animals AND (barn OR farm)
```

```
animals & (barn | farm)
```

Advanced display options

When you move to the Advanced Query page, one more display option is added to the Standard, Detailed, and Compact choices that are offered for a Simple Search. (Just what you need at this point — yet another option.) It is the *as a Count only* selection. (Hey, it's a Dracula option! Not really, unfortunately.) Choosing this option before your search creates a search results page that doesn't contain any links at all — just a number indicating how many links you would have seen with one of the other choices (see Figure 9-6). Why in the world would anyone want to do that? Well, the main reason is that this option is quicker than the others. The Count page zips up pretty fast, and you can see at a glance whether you need to narrow your search. To try it, just select as a Count only and click on the Submit Advanced Query button.

Ranking your results

AltaVista provides an innovative and handy option that enables you to determine how the results of your keyword search are ranked and, therefore, the order in which they are listed. This feature is tremendous, when you think about it, because it gives you a way to cut through voluminous results. If the best sites are near the top of the list, you don't have to burrow through hundreds of links trying to find them. Unfortunately, the feature has a terrible name: Results Ranking Criteria. The folks at AltaVista must have worked long hours to come up with the most unpronounceable, least memorable name for a terrific option.

As far as your search is concerned, *Results Ranking Criteria* basically means *Important Words.* This option takes some of the pressure off choosing exactly the right keywords. It also gives you a way to toss your results in the air and have them settle back down in a different order. Here's how it works:

1. Enter more than one keyword in the Selection Criteria field.

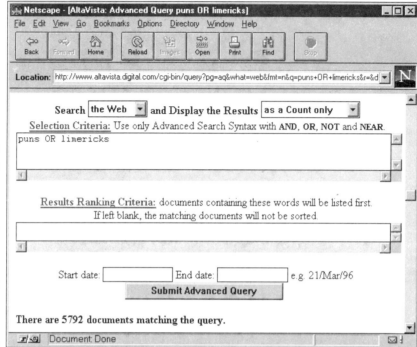

Figure 9-6:
You can
receive a
count of the
results list,
below the
keyword
fields,
without
actually
seeing
the list.

2. Enter a single keyword in the Results Ranking Criteria field.

For the clearest results, use one of the keywords that you entered in the Selection Criteria box.

3. Click on the Submit Advanced Query button.

On the results page, your hits will be grouped in the order you have determined — matches to your ranking keyword will be at the beginning of the list.

You can use the Results Ranking Criteria field when you use the Usenet search option. Just click on the Usenet option and enter your keywords exactly the same way. (Or leave the keywords in place if you've already used them to search the Web.)

Using the Results Ranking Criteria feature doesn't change the *results* of your search; it changes only the *order* in which those results are listed. If you don't put any words in the Results Ranking Criteria field, AltaVista simply doesn't bother to rank or list your results in any particular order. (Thanks a lot for nothing.)

Tossing your salad

Here's how to make the rankings useful:

1. **Enter three keywords in the Selection Criteria form.**

   Following the example in Figure 9-7, your keyword string is **vegetables OR sprouts OR seeds**.

2. **As in the illustration, type** sprouts **in the Results Ranking Criteria form.**

3. **Click on the Submit Advanced Query form to begin the search.**

   The results page indicates how many matches were found (about 60,000 at the time this was written) and presents a list of links with matches to **sprouts** at the top.

4. **Now change the word in the Results Ranking Criteria form from** sprouts **to** seeds **and resubmit the search.**

   (Leave your searching keywords intact.) The results page indicates the same number of overall finds, but the list is now in a different order — Web sites that match the **seeds** keyword come first.

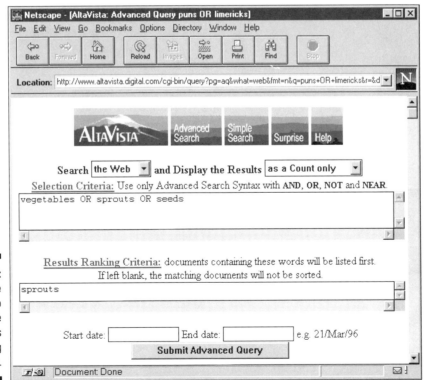

Figure 9-7:
An example
of how to
use the
Results
Ranking
Criteria.

In this way, like digging down to toss the cucumbers up from the bottom of a salad, you can reshuffle your search results and organize the results in various ways. The more words your search string contains, the more useful the feature is.

Adding a new ingredient

You can even use a ranking word that isn't part of your keyword string. Seem confusing? This method is a clever way to narrow your search and, with a little foresight, it's easy to use. Here's how, using a modification of the previous example:

1. **Enter the following search string in the Selection Criteria box:**

   ```
   vegetables AND sprouts
   ```

2. **Click on the Submit Advanced Query button.**

   The search results page informs you that about 2,000 matched Web sites were found, and it lists the first ten links to them. Each site contains both keywords, and they are listed by importance, according to how many matches were found and whether the keywords were found near the top of the site.

3. **Now enter** alfalfa **in the Results Ranking Criteria box.**

   You have asked the search engine to rank the search results toward matches of a word that doesn't appear in your keyword string. It stands to reason that the word *alfalfa* would appear in some Web sites that contain the words *vegetables* and *sprouts*. And you have slanted the results this way because you want to see sites that contain alfalfa information at the top of the list. (Also because you think that having *alf* appear twice in a word is peculiarly funny.)

4. **Click on the Submit Advanced Query button.**

   Your results come back with Web sites that contain all three words (**vegetables** and **sprouts** and **alfalfa**) listed first. Time to get the salad dressing.

Making dates

AltaVista has a few more tricks up its sleeve. You can, for example, define the dates within which it will search for Web pages. But what does this mean? Web sites do not have publication dates, as magazines have. However, the AltaVista software scours the World Wide Web repeatedly, indexing changes made to millions of Web pages. Every time it adds a page (or a modification to a previously existing page) to the index, it stamps the change with a date. You can determine a time range within which your search will be conducted. Here's how:

1. **After entering your keywords and ranking requirements (if any), place your mouse cursor over the Start date box underneath the keyword forms.**

2. **Type a date in Day/Month/Year format, according to the example provided next to the form.**

   You can abbreviate the month or not, as you like (see Figure 9-8).

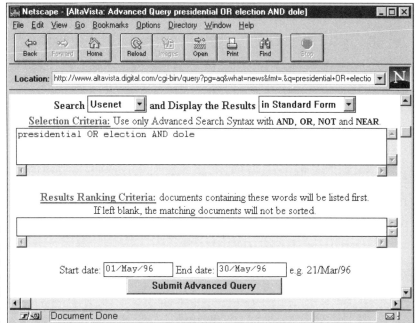

Figure 9-8:
Using the date feature in a Usenet search.

3. **Proceed to the End date box and enter another, later, date.**

   In most cases, it will be close to the present date.

4. **Click on the Submit Advanced Query button.**

   Almost always, the result will be fewer hits than if you left the date boxes blank, because you're restricting the search to a certain time period.

 Don't underestimate the date fields! This feature may not give you the same thrill as winning the lottery, but it is good for finding up-to-date information on topical subjects while avoiding the clutter of old Web pages. One of the big challenges of Web searching is narrowing down the results. And the other big challenge is finding high-quality results. When you're looking for up-to-date information, the date feature solves both problems by reducing your results list and limiting it to a certain time period. The odds of finding good Web pages suddenly becomes much better than the chance of winning the lottery.

You can use dates whether searching the Web or Usenet. But this feature's usefulness really shines when you are doing Usenet searches, because newsgroup postings are more time sensitive than Web pages. And there are more of them, so the need to narrow down search results is greater.

Constrain yourself

AltaVista provides a very specific type of searching that it calls *constraining searches.* If you think that I'm getting too technical, suppress that reaction. Constraining searches are not activated with drop-down lists or button selections. Instead, you simply type certain "tags" into the Search Criteria field on the Advanced Query page. Then you follow the tag with a keyword. The tag determines how the search will be constrained, and the keyword activates the search engine, as does any other keyword. Here's an example:

```
title:NASA
```

In this example, AltaVista would search Web page titles *only,* using the keyword **NASA**. The result would most likely be "constrained" to official NASA pages, instead of a large search result of all pages containing *NASA* somewhere in their text.

Using constraining searches does require a learning curve — and AltaVista doesn't make it easy by providing built-in selectors for the tags. But it's worth it! A constraining search tells the search engine to pay attention only to certain portions of the Web sites in its index. This feature can be very useful (upon occasion) if you remember to use it. The AltaVista search indexing software has already catalogued every bit of millions of Web pages — from their titles to their URLs, from their text content to the names of their downloadable graphic files. You can constrain your search to any of these areas. This tool is nifty when you want to find pages under a certain domain name or pictures that have a certain word in their filename. Here are some of the specific possibilities, listed by the tag that you use to activate them:

✔ **Finding pictures:** If you know the filename of a graphic and want to find it on the Web, you can constrain your search to image files by using the `image:` tag. Here's an example:

```
image:simpsons.jpg
```

In this example, AltaVista searches for all picture files in its database that have a `simpsons.jpg` filename. (JPG stands for a common type of picture file that is often found online.) Even if you don't know the exact filename, you can make an obvious guess that will generally yield results. You can substitute `.gif` for the file extension or leave the extension off completely. (The latter option increases the size of your results dramatically and takes longer to display them.)

✔ **Finding links:** If you know a Web site and want to discover other Web pages that link to it, you can use the `link:` tag. Remember, you're not uncovering links *from* a particular site, you're searching for links that go *to* a particular Web site from other pages. The keyword following the `link:` tag indicates the Web page that you want to find links *to*. This method is an unusual and fresh way of finding related sites. You'll get some surprising results! Try this feature with the following example:

```
link:whitehouse.com
```

In this example, AltaVista finds pages that contain hyperlinks to any URL that includes `whitehouse.com`.

✔ **Finding titles:** Just about every Web page has a title. Every self-respecting one, anyway. You can limit (constrain) your search to the words in World Wide Web titles with the `title:` tag. This method is good for obtaining a smaller set of search results than normal, usually containing highly relevant links. Try it with this example:

```
title:abortion
```

This example finds sites containing the word *abortion* in the title bar.

Using constraining searches in conjunction with the date feature is a dynamite way of finding current, relevant Web material. Just set the Start date for one month preceding the current date and the End date for the current date. Then type in your tag and keyword. After you get the hang of using the powerful constraining search feature, you may wonder how you ever lived on the Web without AltaVista. Then you will know, beyond all doubt, that you are a Webaholic. Welcome to the club.

Here's a little tip for all you Webmasters out there. (*Webmaster* is a politically correct, cyber-hip term for a person of either gender who has a Web server, or even a single page on someone else's Web server.) Use the `link:` tag to perform a constraining search on your own Web page. Keep in mind that this tag lists Web sites that link *to* the page represented by your keyword. Doing this kind of search is a great way to find out which sites have a hyperlink to your page. Just type your URL after the tag. This example is a model of how to do it:

```
link:www.yourpage.com
```

Surprise!

No tricks up my sleeve, actually. But AltaVista has a few in store for you if you click on the Surprise button on the Main Page. Use it when you're sick of searching with intelligent precision and just feel like gamboling randomly on the Web. It takes you to the Surprise CyberSpace Jump page — a minidirectory of unusual topics. Links such as <u>Comics</u>, <u>Galleries</u>, <u>Hobbies</u>, <u>Interviews</u>, <u>Parks</u>, and <u>Wheels</u> send you quickly off to Web pages that are scattered around cyberspace. This directory does not have a second level, so get ready for some random jumps around the Web.

A few final points, finally!

Just a few final words of wisdom to help you have a blast in AltaVista:

- **Don't capitalize unless you mean it:** Typing your keywords in all lower-case (non-capital) letters is safest. The search engine will match them with any identically spelled word in a Web site, no matter how it is capitalized in that site. So **clinton** will match with *Clinton* or *CLINTON.* However, if you use a capital letter, it will match only with identically capitalized words in Web sites. Therefore, **Clinton** will match only with *Clinton,* and not with *clinton* or *CLINTON.*

- **Making phrases:** You can turn any sequence of keywords into a connected phrase, which is necessary to avoid matching with every occurrence of the individual words. For example, you could turn *former soviet union* into a phrase to eliminate every Web site that has *former* and *union* in it. The two ways of making phrases in AltaVista are by removing spaces and by using quotation marks. Here is how the example would look in each case:

```
formersovietunion
```

```
"former soviet union"
```

- **Using the wild card:** Placing an asterisk after a word fragment tells the AltaVista search engine that you want to match results with every occurrence of that root word, no matter what the actual word. For example, you could search the Usenet for the following keyword:

```
legislat*
```

You would get results that match all the extensions of that root word, including *legislature, legislative, legislator,* and *legislation.*

Chapter 10

Deja News Keyword Searches

. . . .

In This Chapter

▶ How to search the Usenet newsgroups through your Web browser

▶ A simple query in Deja News

▶ Using the Deja News Power Search

▶ Learning how to use the Query Filter

▶ Making the most of the Query Results page

▶ Respecting privacy on the Usenet

. . . .

*W*eb searching sites are hot news and big business. When a new one appears on the scene, sporting some slick new way of indexing Web pages or a better searching interface for you and me, word spreads fast. There is a site that, in my opinion, is one of the greatest resources for finding information through your Web browser. It's called Deja News, and it specializes in searching Usenet newsgroups — the bulletin boards of the Internet, where anyone can post messages (called *articles*) on thousands of topics.

This news is only good news, of course, if you like the Usenet newsgroups and their discussion-based article postings. If one of these applies to you . . .

  ✔ You're a participant in the Usenet yourself.

  ✔ You want to take advantage of the Usenet's information resources without subscribing to many newsgroups.

  ✔ You'd like to establish e-mail contact with experts in any number of fields.

  ✔ You're bored and have picked up this book by mistake.

  . . . then Deja News is the perfect solution. Not only is it thorough and specialized, but it also provides all kinds of useful searching tools to get the right information quickly. The interface is a good one, too, so that even though there's a slight learning curve, you'll be tracking down articles and experts in no time. (Say good-bye to boredom and hello to geekish fascination.)

The First Query

You can get started right away, just to see how a basic search works. Here's how to begin using Deja News:

1. **Navigate to the Deja News home page (see Figure 10-1) by entering this URL in your browser:**

```
http://www.dejanews.com/
```

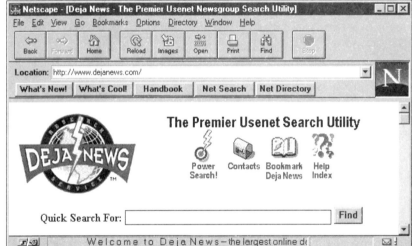

Figure 10-1:
The Deja
News home
page.

2. **Click in the empty Quick Search For box.**

3. **Enter one or more keywords.**

4. **Roll the mouse cursor to the *Find* button and click once.**

When you see the Query Results page (see Figure 10-2) on your monitor, you have a couple of simple choices:

- ✔ Click on any hyperlinked item in the Subject column to read an article that matches your keywords.

- ✔ Click on any hyperlinked item in the Author column to see a breakdown of that person's recent postings, sorted by newsgroup.

For each article listed on the Query Results page, three other columns give you information about that article, in unhyperlinked form.

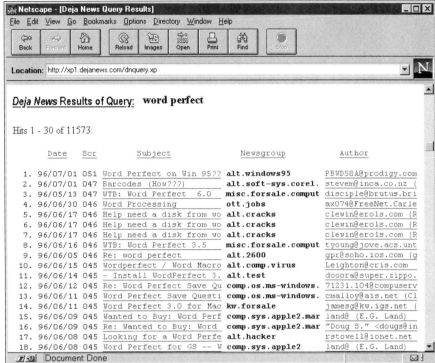

Figure 10-2:
The Query
Results
page in Deja
News.

✔ **Date:** This date is when the article was posted to a Usenet newsgroup.

✔ **Score:** Deja News assigns a relevancy score to each result hit, based on how well it matches your keywords. The score is raised by more matches, a high percentage of matches to the total word count of the article, and more recent posting dates.

✔ **Newsgroup:** This column identifies the newsgroup (bulletin board) in which the matched article was found.

You can get more information about each column on the Query Results page by clicking on the hyperlinked column headings.

The Power Search

When you're ready for more detailed searching, the Power Search icon at the top of the Deja News home page sends you to the Power Search page (see Figure 10-3), called the *Query Form,* or you can go directly there by entering the following URL:

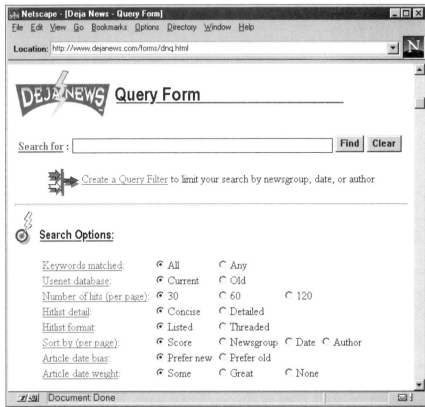

Figure 10-3:
The Query
Form in Deja
News,
where you
perform
Power
Searches.

http://www.dejanews.com/forms/dnq.html

On the Power Search page, you can enter one or more keywords, just as with a simple search from the home page. You get the same results, too, because the default settings on the Query Form match those of the home page form. The real action is farther down the page, under Search Options.

The main function of the Search Options, of course, is to confuse the heck out of you. Besides that, they control how the search engine interprets your keywords and how the Query Results page displays your matches. The interface for controlling these options could hardly be simpler (thank goodness), and you can try it out before beginning a new search. Just place your mouse cursor over the small circle next to any of the choices and click once. A black dot will appear in the circle, indicating that the item is selected. You can go back and forth among the selections as much as you want. The following sections explain the Search Options.

Keywords matched

The two selections for this search option are Any and All. (They sound like twins.) The Keywords matched option is one to consider when you are using more than one keyword. Choosing to match *any* of your keywords will search out articles that contain a single keyword or multiple keywords — but not necessarily all of them. If you want to require the system to match all your keywords and eliminate Usenet articles that contain only one or some of the keywords, select All.

Any and All are the equivalent of the standard search operators OR and AND. In fact, you can use those standard operators instead of clicking on Any and All. Just type the operator between your keywords in the normal fashion.

Usenet database

The two choices for this option are Current and Old. Your choice determines how deeply the search will reach into the Usenet archives. Usenet newsgroups are constantly evolving, with new messages being posted every minute of every day. Considering that there are many thousands of newsgroups and millions of people participating, you can see that the database of all this material can get enormous. You may not want or need to search through the entire thing.

Choosing Current reaches back about one month in time. The Old selection goes back about a year. Choosing to search the entire database results in many more matches, which can be an advantage or a drawback depending on how thorough (or compulsive) you need to be. The Sort by (per page) option enables you to sort the results in different ways, making it easier to make sense of them. (Keep reading, and you'll get to that option a little later in the chapter.)

Number of hits (per page)

This option is simple. It enables you to choose how many links will appear on each Query Results page. The default setting is 30 hits per page, but you can change it to 60 or 120. When the total number of matches exceeds your limit for a page, you can click on a link at the bottom of the page to see the next page. Each Query Results page adheres to your chosen limit.

Hitlist detail

Here, you can decide how the Query Results page will be formatted. Don't let your design sensibilities get carried away, though, because you have only two choices: Concise and Detailed. Predictably, the first option produces results that are more compact (see Figure 10-4). It compresses each hit onto a single line, requiring an abbreviation of some information. The Detailed version (see Figure 10-5) uses a few lines for each match, with everything spelled out fully.

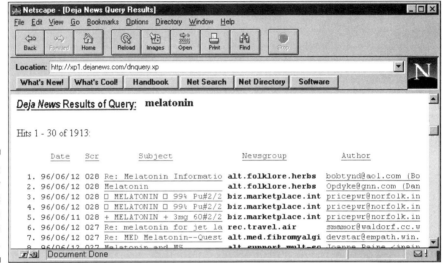

Figure 10-4:
The Query
Results
page in
Concise
layout.

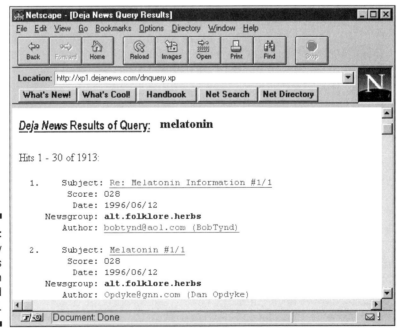

Figure 10-5:
The Query
Results
page in
Detailed
layout.

This option is worth experimenting with. Try performing searches first in one format and then in the other. You must decide whether the extra bits of information are worth seeing, at the expense of a space-saving presentation. Certainly, the Concise view shows you more hits at once, but it may feel overcrowded to you.

Hitlist format

Deja News lets you decide whether to view your search results as a simple list or as a *threaded* list. A threaded list links Usenet messages that are connected by the order in which they were posted in a single newsgroup. Usenet participants often post messages in response to previously posted messages. The response is connected to the original, and any further responses are likewise connected. The connection is called a *thread*.

Your two choices are Listed and Threaded. The first choice presents a list according to the evaluation score assigned to each hit by Deja News. (The evaluation is determined by how often your keywords match words in the article and how close the article date is to the present.) If you choose Threaded, the connection between messages overrides the evaluation score, and you see an indented menu of hits that reflect each article's relationship to other matched articles (see Figure 10-6).

Figure 10-6:
The Query
Results
page in
Threaded
format.

Sort by (per page)

This option is the most complicated Search Option, but with a little experimenting, you'll get the hang of it. You have four choices:

- ✔ **Score:** This choice, which is the default, gives you results that are listed in the order of the Deja News evaluation score of each match.

- ✔ **Newsgroup:** When this option is selected, the Query Results page lists matched articles by newsgroup (see Figure 10-7). All the matches from one newsgroup are clumped together, then all the hits from another newsgroup, and so on. The Deja News score determines which newsgroup goes first.

- ✔ **Date:** Use the Date option to sort your results in chronological order, with the most recent postings first (see Figure 10-8).

- ✔ **Author:** Here, the sorting priority groups together different matching articles from the same author (see Figure 10-9). The Deja News score sorts the list secondarily.

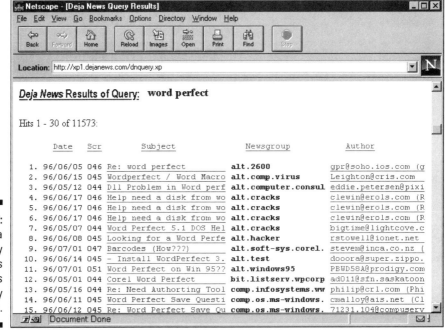

Figure 10-7:
A Deja
News Query
Results
page as
sorted by
newsgroup.

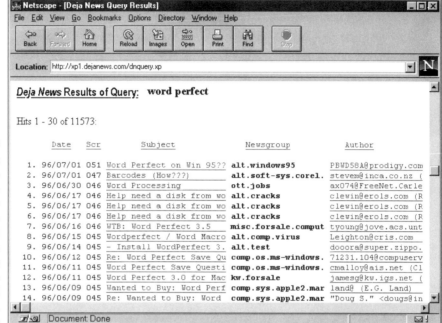

Figure 10-8:
When the results are sorted by date, the left-hand column shows reverse chronological order.

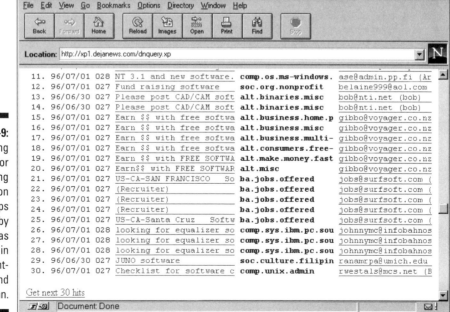

Figure 10-9:
Selecting the Author sorting option groups results by author, as shown in the right-hand column.

Article date bias

This Search Option enables you to set a preference that affects the order in which results are listed. Your choice here does not affect how many hits you receive in the Query Results page — only the order in which you see them. However, the Deja News score ranking still plays a part here, so you don't necessarily get a strictly chronological list.

The two choices are Prefer new and Prefer old. Use the first choice when you're conducting a topical search and the currentness of information is important. Whichever you choose, the effectiveness of this option is controlled by the next option.

Article date weight

You use this option to control how strongly the previous option is implemented. In other words, you can set how important the Article date bias is.

- ✔ Clicking on Great ensures a fairly strict chronological listing, either backward (when Prefer new is selected as the Article date bias) or forward (when Prefer old is selected as the Article date bias).
- ✔ Clicking on Some causes a moderate weighting of the Article date bias. The Query Results page is not strictly chronological.
- ✔ Clicking on None causes the system to disregard the Article date bias selection entirely.

The Query Filter

Now the party really begins! On the Query Form page, immediately below the keyword entry box, is the hyperlink Create a Query Filter. Click on it to go to the Query Filter Form, which is bristling with options and entry forms (see Figure 10-10). This form may look intimidating, but the learning curve really isn't that steep. Besides, the options on this page can narrow your search in a hurry. This page of the Deja News site is one of those great Web resources that come close to the ideal of finding a cyberneedle in the haystack. It's worth learning about.

Three of the things that you can do with the Query Filter Form are

- ✔ Filter out unnecessary newsgroups from your results
- ✔ Set a range of dates within which to search
- ✔ Limit the results to articles written by certain authors

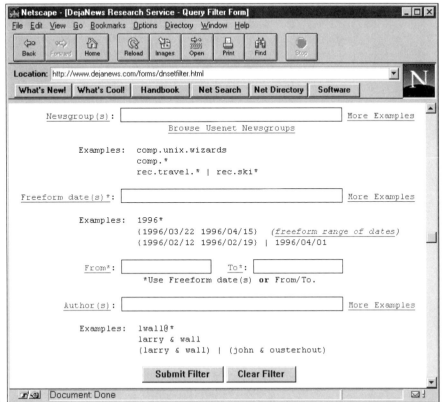

Figure 10-10:
The Deja
News Query
Filter Form.

Filtering newsgroups

If you are familiar with individual Usenet newsgroups, use the Newsgroup(s) filter to define which individual newsgroups (or groups of them) to search. If you're not familiar with the Usenet structure, you can still use this feature to define by subject the newsgroups that you want to search. In either case, you operate the filter by clicking on the Newsgroup(s) keyword entry form and typing your filter command. Here are a few ways that you can enter the command:

✔ **Specific newsgroup:** If you want to search the archives of a single newsgroup, type its full name in the form. Use all lowercase letters, include the periods, and don't put spaces between any letters. An example would be

```
alt.www.hotjava
```

✔ **Specific newsgroup directory:** Newsgroup directories are the first part of the newsgroup address, the part before the first period. The largest ones are alt and rec. If you want to see only articles from a certain newsgroup directory, such as comp for computer-related newsgroups, you can use the directory name followed by a period and a wild card character, like this:

```
comp.*
```

The result will be matches within the entire comp directory of newsgroups.

✔ **Specific directory and topic:** To narrow the search, you can determine a newsgroup directory and a topic within that directory, even if you don't know the names of specific topical newsgroups. Here's an example:

```
alt.religion*
```

This entry finds matches on all kinds of religious subjects in a fairly broad selection of articles from several newsgroups.

✔ **Specific topic:** If you don't know your way around the Usenet, you can simply specify a topic and place wild card asterisks on both ends of it. This kind of entry opens up the search to all newsgroups that contain your word in their name.

```
*movies*
```

When you get the results back, look at the newsgroups represented in the matches and make note of them. You can then narrow your search by inserting the exact name of a newsgroup in this filter.

Filtering dates

The Query Filter Form enables you to specify dates within which the system searches (see Figure 10-11). Any date that you enter must be in the year/month/day form, spelled out like this:

```
yyyy/mm/dd
```

You have two choices:

✔ **Freeform date(s):** Enter any single date in the Freeform date(s) box. Your selection can be as broad as a single year or as narrow as a single day. When entering a year within which to search, just type the year in numerals — nothing else. When typing a date, use the yyyy/mm/dd format. Here are examples of entering a single freeform date:

```
1995
```

```
1996/05/15
```

Figure 10-11:
Using the
Dates feature
to specify a
Usenet
search within
a three-
month period.

The first example searches the whole year, and the second searches only a single day.

You also can enter multiple dates in the Freeform date(s) field when you want to search the chronological period between two dates. But why do that when you can use the Range of dates field immediately below it? Good question, for which I know of no good answer. I suggest that you stick to single dates for the Freeform date(s) field and use the Range of dates field, which is described next, for searching a time period between two dates.

✔ **Range of dates:** Under the Freeform date(s) box are two smaller entry forms that are labeled From and To. Placing dates in these boxes defines a time range within which Deja News will search. Be sure that the From date is earlier than the To date.

Filtering authors

You can use this filter to search for a particular person's Usenet contributions. Knowing at least part of that person's e-mail address is helpful. John Edwards, for example, might have an e-mail name of jedwards, and you would need to enter that name to get matches on his articles. However, using the wild card asterisk gives you some leeway and enables you to guess somewhat. You could try `john*` at first, but that wouldn't work. Persisting, you might then try `*edwards*`, and that would work.

When guessing a person's "electronic" name, remember that an e-mail address is longer than just the name. Usually, e-mail addresses adhere to this format:

```
name@domain.com
```

The domain name that follows the @ symbol is part of the address, but you don't need to know it. Just use the wild card asterisk instead, and all the bases will be covered.

If you don't want to bother with wild cards or with guessing a person's e-mail persona, are you locked out of searching for a Usenet author? Not at all! Deja News permits you to type simple names, and it will do its best to find them. For example, to search for my newsgroup messages (though I can't guarantee you very interesting results), you could try this:

```
brad & hill
```

Since most of my e-mail addresses contain one of my two names, this search string would get results (assuming that I posted any messages within the time frame that you're searching). You can expand this type of search to more than one author by using parentheses and a vertical line to separate the authors. Here's an example:

```
(brad & hill) | (frederick & splatz)
```

In this example, *Frederick Splatz* is a fictional name, and probably doesn't yield any results. But if such a person did exist, you would find messages from both him and me. (Last time I checked, I was still a nonfictional person.)

CompuServe e-mail addresses present a problem because they are numbers, not names. CompuServe is in the process of changing its system of e-mail identity, but until that goal is finalized, you need to know the CompuServe ID number of people who post newsgroup articles with their CompuServe accounts.

The Query Filter in action

You can use any or all of the filter options simultaneously. Load up the Query Filter Form with commands and fire away.

1. **After entering your choices, scroll down to the bottom of the page and click once on the Submit Filter button.**

   The Query Form page appears on your screen again. This page is the main keyword entry page from which you linked to the Query Filter Form. You're returning to the page you left.

   The filter commands that you entered are now summarized just below the keyword entry form (see Figure 10-12).

2. **Enter one or more keywords that you want to search on.**

3. **Click once on the Find button to initiate the search.**

You also may want to fiddle with the Search Options. However, any filter dates that you enter neutralize the Usenet database option. The main thing to remember is that you can't make any serious mistakes, no matter what you do. If, for some reason, a search doesn't work, you can readjust your settings and push it through again. It makes more sense to click on that Find button without hesitation — don't labor too long over your options.

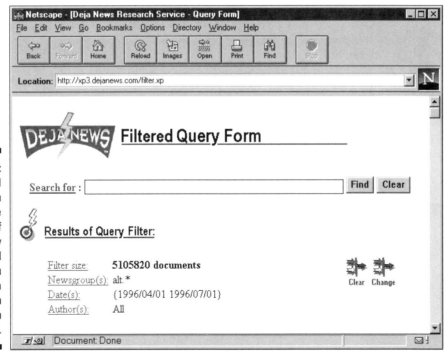

Figure 10-12:
The Filtered Query Form shows the result of your Query Filter, and lets you begin a search with the filter in effect.

Be careful of the Clear Filter button! Clicking it has the drastic result of wiping out everything that you've painstakingly entered in the Query Filter forms. (No, it doesn't clarify the Query Filter, sorry.) It's handy if you've made a few entries and now want to start fresh, either because you've performed your search or changed your mind. But other than that, don't let your mouse near it.

Exploring the Query Results Page

Unlike many results pages on other Web searching services, the Deja News Query Results page has several levels. This is because the result of a Deja News search is not a Web page, but a Usenet article posted by an individual on a newsgroup message board. As such, each item that's listed has three elements: the article itself, the newsgroup in which it appeared, and the author. Deja News gives you ways of exploring all three parts.

Reading articles

When you conduct a newsgroup search, you don't want to just know about Usenet messages that are relevant to your keywords; you want to read them. Here's how to do it:

1. Wait a few seconds for the Query Results page (see Figure 10-13) to display on your screen. The matched newsgroup articles are listed by title under the Subject column. Each item is hyperlinked.

2. Click on any article title and wait a few seconds for the Retrieved Document page to display.

The Retrieved Document page (see Figure 10-14) shows the newsgroup article, complete with the header as it would appear in a newsgroup reader. A toolbar of buttons across the top gives you a few choices:

✔ **Previous Article and Next Article:** Clicking on either of these buttons moves you backward or forward through the articles on your hitlist (the Query Results page from which you linked here). This feature is convenient for reading all the articles on the list without having to dart back and forth between the page with the article on it and the Query Results page.

✔ **Current Hitlist:** If you do want to dart back to the Query Results page, click on this button.

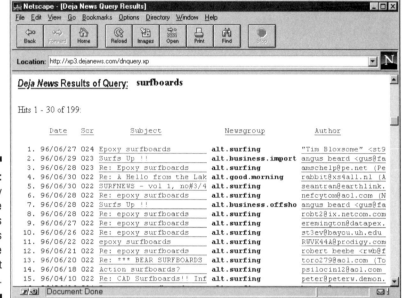

Figure 10-13:
The Query
Results page
shows
articles
under the
Subject
column.

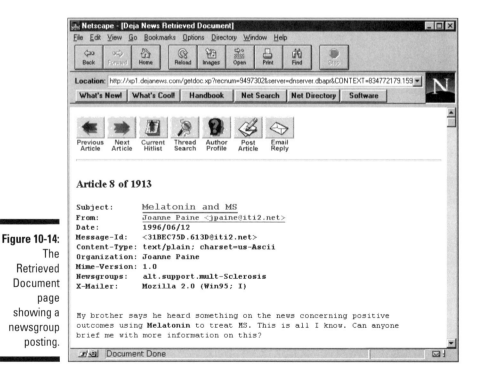

Figure 10-14:
The
Retrieved
Document
page
showing a
newsgroup
posting.

✔ **Thread Search:** Clicking on this button delivers to your screen a list of messages that are connected to the matched article that you're examining. If the matched article was posted very recently — say, within the past three days — you may not see much of a thread. Usenet postings take a few days to make it into the Deja News archive. However, for older articles, using this feature is a nice way to see related discussion posts that may not match your exact keywords.

✔ **Author Profile:** This feature is one of the most intriguing (and a little bit controversial) features of Deja News. (Why controversial? If you're interested, take a look at the sidebar, "Peeping [cyber-] Toms.") Clicking on this button (or the hyperlinked address of the author in the article header, just under the title) takes you to the Author Profile page, which lists a summary of all the Usenet postings of that individual, in every newsgroup he or she has participated in (see Figure 10-15). The list is divided by newsgroup, and clicking on any item sends you to a results page from which you can read any of those messages. This feature offers you a great way to read all the archived Usenet articles of an expert in any field.

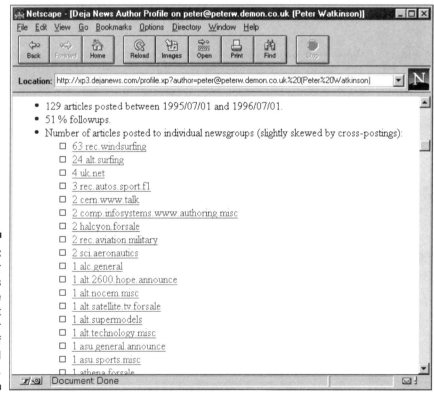

Figure 10-15: The Author Profile lists all the Usenet postings for the author of the selected message.

✔ **Post Article:** If your Web browser is part of an integrated suite of Web programs, clicking on this button opens your newsgroup window and automatically downloads the entire newsgroup in which the matched article appears. (The article itself may no longer be on the newsgroup bulletin board, if it was posted more than a couple of weeks ago.) Now you can write a message yourself and post it in the relevant newsgroup.

✔ **Email Reply:** This button pops open an e-mail response window in your Web browser, automatically addressed to the person who wrote the article you're looking at. If you send this person a communication, it will go to his or her private e-mail box and will not be posted publicly in a newsgroup. But be nice anyway.

Getting author profiles

You can go directly to the Author Profile page without stopping to read the author's message by clicking on the hyperlinked e-mail address under the Author column. As shown in Figure 10-15, the Author Profile page provides a list of the author's newsgroup contributions that are in the Deja News database (about a year), and enables you to hyperlink to individual messages.

Peeping (cyber-) Toms

No question about it — the Author Profile feature of Deja News is hip, cool, and useful. You can find people whose opinions you like and read all their messages, without having to scour several newsgroups to find them. You can track down experts in almost any subject and study what they have to say without drilling through endless discussion threads. So why are some people upset about it?

Deja News enables you to get a Usenet profile instantly on any individual who has posted a message in any public newsgroup. The profile doesn't tell you about that person's personal hygiene or political inclinations, of course, but it does tell you about the person's newsgroup habits. It shows where the person has posted messages and allows you to see them. You can then address e-mail directly to that person.

In most cases, this feature isn't a problem. But as Deja News becomes more well-known and more widely used, some people might be distressed to learn that anyone can track their messaging activity across all newsgroup subjects. A doctor who provides valuable information to a public medical newsgroup and also posts comments in a sexually-oriented newsgroup under a different screen name (but the same e-mail address) will most likely be upset if people are stumbling across that connection.

This feature is yet another aspect of the privacy issues that inflame opinion in the online world. What to do? Privacy is a community ideal that we each must respect individually. Be discreet with what you find in the Author Profile. Also, be aware that your Usenet activity can be tracked by anyone who comes across any single message that you author in a Deja News search. If you want some of that activity to be truly anonymous, use a separate e-mail address for it, and use it incognito.

Using the column headings

If you look on the Query Results page, you can see that the column headings are hyperlinks. Click on them to get instructions for using that column's contents. Of course, you don't need to do that because you've got this book by your side. But it never hurts to get onscreen help. Don't worry about my feelings. Really. I'll be fine.

A final tip

Just in case this chapter has left you with any unanswered questions — inconceivable though that may be — you can get personalized help from the folks at Deja News. Click on the Contacts icon at the top of the home page, and the Deja News Contacts page is displayed. At the bottom of that page are three e-mail hyperlinks. You can use them to do the following:

- ✔ Make a comment (about the weather, perhaps)
- ✔ Get technical help (but don't ask about your car's spark plugs)
- ✔ Report bugs (if you live in New York, don't bother reporting your cockroach problem)

Getting a personal response proves that humans actually exist in cyberspace.

Chapter 11
Other Useful Search Engines

*T*he World Wide Web is crawling with search engines. It's a race, really, to see who can create the best Web index, the most friendly user interface, and the most popular search site. Some of the chapters in this part of the book show you in detail how to work the search engines that are in the forefront of that race. This chapter rounds up a few of the others.

WebCrawler

WebCrawler began as a student project in 1994 and was one of the first Web search engines to appear. Though other companies have advanced beyond its basic functionality and appearance, it remains a solid search site, with a few especially useful features.

WebCrawler scores points for cuteness with its mascot, Spidey, who appears at the top of every page and is referred to in all the Help text. This cartoon spider presumably will keep you from being grossed out by a search service that's fashioned after a spider. To see the adorable arachnid in action, type this URL into your Web browser:

```
http://webcrawler.com/
```

WebCrawler is a service of GNN, a sprawling Web site and Internet service provider. The home page (see Figure 11-1) contains the keyword entry form. It works in the usual manner: Just enter one or more keywords in the form and click on the Search button. Above the keyword search form are two other forms that give you some choice in how the results are presented:

Figure 11-1:
The
WebCrawler
home page.

> ✓ **Summaries or titles:** Summaries, the default selection, provides search
>   results with summaries of each matched link (see Figure 11-2). The
>   alternative is Titles, which provides only the titles of Web sites that match
>   your keywords, hyperlinked to the actual sites (see Figure 11-3). To make
>   your selection, click on the small arrow next to the box and then click on
>   either summaries or titles.

Link for titles only

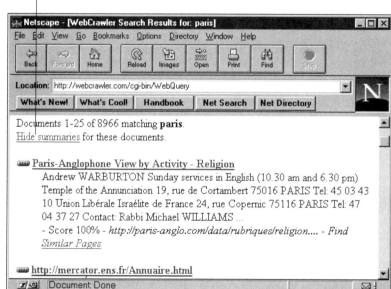

Figure 11-2:
WebCrawler
results
when
Summaries
is selected.

Link for summaries

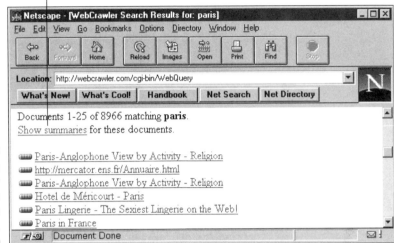

File Edit View Go Bookmarks Options Directory Window Help

| Back | Forward | Home | Reload | Images | Open | Print | Find | Stop |

Location: http://webcrawler.com/cgi-bin/WebQuery

| What's New! | What's Cool! | Handbook | Net Search | Net Directory |

Documents 1-25 of 8966 matching **paris**.
Show summaries for these documents.

- Paris-Anglophone View by Activity - Religion
- http://mercator.ens.fr/Annuaire.html
- Paris-Anglophone View by Activity - Religion
- Hotel de Méricourt - Paris
- Paris Lingerie - The Sexiest Lingerie on the Web!
- Paris in France

Document: Done

Figure 11-3:
WebCrawler
results
when Titles
is selected.

✓ **Number of hits:** You can make the search results page small, medium, or large by selecting 10, 25, or 100 matches per page. A button at the bottom of each search page brings up the next 10, 25, or 100 links when you click on it.

You can toggle back and forth between summaries and titles right on the search results page. When viewing summaries, click on the Hide summaries link; conversely, when viewing titles, click on the Show summaries link.

Like most other search engines, WebCrawler automatically uses an *implied OR* setting when you enter multiple keywords. The *implied OR* means that the search engine finds matches to any one (or more) of your keywords. It does not limit the results to matches of all your keywords. (That would be an implied AND.) Say you are searching with this keyword string:

```
michael keaton batman
```

WebCrawler interprets this string as:

```
michael OR keaton OR batman
```

Accordingly, it searches for Web sites that contain any of the words and brings up a huge number of matches. However, it has the smarts to group the best hits at the top of the list. What are the best hits? The ones that contain all of your keywords, as if you had placed the AND between them. Then farther down the list, sites appear that match two of the three words, while poor matches of only one word are near the bottom. A little bar graph appears next to each link, indicating on a 1–5 scale how accurate the match is.

The advantage to this system is that you can rattle off a few keywords without worrying about proper keyword syntax or using search operators such as AND, OR, and NOT. However, WebCrawler understands search operators if you care to use them. (They are described in detail in Chapter 3.) The usual AND, OR, NOT, and parentheses operators work well (you don't have to capitalize them), in addition to the following specialized operators:

✔ **Near/xx:** The NEAR operator enables you to specify the proximity of two words by specifying the maximum number of intervening words. That is, the two words must appear within a certain number of words of each other in either direction, and you specify the number of words after the slash. So, the keyword string **salad NEAR/10 dressing** matches Web sites that contain phrases such as, "A salad should always be topped with dressing" and "Dressing often makes a salad better."

✔ **ADJ:** This operator requires Web pages to contain two keywords right next to each other, in the same order that you entered them. For example, the search string **wall ADJ street** matches only sites containing those two words exactly as written. It does not match with Web sites that contain simple instances of either word by itself.

✔ **Quotes:** Using quotation marks to surround a phrase keeps that phrase intact and literal for matching purposes. This operator enables you to search for specific and complex combinations of words, such as **sexual harassment in the workplace**, without turning up miscellaneous hits on sites that contain the individual words. Of course, this operator limits your search results drastically, but it is very helpful when you search for document titles and logos.

Inktomi

You may be wondering where in the world this strange name came from. *Inktomi* is a Native American word for a mythological spider. This clever reference takes on significance when you consider that many search indexes are called spiders or crawlers. You can also remember it as a play on the words *ink to me,* except that there's no ink in cyberspace . . . so never mind.

Inktomi began as a project of the University of California at Berkeley and is evolving into a full-featured commercial service. For now, it's open to the public and uses something called *scalable Web server* technology. Basically, as far as the user is concerned, this description means that Inktomi can handle great amounts of traffic while delivering good, fast performance.

Inktomi keywords

You can enter keywords on the Inktomi home page. Go there by using this URL in your Web browser:

```
http://inktomi.berkeley.edu/
```

The keyword entry form is near the top of the home page (see Figure 11-4). Simply click on it, type in one or more keywords, and click on the Start Search! button. Inktomi accepts up to ten keywords, which should be enough for even the most specific quest. The forms under the keyword form give you a few choices:

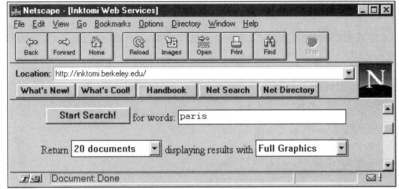

Figure 11-4:
The Inktomi
keyword
entry form.

✔ **How many documents?** When you first arrive on the page, the number of documents is set to 20. The search results page will show you only the first 20 matches on your search. You can change this entry to 10, 30, 50, or 100. Just click on the small arrow next to the window and click again on your selection from the drop-down list.

✔ **Display format:** Here is where you determine what the search results page looks like. The automatic selection is Text Only. This selection gives you a one-paragraph description of each link that matches your keywords. (The paragraphs are written by the remote Web site, not by the Inktomi staff.) Choosing Full Graphics gives you everything in Text Only mode, plus cute little blue ovals that indicate how strong a match each link is (see Figure 11-5). Considering the delay that using graphics causes in the display of the search results page, Full Graphics may not be worth selecting. The Terse Text Only choice (not the same as Text Only) gives you a raw list of links (see Figure 11-6).

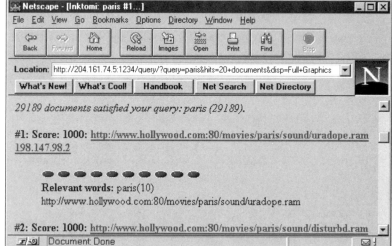

Figure 11-5:
Inktomi search results with Full Graphics.

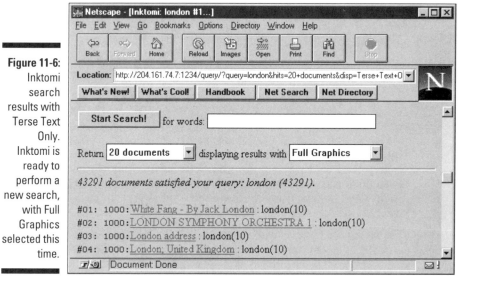

Figure 11-6:
Inktomi search results with Terse Text Only. Inktomi is ready to perform a new search, with Full Graphics selected this time.

Every search results page in Inktomi contains a duplicate of the keyword entry form, plus boxes for the number of documents and the display format. This setup enables you to switch easily among the display formats, viewing your results in Terse Text Only mode first, if you like, and then switching quickly to Full Graphics mode. You need to reenter your keyword(s), however, because Inktomi doesn't carry them over from the query page. Enter the keywords again, select the display mode, and click on the Start Search! button. The search results page then shows the same links in the new display mode.

Keyword operators in Inktomi

Though the instructional text (such as it is) doesn't make a big deal about it, you can use a couple of search operators in Inktomi. The AND and NOT operators are reported to work, and you can activate them with the + and - symbols. Here's how to use these operators:

✔ **AND:** When you want the search engine to match *all* of your keywords, use the AND (+) operator. Here's an example of what to enter:

```
anatomy +blood +artery
```

This entry matches only with pages that contain all three words.

✔ **NOT:** Use the NOT (-) operator when you want to exclude certain words from matching your search. It's a way of eliminating matches with words commonly associated with your keywords. Here's how you enter it:

```
dolphins -miami
```

This entry would match with pages about dolphins but not with the Miami Dolphins football team.

World Wide Web Worm

The WWWW, as the World Wide Web Worm is sometimes known, is an older search engine. Once considered a pioneer, it now rests on its laurels (still advertising an award it won in 1994) while providing a unique service. The WWWW database contains only two kinds of listings:

✔ Underlined hypertext items

✔ URLs

As a result, any Web page, when scouted by the World Wide Web Worm, yields to the WWWW index only its own URL and the URLs of any hyperlinks contained in the page. This discriminating indexing plan makes for a small and peculiarly useful database for searching. It narrows down the search right from the start. Furthermore, it gives you an easy way to look for certain kinds of Web-based files, such as .MPG movie files, because the file extension (such as .MPG) is always included in the URL that links to it.

The WWWW is located at this URL:

```
http://www.cs.colorado.edu/wwww/
```

After you are on the WWWW home page (see Figure 11-7), you can enter keywords and click on the Start Search button to initiate the search engine. In the form immediately above the keyword entry box, you can choose whether to match all your keywords or any of them (by using the AND or OR keyword operators). In the box to the right, select whether you want to see 1, 5, 50, 500, or 5,000 matches at a time.

Selecting a higher number of matches at one time definitely slows down the search results page. Selecting just 1 match per page is frankly useless, and 5,000 will keep you tapping your fingers interminably. The best choices are 5 and 50, depending on how much of an overview you want to see at a time.

Now look at the topmost selection form. If you click on the small arrow, a list of four selections springs downward and at first glance it appears to be baffling. The choices enable you to determine which portions of the WWWW index to match your keywords against. Here's what they mean:

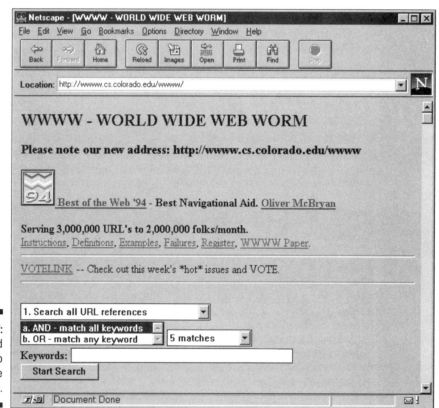

Figure 11-7:
The World
Wide Web
Worm home
page.

✔ **Search all URL references:** When you choose this selection, your keywords are compared to all underlined hyperlinks on every Web page in the WWWW index. Your keyword(s) must appear in the actual hyperlinked text.

✔ **Search all URL addresses:** With this choice, your keywords are matched against the URLs of all Web page hyperlinks. Your keyword doesn't need to match the actual words of the underlined hyperlink, but it does need to match a portion of the URL that the hyperlink goes to.

✔ **Search only in document titles:** Your keywords are matched against the titles of Web pages. Titles are different from URLs. They are not the Internet addresses of the pages; they are what appears in the top (title) bar of your Web browser when you've reached the page. The person who created the Web page assigns the title.

✔ **Search only in document addresses:** This selection tells the WWWW to match your keyword(s) against the URLs of Web pages. It ignores the URLs imbedded in the hyperlinks of Web pages — that's the job of choice number two, Search all URL addresses. This selection is interested only in the database of Web page URLs.

Notice that the first two choices deal with matches that are imbedded in Web pages. The Search all URL references selection tells the WWWW to look at the text of imbedded hyperlinks, and the Search all URL addresses selection tells the WWWW to look at the URLs of those imbedded hyperlinks. Accordingly, the search results page shows not only the match but also the Web page in which the match was found (see Figure 11-8). You can click on either one and go straight to that page.

Figure 11-8:
WWWW
search
results
showing the
matched
citation and
the host
page.

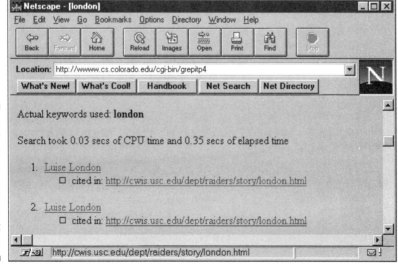

EZ-Find

EZ-Find lives up to its name by giving you centralized access to several popular keyword searching services. It's not exactly simultaneous because you can use only one service at a time. But because you can access several services from a single page, the EZ-Find keyword page is an ideal spot from which to make quick, simple requests of a number of search engines. You can see how EZ-Find works by surfing to the EZ-Find home page (see Figure 11-9), which is located at this URL:

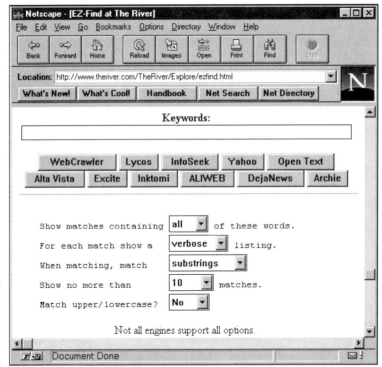

Figure 11-9:
The EZ-Find keyword entry form.

```
http://www.theriver.com/TheRiver/Explore/ezfind.html
```

The keyword entry form on the home page is accompanied by eleven buttons, one for each search service represented in EZ-Find. To use this array, just follow these two steps:

1. **Type one or more keywords into the Keywords form.**

2. **Press the button for the service that you want to use.**

At this point, EZ-Find throws you unceremoniously into the site of whichever search service you chose. If you click on the Lycos button, for example, the search results page will come directly from the Lycos system, with all the same attributes as if you had started the search from the Lycos home page. Same deal with all the other buttons.

Why use anything else?

Because so many great search engines are available from a central location, the question arises of why anyone would go somewhere else to conduct a search. The answer is that each searching service has individual features, strengths, and design options. The big ones, such as Lycos, Excite, AltaVista, and Open Text, enable you to tailor the searching experience to your needs, at least to some degree. They all have specific keyword entry options. Many of them offer miscellaneous benefits that turn them into small online services — one-stop headquarters for a Web session.

EZ-Find is convenient for a quick, down-'n'-dirty search session, but it necessarily leaves out most of the features found in the individual services. However, using EZ-Find is a great way to compare the various search engines. Try entering the same keyword string, pressing each of the search buttons in turn. Do that a few times, and you begin to learn which services give you the best results. Then you can proceed to that service's home page to check out its full range of features.

EZ-Find options

Despite the built-in limitations of providing instant searching through different engines, EZ-Find does its best to provide some generic features that apply to most services. You can change five variables:

- ✓ **All/any:** Choose all to force the chosen service to match all your keywords. You will get back links only to sites that contain every one of your words. Choose any to allow matches to just one of several entered keywords. All and any are equivalent to the standard AND and OR keyword operators.

- ✓ **Verbose/terse:** This option determines what your search results page will look like. The verbose selection yields a full text rendition of the results, including any descriptions that your chosen service normally includes with its matches. The terse selection returns whatever brief version the service provides, which is usually a simple list of matched links.

- ✔ **Substrings/whole words:** When your keywords are treated as substrings, they will match against longer versions of the same root word. For example, plurals will match with singular keywords, as will words with suffixes such as *-ing*. This feature varies among the search engines — some may not have it at all. Choosing whole words requires the search engine to find exact matches to your keywords, as entered.

- ✔ **Number of matches:** Use this drop-down list to select how many matches will be displayed on each search result page. No matter which service you choose, a button or hyperlink at the bottom of each result page takes you to the next page unless you choose the *all* option, which is never recommended.

- ✔ **Match upper/lower case.** Some services may not understand if you choose Yes. Doing so forces the search engine to look at whether you typed any capital letters and to match only with identical capital letters in Web pages. It's usually best to leave this on the default No setting.

HotBot

HotBot is the latest and the coolest. It is the hippest and the boldest. It also is the most broken, but I won't linger over that because it's brand new.

HotBot is a search service from the creators of Inktomi (a keyword engine covered earlier in this chapter) and HotWired (a multimedia, online magazine for the cyber-generation). The synergy of these two organizations promises to merge hi-tech innovation with striking visual design. As I write this paragraph, HotBot is in a *public beta* stage, which means that everyone is invited to test it and e-mail complaints and praises to the designers. I have not been able to successfully initiate a search, and if I wait any longer, this book will be missing this entire chapter.

HotBot is a search site to watch. By the time you read this, it may be performing flawless (and eye-catching) searches. Check it out at this URL:

```
http://www.hotbot.com
```

Part III
Search Expeditions

The 5th Wave   By Rich Tennant

"QUICK KIDS! YOUR MOTHER'S FLAMING SOMEONE ON THE INTERNET!"

In this part . . .

Ready for a field trip? In this part, the chapters take you on eight expeditions to find topics of interest on the Web. Here's where the book puts together everything described in previous chapters — but you don't have to read the earlier chapters first. (This book isn't a detective novel, after all, and the butler had nothing to do with it anyway.)

This part gives you a handle on how to use many different Web-searching tools in the course of research. Whether you're looking for financial information, sports scores, health sites, educational resources, online culture, software, news reports, or e-mail addresses of long-lost friends, one of the chapters in this part will tell you how to proceed and how to expand your searchlight to illuminate all corners of the Internet.

Chapter 12

Finding Finances

• •

In This Chapter

▶ Locating good directory pages about money

▶ Using keywords to find financial sites on the Web

▶ Using Deja News to find Usenet financial communities

▶ Exploring favorite financial sites

• •

*P*ersonal finances are making the jump to cyberspace in a big way. Perhaps your bank has recently sent you a notice offering a modem-based checking account that would enable you to balance your checkbook by accessing the bank's records through your computer. Or maybe you've submitted your tax return through an online service. If you're an investor, you may have considered transferring part of your portfolio to a virtual brokerage and trading stocks through the Web.

The two basic kinds of financial Web site are

✔ **Informational:** Information sites range from outright advertisements to online schools. You can read the Web edition of a finance magazine, browse a multimedia brochure for a bank, or check the performance of your favorite stocks. Informational Web pages are almost always free sites.

✔ **Service:** Service sites transfer some kind of real-world service into the virtual world of the computer, and they usually charge money. The most common type of online financial service site is the online brokerage. These services enable you to establish an account, maintain an interactive portfolio, and trade securities through your computer. Other service sites provide information, such as a magazine database, for which you pay an access fee.

It has never been easier for the financial novice to learn the ropes or for a veteran to expand financial options. The Web brings a great deal of information and a constantly evolving set of tools directly into your home.

Finance Directories

Directories are a good place to begin looking for financial Web sites, as they are for any other topic — especially if you want to see the broadest overview of all the subtopics. Naturally, if you are looking for something quite specific — the online edition of your favorite money magazine, perhaps, or a particular online brokerage service — using a search engine to hone in on your target makes more sense. But general finance is a huge topic, and looking in the directories is a good way to see how it is subdivided and categorized.

Excite

On the main Excite directory page, the Business topic is separated from Money & Investing. Separating them is a good idea, and it makes a useful distinction because many people who are interested in personal finance don't want to shuffle through pages devoted to self-employment, corporate business issues, or entrepreneurialism. Here's how to check out the Money & Investing topic for yourself:

1. **Go to the Excite main directory page by entering this URL in your browser:**

   ```
   http://www.excite.com/Subject
   ```

2. **Click on the <u>Money & Investing</u> topic heading.**

You're now in browsing heaven for personal finance (see Figure 12-1). Most of the topics on the second level of Money & Investing go down at least two more levels and provide good, focused links to investigate. The categories make sense and are of interest. I especially recommend <u>Consumer's Corner</u> and <u>Personal Finance</u>. But, of course, you need to follow the links that interest you. Whatever you're looking for under the general subject of finances, Excite furnishes the best directory balance of thoroughness, quality, and editorial comment on its links.

Yahoo!

Yahoo! is a great directory for seeing the big picture. The really big picture. More of a mural, really, from which you can get a grip on what sorts of Web pages are available to you. The Yahoo! directory is more overwhelming than the Excite experience, thanks to its size, but you can track down some obscure and interesting Web pages by rummaging deeply in the seemingly inexhaustible Yahoo! directory vault.

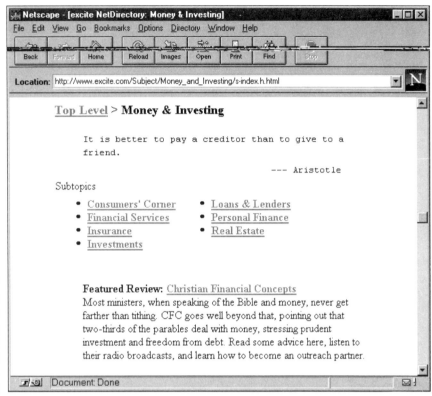

Figure 12-1:
The Money
& Investing
directory
page in
Excite.

You don't want to waste time by getting off to the wrong start. Here's how to get directly to the most useful finance link page on the Yahoo! directory:

1. **Go to the Yahoo! home page by typing this URL in your browser:**

```
http://www.yahoo.com/
```

2. **Click on the <u>Business and Economy</u> link.**
3. **On the next page, click on the <u>Markets and Investments</u> link.**

From this page (see Figure 12-2), clicking on <u>Personal Finance</u>, <u>Stocks</u>, <u>Mutual Funds</u>, or <u>Brokerages</u> brings up lists of hyperlinks to Web information and further subdivisions of the directory. As is the style in Yahoo!, the links are not accompanied by lengthy descriptions or reviews, so you may spend a lot of time jumping back and forth between the service and various finance pages to find the good stuff. When you locate a page that's worth exploring, bookmark it for later and return to checking out the other links from Yahoo!.

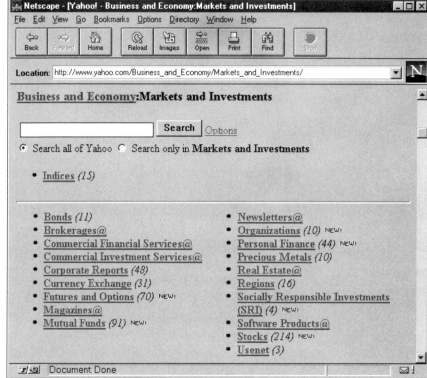

Figure 12-2:
The Markets
and
Investments
page of the
Yahoo!
directory.

Lycos

Lycos is a much weaker directory resource than Yahoo! or Excite for finance and business links. But the links are solid, if few in number, and tend to be weighted in favor of brand-name, recognizable financial institutions. Lycos isn't the place to go when you want a huge directory overview of finance on the Web. But it is worthwhile if you favor a smaller selection of quality hyperlinks. If that's the case, follow these steps:

1. **Go to the Lycos home page at**

    ```
    http://www.lycos.com/
    ```

2. **Click on the Bus/Finance topic.**

You are on a second-level page of broad financial topical links (see Figure 12-3). Personal Finance & Taxes might seem promising, but you may be disappointed. Only a handful of Web pages are represented there. Go back to the second-level page and try a few other topics. The Business & Corporate News & Services link

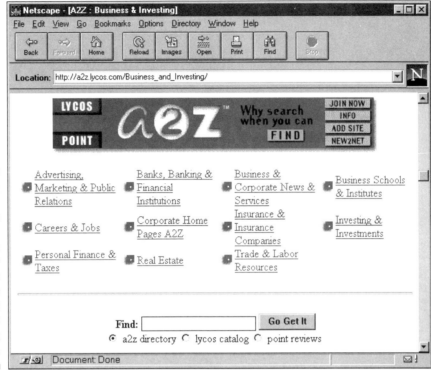

Figure 12-3: The Business and Investing directory page, which you see when you choose the Bus/Finance link.

brings up a healthy page of recognizable, big-name links, as does the Banks, Banking & Financial Institutions link. The Careers & Jobs topic offers good leads for people who are pounding the pavement.

The Lycos directory goes down only three levels under the Bus/Finance heading.

Financial Keywords

As always with keywords, the first step is to formulate short phrases that represent your interest and search goals. But the trick is not to be too broad. Keywords such as **money, finance,** and **banking** deliver gigantic search results, many of them irrelevant. Think how often any of those words could be found in Web pages that don't have anything to do with finances, and you get the picture.

Here are a few basic keyword combinations that work well:

✔ **Interactive finance:** This string yields particularly good results in the Open Text service. When you are using this string, be sure to put the AND operator between the words (AND is sometimes represented by a + sign) to avoid having nonfinance pages match the word *interactive*. Most services, though, list matches to both words first, so you'd have to scroll through a lot of links before hitting the unwanted matches.

✔ **Personal finance:** Lycos and Open Text deliver many of the same matches to this search string, so don't waste your time trying both of them.

✔ **Financial services:** Using this keyword combination tends to result in a lot of company home pages. Financial service companies in the real world design such Web sites to use the Web as an advertising medium. Accessing them provides a way for you to find out about a company and also get an idea of what to look for in other companies.

✔ **Stock trading:** Surprisingly, this combination sometimes works better than keyword strings using the word *brokerage*. Be careful about inadvertently getting matches on the word *stockholm,* though. Choose exact matching features, whenever possible, on the word *stock*.

One great way to get new keyword ideas involves a bit of harmless thievery. When you see a word or word combination that catches your eye in a good Web site, use those words in your next search. Chances are good that they will be matched with other, similarly useful, sites. If, for example, a site charts dividend results for various stocks and you'd like to find other pages with that feature, try the keyword string **chart dividends.**

Finances in the Newsgroups

The Usenet newsgroups — the thousands of bulletin boards that make up the community portion of the Internet — are a great information resource for money and investing. They are especially rich in information about securities trading, with investors from all over the map asking questions about individual issues, sharing experiences and information about companies, and pointing each other to various resources. Even though stock trading is the most competitive area of the financial world, the newsgroups embody a feeling of camaraderie and mutual support.

There are many newsgroups, and they are divided by topic and Usenet directory. The most popular financial bulletin boards are in the `alt` and `misc` directories. They include the following:

```
misc.invest.funds
```

```
misc.invest.stocks
```

```
misc.invest.futures
```

```
misc.invest.canada
```

```
misc.invest.real-estate
```

```
alt.invest.penny-stocks
```

```
alt.invest.technical-Analysis
```

Deja News is a keyword search engine for searching the Usenet. When using Deja News to find financial articles in newsgroups, you will be more successful if you choose keywords a little differently from the way you choose them in a Web searching service. Remember that you are searching the text content of bulletin board messages. The writing is conversational, informal, and colloquial. You need to think in those terms when you formulate keywords. Keyword strings that work well for Web pages may not turn up many matches when Deja News searches newsgroup messages. Here are a few examples:

If These Keywords Don't Work . . .	*. . . Try These*
online banking	computer checking account
interactive finance	stock quote service
financial services	money help

Favorite Financial Sites

The Web has so many great sites about money and finances that highlighting examples is almost pointless. Almost. I can't resist, though, showcasing a few particularly excellent ones. These sites are nothing more than examples of personal favorites. With a little dedicated searching, you can build your own list.

Business World Online Edition

```
http://bizworld.globe.com.ph/
```

An online edition of the well-known business daily lets you browse today's issue, as well as rummage through back issues (see Figure 12-4). It even has a weekly summary of business events. You need to register in order to use the site, but it's a free deal for now. A question on the registration page asks how much you'd be willing to pay for access to the online edition, indicating that payment may soon be required.

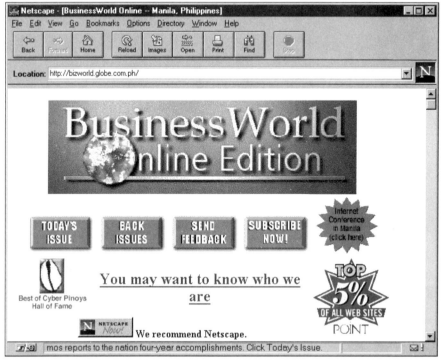

Figure 12-4:
The
Business
World
Online home
page.

Personal Finance Web Sites

    http://www.shore.net/~ikrakow/financew.html

A rather large page (okay, a huge one) containing classified lists of financial Web sites: from mortgages, to taxes, to job listings; from college planning, to insurance, to real estate. This stripped-down page has no graphics to slow you down. In fact, I have rarely seen such a purely utilitarian site — it's a real find.

The World Wide Web Virtual Library: Finance

    http://www.cob.ohio-state.edu/dept/fin/cern/cernnew.htm

If you cruise to this site and maximize your Web browser so it fills the entire screen, there are roughly 20 screens worth of links here. The down side is that the links are not organized or classified in any way — kind of fun if you're browsing, but purgatory if you're searching. (But in that case, you should be using a keyword site.) The upside is that some of the links contain paragraph descriptions.

Finance World

```
http://www.imsworld.com/yp/finance.html
```

Sounds like an amusement park for precocious little investors, right? It's part of the Virtual Yellow Pages, and it features hyperlinks for Web sites that are related to banking, credit, finance, insurance, investment, loans, mortgages, and stocks.

GNN Personal Finance Center

```
http://www.gnn.com/gnn/meta/finance/index.html
```

Essentially a Web-based magazine, the Personal Finance Center has columns and feature articles of interest. Guest experts contribute to GNN (Global Network Navigator) forums, which are browsable. If you like it, you can get a free subscription delivered to your e-mail box just by asking for it. The home page describes how.

Financial Solutions On-Line

```
http://www.rpifs.com/fsp005.html
```

Promoting itself as offering "Complex financial concepts in plain English," Financial Solutions On-Line is a suite of Web pages that delivers on its promise. It's a directory of topics, each thread of which ends up as an article explaining some aspect of financial planning in terms that even I understand. You should have no trouble. This site is even useful for the veteran financier when researching certain money topics for the first time.

DBC Online

```
http://www.dbc.com/
```

This site is wonderful for both the experienced investor and the beginning investor. For the beginner, a financial glossary provides an invaluable education in Wall Street terminology. For the veteran, the site offers Major Market Indexes, an Options Market Summary, and specific exchange roundups. Everyone can use the financial news headlines and, the centerpiece of the site, a stock quote service that gives slightly delayed market prices on stock symbols that you type in. Most of these features are found on the Quotes & Charts link that is located on the home page.

Investor's Business Daily

```
http://ibd.ensemble.com/
```

The Web edition of Investor's Business Daily (IBD) — a well-known daily business newspaper that is available on most newsstands — is well designed, informative, and (best of all) free. You need to register to see articles, but registering just involves filling out a form. After you register, a Web design that is heavy on *tables* — the individually scrollable windows that operate simultaneously on a single Web page — makes reading different sections of the publication easy. In addition to the Web version of the newspaper, you can search the IBD database by keyword.

The Wall Street Journal

```
http://interactive.wsj.com/
```

The interactive edition of the famous financial newspaper is a bit cumbersome in its design, but it contains almost all the articles appearing in the print edition, and they are continually updated throughout the day and night. Hyperlinks take you to the home page of any company that is referred to in the publication. Word is that the site will begin charging an access subscription rate soon. For the time being, it's a free ride, and a good one — though it would be a faster read if a text-only link enabled you to bypass the intensive graphics.

Chapter 13

Searching for Sports

. . . .

In This Chapter

▶ Finding sports in the Web directories

▶ Using Deja News to search the Usenet for sports

▶ Browsing for sport newsgroups

▶ Sampling some great Web sports sites

. . . .

*T*he three things that fans enjoy most about sports translate very well to the computer-based world of the World Wide Web:

✔ **Immediacy:** When you have a favorite team, you want to know the results of their games right away. You don't want to wait for tomorrow's newspaper or the nightly news.

✔ **History:** Sports thrive on comparisons to the past, and a history of any sport relies on statistics.

✔ **Community:** Fans like to talk, argue, reminisce, and make predictions with other fans.

Today's results and yesterday's stats both thrive in the computer network environment of the Internet. And the large number of people online certainly fosters that warm sense of cyber-community. Well, maybe not as warm as standing around a barbecue. . . . But newsgroups and Web pages combine to give fans a vital informational and communal sports experience. You just have to know where to look.

Sports Directories

In a topic as broad and multifaceted as sports, a good directory system can help you get your bearings before you hunker down to do keyword searches. All directories offer a top-level Sports category and then divide Web pages into the different major sports in the lower levels, but the three main directories offer some interesting features that go beyond what the others include.

Yahoo!

Only the vastly detailed Yahoo! directory would go so far as to include links for <u>Lumbering</u>, <u>Korfball</u>, and <u>Cheerleading</u> in its sports directory. The Yahoo! sports directory is an incredibly thorough place to begin a search expedition for sports sites. Follow these directions to begin exploring the directory:

1. **Go to the Yahoo! home page at this URL:**

   ```
   http://www.yahoo.com/
   ```

2. **Look for the <u>Recreation and Sports</u> link and then click on the <u>Sports</u> link just below it.**

3. **Click on the <u>Indices</u> link.**

   You're now confronted with a long list of links to pages that will splash yet more links on your screen. Basically, this Yahoo! page is a list of sites that have good lists of sports sites. Your best approach is to bounce back and forth between this Yahoo! page and all the links that appeal to you, pausing only long enough to bookmark any Web site that you want to return to later.

   When you're done with this page, check out some scores.

4. **Use the Back button on your browser to return to the Sports directory page.**

5. **Click on the <u>Scoreboard</u> link.**

6. **On the Yahoo! Scoreboard page, click on any sports link that interests you.**

   You now have quick access to yesterday's final scores (with game summaries), previews, schedules, statistics, and standings (see Figure 13-1). Okay, you need to explore one more avenue.

7. **Use the Back button to return to the Sports directory page.**

8. **Click on the <u>Current Sports Headlines</u> link.**

   You now see up-to-the-minute wire service headlines. When you finish catching up on today's news, go back to the Sports directory page to pick a search path from among the many sports listed. Yahoo! has the most extensive sports directory available.

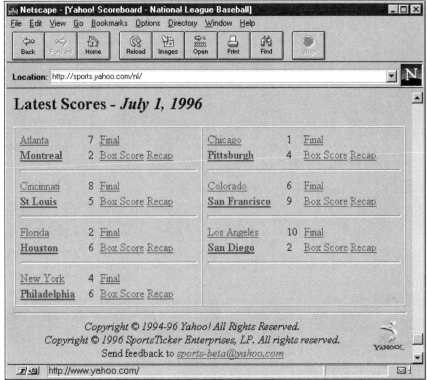

Figure 13-1:
The Yahoo!
Scoreboard
is a good
place to get
quick sports
updates.

Excite

When you get into the Excite sports directory, you'll see many individual sports on the second level. Rummage through those subdirectories according to your particular interest. One section provides links that will appeal to all kinds of fans, and it is a good place to begin searching. Here's how to get to it:

1. **Go to the Excite directory home page by typing this URL into your Web browser:**

```
http://www.excite.com/Subject
```

2. **Click on the <u>Sports</u> link.**

3. **When the second-level page appears, click on the <u>Sports Indexes</u> link.**

4. When the third-level page comes up, click on <u>Links & More Links</u>.

You are at the bottom level of this directory path, and you see an alphabetical list of reviewed, general-purpose sports Web sites (see Figure 13-2).

5. Click on any title to visit that site.

Lycos

Lycos comes through with an unusual and varied assortment of sports. Here's how to position yourself on the directory of sports sites:

1. Go to the Lycos home page at

```
http://www.lycos.com/
```

2. Click on the <u>Sports</u> link.

3. Click on the <u>Individual & Team Sports</u> link.

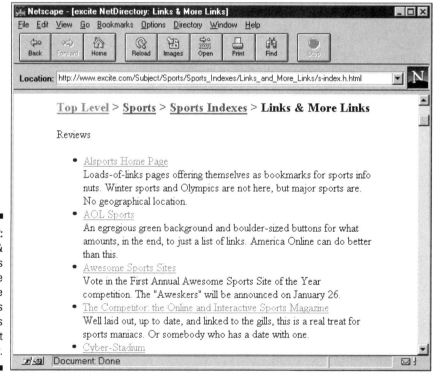

Figure 13-2:
The Links & More Links page of the Excite Sports directory is a good spot to start.

4. When the third-level page displays on your screen, gape at the selection and start linking.

Fans of frisbee, martial arts, aviation, orienteering, table tennis, darts, shooting, and rollerblading will be gratified to see their passions represented here (see Figure 13-3). The number of links to Web sites representing these unusual sports may be few (How many Web sites about orienteering would you expect to see?), but this page is the place to find them.

Sports Keywords

When you are looking for sports sites, general, all-purpose keyword searches work well enough, but they are not the best way to use the resources of Web-searching services. For example, **sports scores** is a good keyword string (although it doesn't work that well in the Open Text service). But because you can so easily find sports scores through the directories, right off the top-level page, performing a keyword search to get the same information is hardly worth the effort.

Figure 13-3:
The Individual & Team Sports page offers an astounding directory of athletic categories.

Instead, use keywords to find pinpoint information about individual teams or athletes. Searching on an athlete's name gets great results for a couple of reasons:

✔ Names are not often confused with other words in a keyword match, so the results are likely to be on the mark.

✔ The results often point you toward useful general-purpose sports sites that you might want on your hotlist. For example, searching on **rickey henderson** (a major league baseball player) in Lycos brings up references and hotlinks to major television and newspaper Web sites that include his name in their current text.

If you don't want to trudge through directory levels, using the name of a sport as a keyword works well. This method saves time but doesn't necessarily provide you with better quality sites.

Sports Newsgroups

The Usenet has too many sports newsgroups to list individually, but two methods can help you find newsgroups that you'll be happy with.

Locating newsgroups with Deja News

Chapter 10 describes the Deja News Usenet searching service in excruciating detail. (It also tells you more about the Usenet and newsgroups in general.) The normal use for this service is for finding particular newsgroup articles that relate to a search topic. However, following these steps will bend it to your purpose of finding good newsgroups to subscribe to:

1. **Go to the Deja News keyword entry page at this URL:**

   ```
   http://www.dejanews.com/forms/dnq.html
   ```

2. **Enter one or more keywords that describe your interest.**

   Ideally, the keywords should be neither too broad nor too specific. A team name, such as **yankees**, usually works well. But a more general word, such as **baseball**, also works.

3. **Set Number of hits (per page) to 60.**

4. **Set Hitlist format to Threaded.**

This selection creates a particular Query Results page format. If several messages from one newsgroup discussion (called a message thread) match your keywords, those messages are presented together, in "discussion" order (the order in which they were posted). This way, you can see how the discussion evolved, rather than having the pertinent messages scattered through a strictly chronological list of search results from many newsgroups. However, if messages from a newsgroup's discussion thread don't match your keyword, they will not appear on the Query Results page.

5. **Set Sort by (per page) to Date.**

6. **Leave all the other Search Options the way they are and click on the Find button (see Figure 13-4).**

7. **When the Query Results page appears on your screen, select from the list of articles.**

With the articles listed in threaded format and the most recent ones toward the top, you can get a preliminary indication (from the article titles) of which discussions are of interest to you.

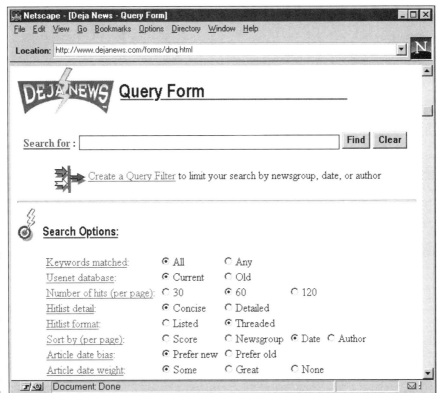

Figure 13-4: Use these settings in Deja News for good search results on a sports team.

8. **Click on the links for the articles that you want to see.**

   Now that you're actually reading the articles, and not just their titles, you can really hone in on discussions of interest and on newsgroups that you may want to subscribe to. It takes some time to select and read many articles, so if your Query Results page contains many matches, be prepared to settle into some message-scanning. (With a little luck, it'll be good reading.)

9. **When the Retrieved Document page appears on your screen, note the newsgroup in which it is posted.**

   In this fashion, you can build a list of newsgroups that seem worth subscribing to. Another method is to click on Post or Reply from the Retrieved Document page if you are using an integrated Internet suite of programs, such as Netscape Navigator Version 2.0 or later. Clicking on Post Article or Email Reply opens the newsgroup portion of the program and automatically displays a list of all the current articles in that group, by message title. Clicking on any message title in the list displays the complete message. You don't need to post a reply.

10. **After making a list of interesting newsgroups, subscribe to them according to the instructions in your newsgroup program.**

Browsing for sports newsgroups

Another method of finding sports newsgroups is by browsing from the directory list of the entire Usenet. This method is less complicated and more direct than using Deja News, but it may be more time-consuming. Using this method can seem like looking for a needle in a haystack because of the large number of newsgroups — even just sports newsgroups.

On the other hand, if your newsgroup program gives you an article count for each bulletin board (newsgroup), you can see at a glance which boards are most active. That information is helpful, since the popular groups are often the most worthwhile. (But not always! When you have some free moments, check out the more obscure groups. Small communities can be gems, too.) If you find a newsgroup that attracts you, whether it's an information highway or a backroad, you can dive right in to the message board to find out whether it meets your needs.

Here's how to find sports newsgroups from the directory list:

1. **Get your newsgroup reader to display a list of every newsgroup to which you have access.**

The procedure for displaying the list of newsgroups varies among browsers, so you may need to poke around your menus or read the instructions. (In Netscape Navigator Version 2.0, you open the News Reader window, pull down the Options menu, and select Show All Newsgroups.)

2. **From the long list of newsgroup directories, select the ALT directory.**

3. **Scroll down the list of ALT newsgroups, looking for sports-related titles.**

When you encounter subdirectories on sports subjects, such as `alt.sports`, double-click on those directories to see a list of newsgroups tucked within them. You may find folders within folders; if so, just repeat the process.

4. **Repeat this process with the REC newsgroup directory.**

5. **As you go, subscribe to any newsgroups that look interesting.**

The subscription process differs depending on your software. In some programs, you can subscribe "on the fly" like this; other programs may require another procedure. Check the Help menu of your program if you run into trouble.

The Hot Sports Sites

Here are a few good, basic, and all-purpose sports sites. Finding a Web sports site that you want to visit time and again is just as personal as developing a loyalty to a newspaper's sports section. It all depends on how it is laid out, who the writers are, and how current the news is. You also want the right balance of raw information and commentary.

These sites are just a small sample of what's available. Search around, chat with other wired sports fans, and pretty soon you'll have your own hotlist of personal favorites.

ESPNET SportsZone

```
http://espnet.sportszone.com/
```

ESPNET SportsZone is one of the great Web sports sites (see Figure 13-5). Every wired fan knows about this one, and you should, too. It's a complete publication, with terrific graphics, updated scores, feature articles, contests, reader participation, columns, and live audio. Of course, the traffic crunch at such a popular site can be a problem, but I haven't had any significant delays. Two links lurk quietly at the top of the front page:

Figure 13-5:
The high-graphics home page of ESPNET SportsZone. A "mostly text" version is also available.

✔ **Mostly Text Front Page:** This link takes you to a site "path" in which the graphic magazine format is replaced with, as advertised, mostly text. A few pictures are sprinkled in. Navigation through the magazine in this mode is much quicker, especially for users who have 14.4 bps modems.

✔ **Index:** This link takes you to an astonishing list of everything available at the site. It's enormous. Take note — the Index is not a link page to other sites.

ESPNET SportsZone is a hybrid subscription/free service. Anyone can visit the site, but some elements of it are available only to users who have registered as online subscribers by using a credit card. The monthly fee enables them to read the columns, access summaries of games, and enjoy some other features. Raw scores are available to anyone, and, in fact, most of the publication is free. Naturally, some of the best stuff is available only to subscribers. This site is on my bookmark list on a nonsubscription basis.

GNN Live Sports Feeds

```
http://gnn-e2a.gnn.com/news/sports/
```

If you want a good, quick, free site that delivers sports scores without a lot of commentary, add this page to your hotlist. Unburdened by fancy graphics, it moves you quickly through news, transactions, injuries, and scores.

ALSPORTS

```
http://www.branson.com/branson/alsports/alsports.htm
```

Claiming to be the "perfect bookmark opportunity," the ALSPORTS site is well organized and easy to use. It is divided into 16 sports, including <u>Body Building</u> and <u>Weight Lifting</u> as separate athletic endeavors. Its typical directory format enables you to choose a sport and then link from lists of related Web sites.

World Wide Web of Sports

```
http://www.tns.lcs.mit.edu/cgi-bin/sports
```

This page looks a little peculiar in a browser that doesn't understand Netscape extensions, but it will work nonetheless — and it works very well, in fact, thanks to its no-nonsense approach. Its absence of graphics means that the site moves very quickly, delivering thousands of links to other sports sites for the eager searcher. Dividing sports into dozens of categories, the World Wide Web of Sports can link you to pages in such esoteric athletic pursuits as checkers, curling, croquet, billiards, kite flying, lawn bowling, hydroplaning, jump rope, korfball (if anyone knows what this is, please email me), paint ball, rodeo, and others too numerous to list.

SportsLine USA

```
http://www.sportsline.com/index.html
```

SportsLine USA is one of the most comprehensive Web sports magazines (see Figure 13-6). One of its claims to fame is an up-to-the-minute approach that rivals the broadcast media. During the baseball season, "live" reports update certain pages almost constantly, and users armed with Shockwave plugins are treated to a multimedia experience. (If you don't have Shockwave or don't want to use it, an alternate site path is available.)

A dynamic mix of feature writing and statistical reporting is the hallmark of SportsLine USA. However, not all of the features are available for free. You can register for a free trial month, after which a monthly fee kicks in and is billed to your credit card.

Figure 13-6:
Sportsline USA is a great Web sports magazine.

Chapter 14

Hunting for Health

*O*bviously, the computer is no substitute for a doctor. Or even for taking your own temperature. But living in the information age has health benefits, if only helping you understand what in the world your doctor is talking about or researching possible alternative therapies for a medical condition. Health and medicine are represented on the Internet in a couple of primary forms:

✔ **Web sites:** More medical Web sites are appearing all the time. Some of them, I must admit, are on the other side of comprehensible if you haven't done your internship. But others are terrific resources for lay people who want to take responsibility for understanding their own medical conditions or are researching on behalf of someone else.

✔ **Communities:** The message board of the Usenet, which is available through most Web browsers, provides a rich vein of information and group support. Staying current with a certain medical or health newsgroup is often the best way to get pointers to the newest Web sites on that subject.

Health Directories

If you want an overview of how health subjects are categorized on the World Wide Web, the best plan is to start with the directories. You can go down a couple of broad search avenues, and the directory menus of Web pages provide a map of the terrain.

Yahoo!

You can get started quickly with a roundup of health sites in Yahoo! by going to the directory home page at this URL:

```
http://www.yahoo.com
```

After you arrive at the home page, click on the <u>Health</u> link. Alternatively, you can cut right to the health page by entering this URL in your Web browser:

```
http://www.yahoo.com/Health/
```

Either way, you're now on the top level of the Yahoo! Health directory (a second level of the overall Yahoo! directory). Here you can see many broad choices (see Figure 14-1). Click on any one of them to proceed downward in the directory along a certain path. Here are some of the main paths:

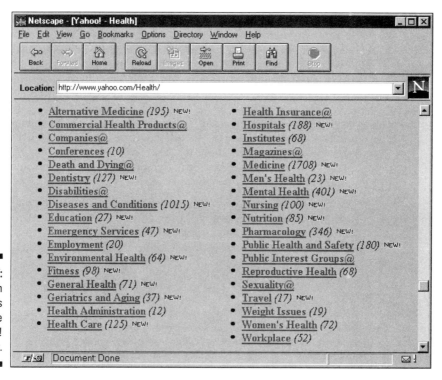

Figure 14-1: The Health categories of the Yahoo! directory.

✔ **Medicine:** Clicking here takes you to a page of medical disciplines. You can choose one of them, such as <u>Chiropractic</u>, <u>Preventive Medicine</u>, <u>Physical Therapy</u>, or <u>Dermatology</u>. Below these choices are a couple of dozen links to outside pages, mostly general information sites for finding more links to specific medical practices. The Medicine page is not where you find particular diseases, though.

✔ **Diseases and Conditions:** Clicking here takes you to a directory of diagnosable conditions. It's a big list, from <u>Acoustic Neuroma</u> to <u>Vitiligo</u>. Below this list is an assortment of outside links for even less common ailments, such as stuttering and silk road disease, as well as general clearinghouse sites for various pathologies. Follow the <u>Diseases and Conditions</u> link if you're tracking down information on a specific ailment, not a type of medical practice.

✔ **Fitness:** If your search emphasis is more on preventing illness than on healing it, this path points you in the right direction (see Figure 14-2). You can drill down in a number of different directions from here by using links to <u>Institutes</u>, <u>Organizations</u>, <u>Yoga</u>, <u>Walking</u>, and <u>Bodybuilding</u>. A selection of outside links can spin you off to various health and fitness sites.

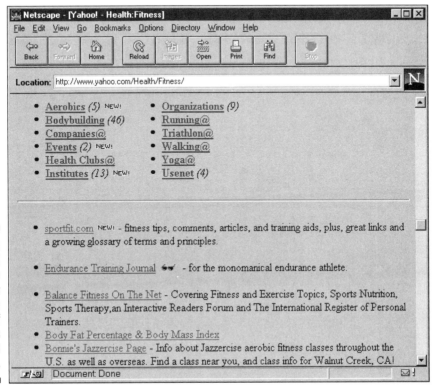

Figure 14-2:
The Yahoo!
Fitness
directory
page is a
good mix of
subtopics
and linked
Web sites.

✔ **Mental Health:** This is another main directory path on the search for health sites. On this page, you see a <u>Diseases and Conditions</u> choice that takes you to the next level down where you see links to a broad selection of mental health conditions, such as <u>Alzheimer's Disease</u>, <u>Mood Disorders</u>, <u>Schizophrenia</u>, and <u>Substance Abuse</u>. Or link your way to directories (outside Yahoo!) of organizations, therapies, and institutes.

✔ **Health Care:** If your focus is on the financial coverage of medical treatment, this link takes you to a directory of companies, institutes, and rural health organizations.

Excite

The Excite directory is less extensive than Yahoo! for health subjects, but it contains interesting menu choices and is definitely worth checking out. It also lists topics in a less scientific, more familiar way, and you may find what you're looking for with less need for interpretation. Follow these steps to get started with the Excite health listings:

1. **Go to the home page of the Excite directory by giving your Web browser this URL:**

```
http://www.excite.com/Subject/
```

2. **Click on the <u>Health & Medicine</u> link.**

You are now looking at the main health directory menu for Excite (see Figure 14-3). You should follow your own search path, but here are a few of the basic choices to make at this point:

✔ **Diseases:** <u>Chronic Fatigue</u>, <u>Joint Problems</u>, and <u>Skin Disorders</u> are the more unusual directory selections when you follow this link.

✔ **Medicine:** An interesting link called <u>Body Human</u> is found here, leading you to a directory page that features parts of the body — click on <u>Brain</u>, <u>Eyes</u>, or <u>Heart</u>, for example, to see lists of links related to those aspects of human anatomy and medicine.

✔ **Children's Health & Disabilities:** Here you can link to resources for learning disabilities, camps for disabled kids, children's blindness, child safety, and many other pediatric and family sites.

✔ **Nutrition:** Clicking on this link takes you to a directory page for tracking down information on diets, vitamins and other supplements, and vegetarianism.

Figure 14-3:
The Health
& Medicine
lineup in the
Excite
directory.

Lycos

To get on the right page for health concerns in the Lycos Web directory, you can go to the Lycos home page by using this URL:

```
http://a2z.lycos.com/
```

After the page appears on your screen, click on the <u>Health & Medicine</u> link. Or go directly to the Health & Medicine directory page (see Figure 14-4) by using this URL:

```
http://a2z.lycos.com/Health_and_Medicine/
```

Figure 14-4:
The Lycos
Health &
Medicine
directory
contains
quality
topics and
links.

Lycos points the way to extremely high-quality health links. As with other subjects, Lycos stands between the sheer voluminous wealth of links in Yahoo! and the sparse, yet well reviewed, resources of Excite. This directory has a good range of health pointers, and they are interestingly organized, with some surprises. From the Health & Medicine page, the following links make for interesting exploring:

✔ **Alternative Medicine:** From new methods of giving birth to massage therapy to chiropractic, going down this directory path puts you in touch with links to the world of less standard, quasi-medical therapies. Links to pages of indexes, publishers, and organizations are especially helpful.

✔ **Disabilities:** If you or someone you know is physically challenged, this subdirectory puts forth a surprising number of links to Web pages for organizations, information archives, and commercial services. From links related to blindness to help finding a seeing-eye dog, this directory is a great resource for Web searching.

- **Family Medical Almanac:** This category is good browsing territory for the whole family, as you might guess. Subtopics on the next level include <u>General Wellness</u>, <u>Emergency Medicine</u>, <u>Libraries</u>, <u>Databases & Indices</u>, and <u>Travel Medicine</u>. Follow this link rather than the similarly titled Family Medicine, for the simple but sound reason that Family Medicine contains no links whatsoever.

- **Illnesses & Disorders:** You expect to find a category such as this one in any health directory, and Illnesses & Disorders contains the typical divisions of ailments. Its links are not nearly as extensive as the ones on the corresponding Yahoo! page.

- **Parenting:** This link is a surprise, and a pleasant one. It leads to a modestly sized, useful resource of links to associations, newsletters, and parenting sites.

Health Keywords

You can, of course, duplicate basic directory topics as keywords to find sites for medical conditions, illnesses, and treatment types. But the directories do such a good job of categorizing the basic information that you would do better using keywords to zero in on highly specific information. Here are some examples of the kind of information that you can find more quickly by using keywords than by using directories:

- **Technical names of illnesses:** If you know the scientific name for a disease, searching with the technical name as the keyword is a shortcut to Web pages that deliver information you need. Examples are **hypothyroid, scoliosis**, and **ischemic heart disease.**

- **Drug names:** Searching on drug names is a good way to get information about side effects, protocols, and alternatives. You must know how to spell the drug's name, though, or you waste a lot of time guessing. If you already have the drug, just type the name as it appears on the container.

- **Body parts:** Using the names of body parts (especially the smaller ones), and other body elements, such as enzymes, hormones, glands, cell types, and so forth, generally gets good results (see Figure 14-5). Searching on **pituitary,** for example, can lead you on a highly educational tour of the human endocrine system, just by following links that you encounter. If you or someone you know has been diagnosed with a medical condition (hypoglycemia, for example), searching on a relevant body part (**pancreas**) would shed light on the condition from a physiological perspective.

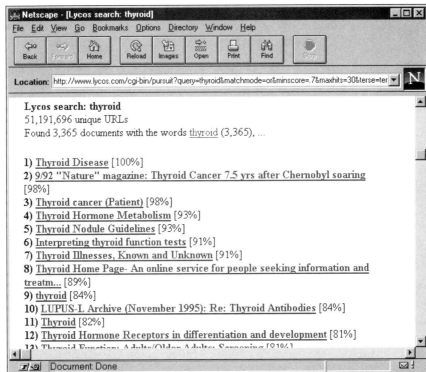

Lycos search: thyroid
51,191,696 unique URLs
Found 3,365 documents with the words thyroid (3,365), ...

1) Thyroid Disease [100%]
2) 9/92 "Nature" magazine: Thyroid Cancer 7.5 yrs after Chernobyl soaring [98%]
3) Thyroid cancer (Patient) [98%]
4) Thyroid Hormone Metabolism [93%]
5) Thyroid Nodule Guidelines [93%]
6) Interpreting thyroid function tests [91%]
7) Thyroid Illnesses, Known and Unknown [91%]
8) Thyroid Home Page- An online service for people seeking information and treatm... [89%]
9) thyroid [84%]
10) LUPUS-L Archive (November 1995): Re: Thyroid Antibodies [84%]
11) Thyroid [82%]
12) Thyroid Hormone Receptors in differentiation and development [81%]
13) Thyroid Function: Adults/Older Adults: Screening [91%]

Document Done

Figure 14-5:
Using a body part as a keyword (in this case, **thyroid**) yields health-related hyperlinks.

Health on the Usenet

Casting your Web browser into the Usenet newsgroups brings forth the community of the Internet. Here you can find all levels of helpfulness, from dialogs with professionals to sales pitches from cyber snake-oil salesmen. I've seen doctors post entire articles they have authored for medical journals in response to a stranger's question. It's commonplace for people to get quick, helpful suggestions in situations where they need to make treatment decisions quickly.

You should not rely too much on the Internet for guidance on health issues because personal diagnosis and realtime medical advice are essential in any medical situation. Take the Usenet newsgroups as vitamins — they are strictly supplementary. As such, they are a great way to instantly meet many people from all over the globe who share an interest in a specific health subject.

Here are the main directories for health and medical Usenet bulletin boards.

```
sci.med.*
```

```
sci.med.diseases.*
```

```
sci.psychology.*
```

The newsgroups of the sci.med directory are, as the directory name implies, rather scientific by nature. They are not restricted to doctors or scientists by any means, but many health experts frequent them. Shop talk abounds, as professionals bandy about such before-dinner questions as "Does thrombin cleave the fibrinogen which is bound to the platelets or 'free' fibrinogen?"

Sorry to keep you in suspense about the answer, but it hadn't yet been posted. Amidst such scintillating repartee, you also can find regular folks asking about their conditions and taking advantage of a serious, professional environment. Ask a question in one of the `sci.med` groups, and you are answered by other lay people who share your interest, and quite often by doctors who offer advice, detailed information, personal experience, and recommendations. Of course, such dialog is no replacement for an actual consultation with a physician. But for gaining a better understanding of your health or a particular illness, the `sci.med` directory is quite a resource.

A less technical environment reigns in the groups in the `misc.health.*` directory. Here, regular folks gather to share information and support. `Misc.health.alternative` is often the most popular of these groups, and it offers a fine method of finding therapies that are off the beaten path. Exotic mushrooms and magnetic mattresses are discussed as seriously as calcium and nitrites.

Least technical of all are the newsgroups of the ever-popular *alt* directory:

```
alt.med.*
```

```
alt.health.*
```

```
alt.psychology.*
```

Exploring ayurveda (a traditional East Indian healing system) to oxygen therapy, and allergies to better vision (`alt.med.vision.improvement`), a wide range of folks congregate in the `alt` newsgroups to ask questions, seek support, and hold forth on personal agendas.

A Few General Health Sites

Health information is prolific on the Web, and most of it is geared toward specific conditions or fields of research. Here, though, are a few general purpose Web sites that are impressive for their completeness and ease of use.

Hardin MD

```
http://www.arcade.uiowa.edu/hardin-www/md.html
```

A directory of Internet health sources, the Hardin MD page bills itself with the tagline, "We list the sites that list the sites." If you can follow that, it means that this site is one terrific link hub for health resources on the World Wide Web. Basically, it's a list of lists.

Health, Medicine, and Life Extension

```
http://www.physics.wisc.edu/~shalizi/hyper-weird/health.html
```

This dedicated Web health directory is remarkable for the range of resources in its links. You can discover not only Web pages, but also e-mail mailing lists, FAQ (Frequently Asked Questions) files, and health databases with search engines. Its life extension links veer toward the unusual, including oxygen therapy and cryogenics.

Multimedia Medical Reference Library

```
http://www.tiac.net/users/jtward/
```

This health directory is terrific. The point of this site is not to link you to other Web resources but to provide broad information on seemingly all medical conditions. Geared somewhat toward professionals, or at least serious amateur researchers, this site provides a good way to learn what questions you should ask your doctor. Click on Comprehensive Info to start off with a basic menu of medical subjects, such as Cardiology and Endocrinology. Clicking on a topic sends you to the next level, from which you can choose from a list of articles provided by institutes, doctors, and universities.

Centers for Disease Control and Prevention

```
http://www.cdc.gov/
```

This Web domain goes well beyond any brief description. A strong emphasis on disease prevention informs much of the content of this site, and it has an entire section on prevention guidelines and strategies. You can get a history of the Centers, link to traveler's information, and hook into many publications, products, and services. Statistics abound if you want them, and this site has no shortage of links to other Web resources.

Chapter 15

Exploring Education

- -

In This Chapter

▶ Using the education directories

▶ Keying into education with keywords

▶ Finding Usenet newsgroups about learning

▶ Exploring selected education sites

- -

*1*nformation retrieval may seem like a technical field that's only for professionals, but most parents of high school seniors (as well as their college-bound students) have dabbled in the field. Choosing a college requires searching through one heck of a lot of information! Guidance counselors, being education professionals, have had information-age tools to help parents and students since personal computers became prevalent. Now that the information resources of the World Wide Web are equally available to students, parents, and their counselors, anyone who has Internet access can explore many aspects of education. Selecting a college with the help of the family computer might teach a student more about research methods than *going* to college!

Distance learning is one aspect of education that is especially well represented on the Web. *Distance learning* involves telecommuting to school — matriculating through a curriculum without actually showing up someplace. Correspondence courses are one example. Because opportunities for computer-based distance learning are available through the World Wide Web and e-mail, it makes sense that you can search for such opportunities in Web directories and through Web search engines.

Education Directories

Browsing the main Web directories for education topics is a great experience because the World Wide Web includes a great deal of material on education in addition to simple college home pages. As a matter of fact, although you can find those college pages by browsing the directories, using keywords to find them makes more sense because keyword searches save you from endless rummaging through directory levels. Browsing is better for helping you find the types of resources that you didn't know existed and therefore couldn't search for with keywords. Just read on to find out how the main Web directories stack up in the education department.

Lycos

Lycos has chosen practical and useful sites for its education directory. The Yahoo! education directory is larger (What else is new?), but the Lycos sites are well chosen and reviewed. You can get started by surfing to the top level of the Lycos directory at this URL:

```
http://a2z.lycos.com
```

When you arrive at the top level of the Lycos directory, click on the <u>Education</u> main topic. Or, go directly to the Education directory page by entering this URL:

```
http://a2z.lycos.com/Education
```

Now you've got some interesting choices (see Figure 15-1):

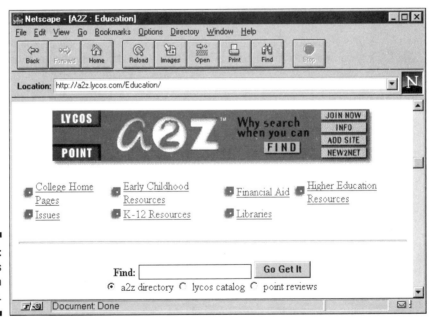

Figure 15-1:
The Lycos Education directory.

✔ **Issues:** Clicking on <u>Issues</u> takes you to a few dozen links that mostly represent organizations that deal with ongoing educational questions and challenges. From the <u>Commonwealth of Learning</u> to the <u>Consortium of Language and Teaching</u>, these links appeal to people who are involved in or interested in theories of learning and structures of education.

✔ **K-12 Resources:** Click on K-12 Resources to find one of the best lists of high school Web links. In addition, here's where you can find links that are useful to students, such as the *Encyclopedia Britannica* site. This directory page is good for teenage surfing — teens can see what students in other high schools are doing on the Web and get help with their homework, all in the same session.

✔ **Higher Education Resources:** Far from being a repository of college home pages, this page is a surpassing treasure trove of unexpected sites. These links enable you to peruse annual reports of the American Indian College Fund, various alumni associations, gopher servers for educational journals, resources for college applicants, and much more. All in all, this page is one of the best educational directory pages around.

✔ **Financial Aid:** This directory page lists only about a dozen links, but they are terrific — and when you are looking for tuition money, good links are gold links.

✔ **Libraries:** This list of links is immense. Although physical libraries have an obvious advantage over virtual ones (you can get your hands on a book, mainly), many of these links are worthwhile if you live close to the library that's represented by a Web page. Some of the Web pages are cyber-versions of the library's card catalogue, so you can research titles from home and then make the trip to get the book. If you don't live close to the library, using the card catalogue is still a good way to research what books are out there in a certain field.

Yahoo!

Yahoo! demonstrates its fine tradition of aggressive topic subdivision in its Education directory. (In other words, it has lots of education topics to follow.) Yahoo! does not review its directory listings or even describe them at any length. So browsing the education directory is like swimming in a sea of links. To see your choices, go to the top level of the Yahoo! directory at this URL:

```
http://www.yahoo.com/
```

Then follow the <u>Education</u> link. Or, go directly to the Education directory level by typing this URL in your Web browser:

```
http://www.yahoo.com/Education/
```

At this point, you can browse according to your needs by clicking on subtopics. Of all the choices confronting you (see Figure 15-2), these topics are particularly well represented:

✔ **Math and Science Education:** This Yahoo! topic is new, and it has hundreds of links, including Web pages for science camps and technology fairs and a whole directory of math and science education topics.

✔ **On-line Teaching and Learning:** Click on this link to browse a large list of links to virtual learning environments. A recent visit to this directory showed links to a multimedia retrospective of the 1980s created by a university class, a collection of Internet tools for teachers, an online math tutoring service, and countless others. (At least, I wouldn't want to count them.)

✔ **Organizations:** Professional associations, alumni groups, student organizations, and faculty alliances are all well represented in this part of the directory.

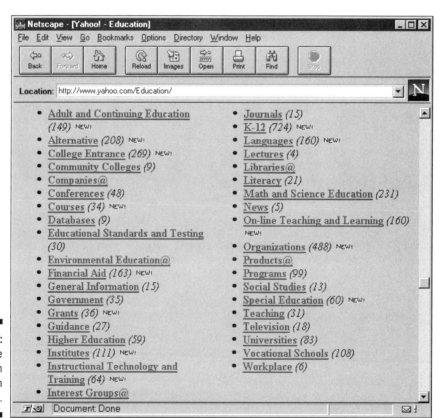

Figure 15-2:
The large Education directory in Yahoo!.

✔ **Vocational Schools:** You probably don't know how many different kinds of vocational schools exist if you haven't checked out this page. From the American Woodworking Academy to the Casino Career Institute and from an advanced hair training institute to the English Nanny and Governess School, you can choose a link and choose a career.

✔ **Special Education:** This directory page is a wonderful collection of links to Web sites that describe programs in all kinds of special education. If schools that offer programs and curricula for disabled and special-needs students have a Web presence, you can find them here.

✔ **College Entrance:** This page contains a few links to sites that are relevant to college search and admissions procedures. Its main value lies in the <u>Admissions Offices</u> subtopic link, which takes you to a long list of college admissions office Web sites. (Brush up on your interview skills!) Such sites offer you a way to initiate contact with a school or review its admissions requirements quickly before sending for applications.

Education Keywords

Searching for education Web sites presents a different challenge from searching for sites for most other topics. The directories do such a thorough job of cataloging many types of educational subjects and institutions that searching with keywords plays a smaller role. However, these keyword searches, like others, are good for getting to specific sites fast.

If you know the name of an organization, association, guild, or school and are looking for a Web page representing that name, try typing it as a keyword string in Yahoo!, Lycos, Excite, AltaVista, Open Text, or any other services that enable you to do keyword searches. Also, you can generally get good results from using the following clusters of keywords in different combinations (see Figure 15-3 for a results page of one of these keyword clusters):

✔ **homework, help, assignment**

✔ **college, admissions, requirements**

✔ **financial, aid, tuition, scholarship**

✔ **distance, learning, online, courses, programs**

✔ **testing, SAT, entrance, examination, college**

Keyword search string

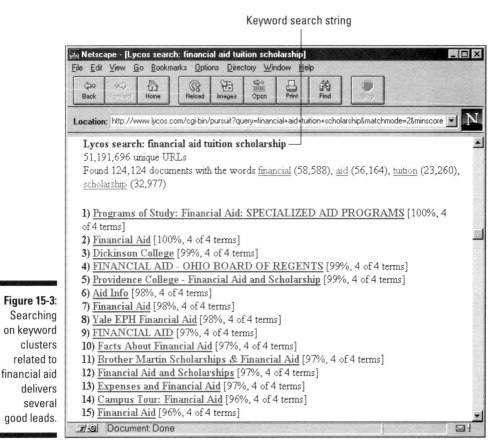

Figure 15-3:
Searching
on keyword
clusters
related to
financial aid
delivers
several
good leads.

Education on the Usenet

The Internet bulletin boards that are known as *Usenet newsgroups* don't contain as much conversation about education subjects as they do on more conversational topics such as sports or money. The newsgroups that are worth checking out can be summarized quickly.

The alt newsgroup directory seems to have a little bit of everything, and you can find most of the education newsgroups there. The first directory folder to look at is

```
alt.college.*
```

Six newsgroups lurk within this folder, including a couple that are devoted to fraternities. The `alt.college.us` newsgroup is an interesting hodgepodge of postings, not all having to do with education in any way.

Moving down the list, another `alt` newsgroup directory to try is

```
alt.education.*
```

Here you have 11 groups to explore, including alternative education, distance learning, education for the disabled, research, and Christian education.

Moving away from the `alt` directory, try scrolling down the list of groups and folders in the `soc` directory. It includes a subdirectory called

```
soc.college.*
```

This subdirectory contains six bulletin boards, and although they are not the most popular, most trafficked areas of the Usenet, they are particularly focused, serious, interesting, and helpful. The `soc.college.admissions` group is a gathering place for trading information and support when applying to colleges; and `soc.college.financial-aid` is a valuable repository of grass-roots tips about affording the high cost of college.

Finally, one main newsgroup directory is completely dedicated to education:

```
k12.*
```

The k12 folder has 34 groups in it, all of them focused on precollege issues. It is an especially good resource for teachers but also interesting reading for anyone who is concerned with educational issues. A recent discussion in `k12.ed.math`, for example, went to great lengths in analyzing concrete and abstract reasoning skills and the development of intuition. Many conversations are less cerebral than that. The `k12.chat.teacher` board is the largest in the whole directory, and it is a nice meeting place for elementary school teachers.

Education Sites

So many colleges and universities have institutional Web pages, and they are so easy to find in the main Web directories, that I have avoided highlighting any of them in this section. Instead, here is a group of home pages that seem especially useful or interesting, and they are geared mostly to online or distance learning. Remember, this is just a handful of personal recommendations to get you started. Keep looking around, and in no time you'll have your own hotlist of education sites.

CyberEd

`http://www.umassd.edu/cybered/distlearninghome.html`

Established by the University of Massachusetts at Dartmouth, CyberEd is an online curriculum offered through your Web browser and e-mail account. With the motto, "Delivering quality education from our desktop to yours," CyberEd strives to create a distance, virtual learning environment that rivals a classroom experience in quality and content. Thirteen courses are offered, only two of which are noncredit — the others are for either graduate or undergraduate credit. CyberEd makes good use of the interactive and multimedia qualities of the Internet, which simply means that if you enroll, you can count on meeting one heck of a lot of people from around the world and receiving sound and video files over your computer that will enhance the learning experience.

To answer the big question: No, it's not free. These are college courses that you take for credit, and the cost for each one runs into the hundreds of American dollars. But just think of the traveling expenses you save!

Integral Link

`http://www.integralink.com/`

This page is nice to add to your hotlist if you're interested in online education or home schooling. The person who assembled Integral Link has done a wonderful job of gathering and reviewing education spots on the Web. The home schooling section alone is a keeper for people who are educating their own children. Likewise, the links to online courses are well chosen and carefully described. The site is updated often, with new sites gathered together for frequent visitors.

Distance Learning Directory

`http://199.125.205.20/webpages/dll/dist-lrn/dld.htm`

This list of links is good if you are interested in distance learning. Distance learning doesn't mean only online courses; it also includes videotape courses, correspondence courses, and any other kind of classroom experience . . . without the classroom. Most of the links on this page lead to college and university sites that offer some kind of distance course work, some of which is through e-mail.

Peterson's Education Center

```
http://www.petersons.com/
```

Peterson's, the famous college guide company, has established a presence on the World Wide Web that enables you to access its database of information related to all kinds of education: from kindergarten, to graduate schools, to distance learning. A slight learning curve is required to make the most of the Peterson's resource, but the time required to learn how to use it is well spent if you're conducting serious research into educational options. Families who need information on colleges — the database area that put Peterson's on the map many years ago — will want to add this site to their hotlist.

You can browse alphabetically, geographically, by college type, and by religious affiliation; and you can even read campus news from many schools. A search engine accepts keywords, and linked instruction pages can help you make sense of all this. Is using this site better than just buying a Peterson's book? It depends. You have more flexible search options with a computer, and it's certainly cheaper. You also can get your hands on high schools, summer pro-grams, careers and jobs, language study, distance learning, continuing education, educational vacations, vocational schools, and testing information — all in one place.

KidLink

```
http://www.kidlink.org/
```

The KidLink Web page represents a grass-roots effort that enables as many kids as possible between the ages of 10 and 15 to network by using a number of special-interest forums on the World Wide Web. All these forums are accessed from the home page. Any child in the right age group can participate by answering four basic introductory questions and then proceeding to any of the forums. KidLink has multilanguage features, a gallery of computer art, and an IRC (Internet Relay Chat) discussion area.

NASA Online Educational Resources

```
http://quest.arc.nasa.gov/OER/
```

If your interest is science, you've hit the jackpot with this page. In addition to NASA's own educational resources, the site offers classified lists of universities and colleges, online museums and expositions, online libraries, collaborative projects, and science education search pages. Every one of these categories provides a useful list of links and could be bookmarked in its own right. For sure, if you or your kids are looking for scientific content online, put this NASA resource page on your hotlist.

Smithsonian Natural History

http://nmnhwww.si.edu/nmnhweb.html

This Web site is for the Smithsonian's famous Museum of Natural History. Geared for the adult or precocious teenage browser, the page links you to various disciplines within which the Smithsonian conducts research, such as anthropology, botany, zoology, entomology, and mineral sciences. Light on the graphics, this page offers mostly articles, newsletters, and research results. It includes a search engine for using keywords (see Figure 15-4).

Figure 15-4:
The Smithsonian Natural History home page. Inside, you can use keywords to search the site.

Teachers.Net

```
http://www.teachers.net/
```

The Teachers.Net page is a one-stop Web resource for educators. Here you can communicate with other teachers, explore lists of resource pages on the World Wide Web, and even put up your own home page. This site even includes a geographical list of Internet service providers, but if you can look at this page, you probably don't need the list.

College Board Online

```
http://www.collegeboard.org/
```

When I first entered this site (see Figure 15-5), I was intrigued by the link to a "Test Question of the Day" from a College Board exam. I went right to it, viewed a picture of a complexly folded piece of paper, read the question about centimeters and edges, puzzled over the impenetrable problem, took a short nap, and awakened with fresh resolve to write this paragraph and get away from the site! Fortunately, my college days are behind me. But for those facing the challenge, this site is a great (and actually nonintimidating) way to get to know how the College Board operates and when its test dates are. You can even register for SAT testing online (though you can't take the tests on your computer). The site also has information geared to counselors, faculty, and admissions staff.

CollegeNET

```
http://www.collegenet.com/
```

A glaringly ill-designed home page is the only downside to this excellent college search resource. Your first experience of CollegeNET will be tempered by a server system that pushes graphics into your computer even if you're running your Web session with graphics turned off (which I generally recommend). So you must wait a bit for the page to display, and then you'll strain your ocular limits reading the white-on-black links. But no matter. After you get past the front page, the design normalizes, and a terrific search engine opens for your use. You can search for colleges by geography (states in the U.S.), enrollment numbers, tuition amounts, and majors offered. You also can search by name, of course. The results link to college Web pages, where available.

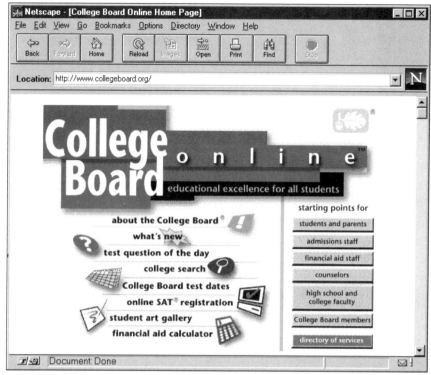

Figure 15-5:
You can try
sample
questions
and learn
test dates at
College
Board
Online.

FinAid

```
http://www.cs.cmu.edu/afs/cs/user/mkant/Public/FinAid/
            finaid.html
```

The Financial Aid Information Page is a clearinghouse of information for college students who need tuition help. Maintained by the author of a book on the subject, FinAid contains an astounding wealth of information. Glossaries; FAQs (Frequently Asked Questions); special topics such as international and disabled students; links to financial aid Web pages, books, videotapes, and consultants; and much more combine to create a one-stop resource page. This one's a keeper.

Chapter 16

Uncovering Culture

Culture is a big word. It can mean different things to different people. An opera fan's idea of culture is likely to differ from a sociologist's or a teenager's. (Not to say that all teenagers dislike opera.) In each of the main Web directories, three main directory paths lead to culture sites on the World Wide Web. Taking this as a cue, we can divide cultural interests into three major avenues of exploration:

- ✔ **Artistic culture:** This group includes painting, sculpture, architecture, classical music, photography, philosophy, and all other refined artistic pursuits.

- ✔ **Entertainment culture:** Entertainment is a huge subject of interest online as well as offline. Popular culture is represented in movies, music, television, books, theater, and magazines.

- ✔ **Societal culture:** Culture is, ultimately, the entire human-made environment in which we live. It includes our religions, sexual ethics, and famous people. It includes our folklore, advertisements, gender issues, and even cyberculture.

Of course, such divisions are not that neat in the real world, or even in the real Web world. Aspects of each group overlap into the others, creating a big, dynamic range of online cultural watering holes. If you're interested in the arts, pop culture, or contemporary cultural issues, you can keep busy surfing and uncovering sites forever. All the more reason to have good searching tools at your disposal.

Uncovering Culture in the Web Directories

You can get an idea of the rich diversity of culture sites by looking in the Yahoo!, Excite, and Lycos directories. In each case, the top level offers three main subject headings that relate to the quest for online culture.

Art in the directories

In Lycos, art subjects are best represented in the Art directory (no surprise there), which you can link to directly with this URL:

```
http://a2z.lycos.com/Arts_and_Humanities/Art/
```

As you can see in Figure 16-1, Lycos takes a detailed approach to art subjects. The Art page links to lower levels of Web sites in such detailed and, in some cases, esoteric fields as calligraphy, body art, holograms, graffiti, cartoon art, and metalsmithing. As usual, Lycos offers interesting subjects, and well-chosen links within them.

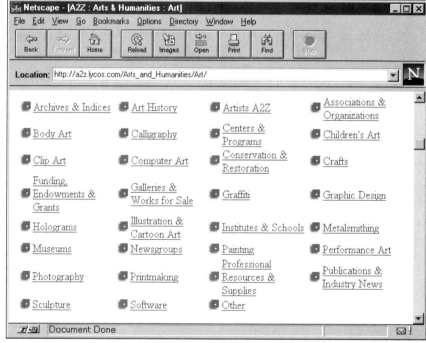

Figure 16-1: The Lycos Arts/ Humanities directory contains lowbrow choices, such as Graffiti and Clip Art.

The Arts directory page in Yahoo! is located here:

```
http://www.yahoo.com/Arts/
```

The range of artistic subjects is broader in Yahoo! (see Figure 16-2), thanks partly to the cross-referencing to fields found in other main topic areas besides Art. (Cinema and Music are two examples.) This setup is not necessarily inconvenient, but you may have to delve deeper into the directory levels to get to the specifics. Two very interesting links from this page are Countries and Cultures and Thematic.

As usual, the Excite directory's contribution to art sites is slimmer, but carefully chosen and reviewed. If you click on the Arts link from the top directory level, you see a short, basic selection menu (see Figure 16-3). You can go directly to it by typing this URL:

```
http://www.excite.com/Subject/Arts/s-index.h.html
```

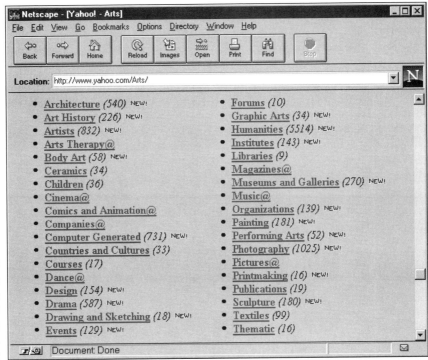

Figure 16-2: The Arts directory page in Yahoo!.

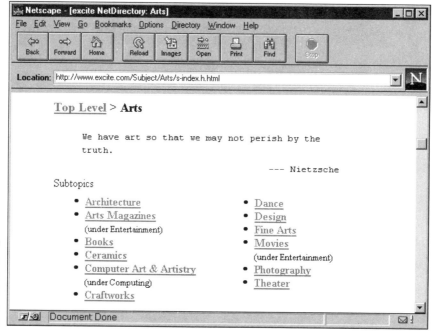

Figure 16-3:
The Arts
directory of
Excite.

The <u>Fine Arts</u> link contains basic art choices, concentrating on sites that have some real-world connection. For example, it includes groups of links to <u>Galleries</u>, <u>Festivals and Events</u>, and <u>Museums Around the World</u>. Using Excite is probably the quickest way to get information about art events that are happening on the outside.

Entertainment in the directories

When you use this URL you see the Lycos Entertainment & Leisure directory page :

```
http://a2z.lycos.com/Entertainment_and_Leisure/
```

Or you can link to it from the Lycos home page. However you get there, you can choose among standard entertainment topics, such as music, movies, videos and books, and somewhat less common links, such as <u>Pets & Animals</u>, <u>Party Central</u>, and <u>Personal Home Pages</u> (see Figure 16-4). Search through the <u>Pop Culture</u> directory path for some of the most hilarious Web sites you've ever seen. <u>Famous & Infamous People</u> contains an entire directory for Elvis. For one of the best collections of humor links in cyberspace, click on the <u>Humor</u> selection. And if you like electronic publications, try out the <u>'Zines</u> link.

The Yahoo! Entertainment directory is at this URL:

http://www.yahoo.com/Entertainment/

It's enormous (see Figure 16-5). Yahoo! is a huge directory, and entertainment is one of the biggest topics on the Web, so the result is a deep, complex directory that you can search productively for hours. The <u>Music</u> pathway is gigantic, and <u>Movies and Films</u> is no slouch either. Here are some of the more unusual portions that are worth checking out:

✔ **Useless Pages:** The name alone almost forces you to see which useless pages are worth listing, doesn't it? Perhaps the most amazing discovery is just how many there are.

✔ **Trivia:** Some fact of the day sites and more useful scientific trivia enliven this directory.

✔ **Drinks and Drinking:** Believe it or not, this link leads to subtopics and still more levels of hyperlinks. Whether your proclivity is beer or Ovaltine, you can probably find a Web page that will tip your mug.

✔ **Hard to Believe:** That's not my opinion; that's the name of the link. But I agree — some of the sites *are* hard to fathom. Shrinking brains and exploding whales? You have to see for yourself. You can also learn to polish your furniture with Spam and shave with peanut butter — but I'm not going to spoil the surprises any more than I already have.

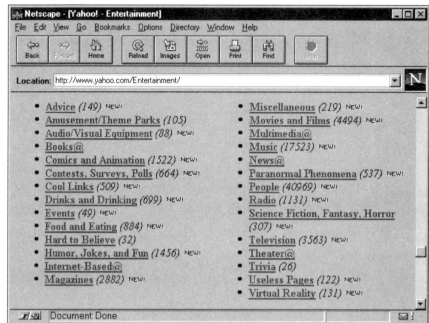

Figure 16-5:
The Yahoo!
Entertainment
directory.

Here's how you get to the Entertainment directory in Excite:

```
http://www.excite.com/Subject/Entertainment/s-index.h.html
```

Whereas Yahoo! throws everything but the kitchen sink in your face (and the sink is probably in there somewhere), Excite is refreshingly concise, brief, and selective. No surprises here, but as always, the Excite reviews lend a valuable hand when you are trying to find quality sites.

Social culture in the directories

In Lycos, social culture topics are found at this URL:

```
http://a2z.lycos.com/Social_and_Community_Affairs/
```

The Social and Community Affairs directory looks pretty slim at first glance, but when you dig deeper you can get some substance out of it. The Advocacy & Activism link is a good place to start because it contains links to all kinds of social issues and is the deepest part of the directory. Other links don't reach down as far into the directory structure, but they are still worth exploring.

In Yahoo!, the Society and Culture topic is the place to go. Get there with this URL:

```
http://www.yahoo.com/Society_and_Culture/
```

The selection is vast; Figure 16-6 shows only part of it. As expected in the fastidious roundup of Yahoo! Web sites, some irresistible tidbits beckon the curious searcher:

- **Cyberculture:** This topic isn't exactly esoteric anymore, but Yahoo! has certainly put together an impressive compendium of sites that are related to virtual living. The directory path has 20 subtopics.

- **Diversity:** The links here celebrate human and ethnic diversity, including the encouraging Bald is Beautiful link.

- **Environment and Nature:** This is the place for thorough environmentalists to start their search. The 971 links catalogued here are divided into zillions (approximately) of subtopics.

- **Folklore:** Sites about dragons, fairies, myths, mermaids and vampires rub URLs in this midsize directory.

- **Holidays:** You will never believe how many Web sites are devoted to various holidays (mostly U.S. celebrations) until you search through this directory.

- **Left-Handers:** This link is too quirky to pass up.

The Excite directory pulls out the stops on its Life & Style page. Start a search session from there by either linking from the top level of Excite or using this URL:

```
http://www.excite.com/Subject/Life_and_Style/s-index.h.html
```

As you can see in Figure 16-7, the topic selections are more extensive than usual for an Excite page. Admittedly, it is more broad than deep — that is, there aren't always very many links when you follow one of the topics. Still, the Excite characteristics of careful selection and thorough reviewing are in full force.

Reviewing culture directory pages

Here's a summary of the relevant main culture directory pages in each of the three big Web directories.

- In Yahoo!, check these main links from the top directory level: Arts, Entertainment, and Society and Culture.

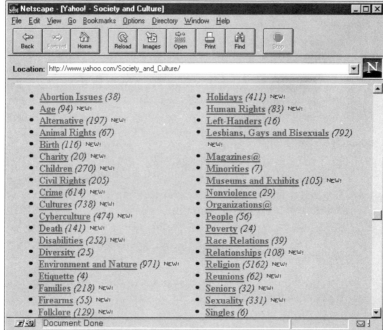

Figure 16-6:
A portion of the large Society and Culture directory in Yahoo!.

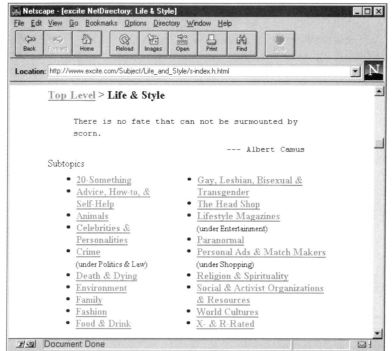

Figure 16-7:
The Life & Style directory is one of Excite's best.

- In Lycos, look under these categories: <u>Arts/Humanities,</u> <u>Entertainment,</u> and <u>Social Issues.</u>
- In Excite, the main culture subjects are <u>Arts,</u> <u>Entertainment,</u> and <u>Life &</u> <u>Style.</u>

As always, when searching in a large subject area, the more specific your keywords are, the better. Using keywords such as **music**, **movies**, **museums**, **books**, and other very broad requests will just overwhelm you with possibilities. However, the names of musical artists, specific movies, museums, book titles, and authors work well.

Culture Sites

The World Wide Web has so many fantastic individual arts and entertainment sites — from the Metropolitan Museum of Art in New York City to the Rolling Stones to Disney Studios — that attempting a best-of list here is impossible. I can, however, point out some of the finest launching pads for culture explorations on the Web. These sites provide links to pages on art, music, entertainment, and other refined subjects. As such, they are like cultural hubs whose spokes radiate into the global Web.

ArtsUSA

```
http://www.artsusa.org/
```

ArtsUSA on the Web brings information about American arts and culture to the Internet community. It is provided by the American Council on the Arts, and it offers an Arts Advocacy section (showing you how to increase your support for the arts); an ACA catalog (with books and other tools to help promote the arts); a discussion area; information on arts education; and a hyperlinks section.

Going straight for the links, you see a directory showing the range of cultural interests represented by ArtsUSA. Dance, film, literature, music, television, and theater all enjoy separate directory paths that lead to a diverse selection of Web links. The entire directory, which is just two levels deep, is contained on a single Web page. You need to wait several seconds for the page to load and display fully, but after the page is on the screen, you can navigate quickly among the sections.

CyberDance

http://www.thepoint.net/~raw/dance.htm

A clearinghouse for ballet on the Net, CyberDance provides links to dance companies, educational sites, news and information, people and organizations, and international dance, as well as many other links. If you like ballet, the links to dance festivals by themselves make this site more than worthwhile. Dance students will love the educational links to dance departments in colleges. The list of links for people is an education by itself, and the list of dance companies that have home pages is mind-boggling. This multilevel directory is a tremendous site, and must be on every ballet-lover's hotlist.

Dave's Arts and Culture Home Page

http://www.neonramp.com/kpowell/

Whoever Dave is, he has done a lot of searching and has great taste in high culture. Leaving aside the regrettable choice of gray text against a black background, this page delivers a terrific range of artistic categories, such as cultural information in different countries; poetry; literary sites; music links (heavy on classical and jazz); world newspapers (take your bilingual dictionaries); and photographic art.

The Film Festivals Server

http://www.filmfestivals.com/

The Film Festivals Server has so much festival information that it can drive a film lover to distraction. The festival information is not link-driven — that is to say, you can't link to festival sites in most cases. This is probably because many of the festivals don't have Web sites. However, you can find out what film festivals are occurring during any particular month of the foreseeable future or look them up from an alphabetical database. Are you going to be in Brussels next month? You could see some exotic movies. While you're there (at this Web site, not in Brussels), check out the coverage of recent festivals.

FineArt Forum Online

```
http://www.msstate.edu/Fineart_Online/home.html
```

The FineArt Forum is almost like a little online service. It has an index, an FAQ, a section for links, and an eZine (electronic magazine). More than a thousand resources are indexed here, with an emphasis on the possible relationship between art and technology. The links lead to all kinds of Internet resources — Web sites, of course, as well as FTP sites (for downloading files), Gopher directories (for finding FTP sites), and electronic mailing lists.

GNN Select: Arts & Entertainment

```
http://gnn.com/wic/wics/art.new.html
```

This directory page is part of the GNN Web directory, and it is a good supplement to the Yahoo!, Lycos, and Excite directories. A typical collection of culture topics is enhanced by a few unusual categories, such as Fashion, Digital Images, Film Studios & Festivals, Serials, and Stars & Famous People.

Musical Web Connections

```
http://www.columbia.edu/~hauben/music/web-music.html
```

This astonishing list of musical links has become justifiably famous for its sheer enormity, but it deserves equal renown for how well organized it is. Recent improvements have made it easier to use, breaking up the previous single Web page into more manageable (and quicker loading) pages for each category. Some of the directory categories that are ready for surfing are Broad Musical Sites, Individual Band Pages, Music Review Sites, Digitized Music, Record Labels, Music Zines and Publications, and the latest unsorted links.

The latest addition to an already knock-out resource enables you to search the database by keyword. Just click on the search link from the home page to get the keyword entry form. Every wired music lover on the planet should know about the Musical Web Connections site.

World Wide Arts Resources

```
http://wwar.world-arts-resources.com/
```

The World Wide Arts Resources (WWAR) site is a registry of arts resources whose work is represented on the Web. A directory format gives you main choices such as <u>Art Market</u>, <u>Artist Index</u>, <u>Art Galleries</u>, <u>Museums</u>, <u>Performance Arts</u>, <u>Art History</u>, <u>Dance Resources</u>, <u>Arts Publications</u>, and <u>Antiques</u>. (And many more category links — check out the impressive list yourself.) Furthermore, a keyword entry form enables you to search the site more specifically. If you enter the keyword **cezanne**, for example, a long list of matching sites is quickly displayed, linking you to outside Web pages that have examples of the great painter's work and information files about art history.

Joining WWAR is free, though you don't have to join to enjoy all the features of this site. The advantage to membership is that members receive e-mail updates of what has been added to the WWAR database.

WWW Virtual Library: Culture

```
http://hirsch.cosy.sbg.ac.at/www-virtual-library_culture.html
```

A truly international list of hyperlinks, this page presents a startling breadth of information. Find out the touring schedule of the Vienna Boys Choir, or link to the longest running film festival in the world. (It's in Edinburgh.) Then again, mixing the ridiculous with the sublime, a link to Disneyland sites is near the top of the list. Festivals, events, exhibitions, and tourist information round out this link feast. Dig deep in this site and become amazed by how richly cultured the Web can be.

Chapter 17

Foraging for Files

· ·

In This Chapter

▶ Discovering files

▶ Using Gopher on the Web

▶ Finding software

▶ Great shareware Web sites

· ·

*1*n the old days of the Internet, before the World Wide Web was born, file libraries were what most people logged on for. (The Usenet newsgroups were also popular.) Internet file libraries contained text files and software programs, and were generally shared for free. (Shareware, the honor system of software purchase, wasn't as prevalent back then.)

In these new days of the Web-centric Internet, files and file libraries are still great things to log on for. And searching for text files and programs is far easier than it ever was, thanks to the Web's simple navigation. Adding to the fun is the greater range of file types. Multimedia has arrived in the computer age, and you can now download pictures, sound recordings, and even short movies from the Web.

Downloading simply means acquiring something from a computer that stores files. The file must be located on a server (a type of computer) that allows downloading. You don't need to know anything to recognize a downloadable file or the type of server it's on — the Web page you're visiting will explain it to you. In fact, downloading was never so easy before the Web. In most cases, the Web site from which you're downloading gives you a hyperlink to initiate the download. Click on it, and within a few minutes (depending on the size of the download) you have your file.

What's So Exciting about Files?

The word *files* brings to mind images of office filing cabinets and endless manila folders. Not exactly what the allure of the World Wide Web is all about, you may think. Although the Web has become popular because of its graphic dazzle and hyperlinked pathways, it's also a great place to augment your computer's supply of manila folders (on your hard drive, that is).

Files are technospeak for the stuff that makes computers fun. Your favorite software program is a file. If you create a party invitation on your computer, that's a file. When you see a video on your screen, your computer is playing a file. Files either make your computer do things, or they are the result of what you do with your computer.

On the World Wide Web, you can find three main types of files: programs, information files, and multimedia files. Read on to find out exactly what these types give you.

Programs

The files that most people search for most of the time are program files. Computer software (programs) turns your computer into a whole new device. When you acquire a new game program, suddenly your computer is an arcade machine or a flight simulator. When you get a graphics program, suddenly your computer is a hi-tech digital painting device. You can download just about any kind of program from the Web by using your Web browser to place it directly on your hard drive. The three main kinds of software that are available for downloading are as follows:

- ✔ **Shareware:** Shareware is commercial software that you try out at no charge and then pay for if you decide to keep it. Its distribution system is run on an honor code, to everyone's advantage. Software authors can distribute their products inexpensively online, and customers can browse shareware products by the thousands right from home and try them at no cost. Some shareware programs are limited in some way, and to get the full version, you need to register and pay for it. Other programs have built-in time bombs (which are harmless to your computer) that kill the program after it has been on your hard drive for a certain number of days. Still others flash registration pleas on your screen insistently until you pay for a guilt-free version. But many programs are full-fledged versions of the commercial program, and you are simply on your honor to pay for them if you use them.

- ✔ **Freeware:** As the name implies, these programs are yours for the download, no strings attached. Download them, use them, keep them forever at no charge. Naturally, the old rule of thumb sometimes applies: You get what you pay for. Freeware programs are not usually powerful, complex, deeply resourceful productivity tools. They tend to be small utilities that fill a small niche for some computer users. However, don't write off freeware! There are some great free programs out there. Some of them are provided by major software companies such as Microsoft (the Internet

Explorer, for example, is freeware). Other excellent utilities are authored by professional programmers who create programs for their own use and then make them available to the public in the traditional Internet spirit of sharing.

✔ **Demos:** Some software houses don't want to distribute their programs as shareware but do want to take advantage of the online customer base. They take a middle road by providing demonstration (demo) versions of their programs for downloading. These programs are never fully functional. Usually, something crucial is missing, such as the Save features. When that is the case, you can test the program indefinitely and try out its many aspects, but you can't save any of your work to a file. Obviously, such software is useless as a productivity tool, but it works well to demonstrate the program.

Information files

The Internet is the world's biggest library, and the World Wide Web offers the easiest way to access information files. I want to emphasize that much of the Web's informational resources are embedded directly into Web pages. In other words, you can learn a lot about almost any subject just by visiting Web pages, without downloading separate files of any sort. However, you can access and download many information files through Web sites, and these files are well worth acquiring so that you can refer to them after you've left the sites from which you got them.

References and links to FAQ (Frequently Asked Questions) files spring up all over the Web. These files are text documents, without graphics, and they usually do a good job of explaining basic information about a topic in question-and-answer format. You can find FAQ files that explain how to navigate the Internet, how to use Usenet newsgroups, what Java is and how to use it, and probably even how to scramble eggs, if you look hard enough. The truth is, there are FAQ files for darn near everything, especially computer-related topics. The three proven ways of finding FAQ files are as follows:

✔ **Stumble across them:** Obviously, this method is the least organized way of finding FAQ files. But it often works when you least expect it, so keep your eyes open for links to FAQ files on Web pages.

✔ **Ask for them:** To ask for a FAQ file, you go to the Usenet bulletin board, find a newsgroup on the topic in which you're searching, and post a message asking whether anyone knows the Internet location of certain FAQ files (you can plug in any subject). You can often get good results within a day or two.

✔ **Use** FAQ **in your keyword string.** If, for example, you're searching for basic information about VRML, the Virtual Reality Modeling Language that is sometimes found on the Web, you can get good results by using **vrml faq** as a keyword string in any of the major search engines.

Downloading: What's the delay?

When you begin a download with your Web browser, you may experience delays, and getting the file may take longer than it should. What is the reason for the delay, and how can you tell if it's happening?

Download delays can be caused by a few things. If you're trying to get your hands on a popular file, such as the latest beta-test version of Netscape Navigator, many other people may be downloading it at the same time. If too many people access the server (the computer storing the file) simultaneously, everyone will experience slowdowns. You have no way of knowing how many other users are reaching for the same file as you, but if you're logging on during Internet prime time (such as late Friday evening), chances are good that you have lots of company.

Other bottlenecks can occur. The file has to travel over the phone line from the server upon which it is stored to your Internet service provider (encountering a few switching points along the way). Then it has to go through your service provider's Internet gateway, over more phone lines, through your modem, and into your computer. Telephone line noise and Internet traffic can interfere with the process at several stages.

How can you tell whether your download is delayed? If you're using an external modem, keep an eye on the RD (Receiving Data) light. If it doesn't blink, nothing's happening. Most people have internal modems, though, and in that case you have to rely on your Web browser to tell you what's going on. Most browsers display a status panel (a small window that opens on top of the main browser window) telling you how big the file is, how much has been received, and how much time remains. If the status panel doesn't show any change for about 15 seconds, you're stalled. Sometimes (like if you have something else to do), the best thing to do is to let it proceed slowly. Alternatively, you can stop the download and try again later. Sometimes trying again immediately works too. No matter what you try, yelling a few choice words can help — or at least make you feel better.

Multimedia files

Multimedia refers to any computer experience that goes beyond reading text. Multimedia files include pictures, sounds, and movies. The Web is a multimedia playground, and most of its multimedia files come bundled right in the Web pages. But there are also stand-alone files of pictures, sounds, and videos that can be accessed and downloaded through your Web browser.

Gophering for Files

Before the Web, there was Gopher. Gopher was big news in its heyday. Before Gopher, there was utter chaos on the Internet. It was a rich resource of information and files, but if you didn't know your way around, finding anything was a nightmare. And who could possibly know the landscape of such an immense cyberspace? Gopher was the Internet's first popular and effective directory system. When it was established, Internet surfers could use directory menus — pretty much like the multilevel Web directories everyone uses now — to travel methodically from a grand overview to a specific file. It was Gopher that first made the Internet a friendly place and first attracted the attention of the general public.

Gopher had a short day in the sun, though. Before long, the World Wide Web was stealing headlines with its superfriendly point-and-click hyperlink navigation. The Web is less organized than Gopherspace, but it has the star appeal of bright graphics and ease of use. Did it spell the end of Gopher? No, it merely relegated that industrious animal to the background.

Gopher directories still work, and you can access them through your Web browser. Gopher has become a Web tool the way that DOS has become a Windows tool that you access through Windows. The difference between a Web directory and a Gopher directory is this:

✔ You search through a Web directory for Web sites.

✔ You search through a Gopher directory for files.

You can find all kinds of files through Gopher: programs, texts, sounds, pictures, and movies. You can view and read the text files directly from the host server, without downloading them. You have to download the others and then view them (or listen to them) from your own hard drive with the correct utility software.

Getting going with Gopher

Getting started at using Gopher on the Web is easy. Just enter the URL for a main Gopher directory (located on a Gopher server) and click your way through the directory levels, just as in Yahoo!, Excite, or Lycos. Gopher menus are stark affairs (see Figure 17-1), completely lacking in pretty graphics and flashy advertisements — I leave it up to you to decide whether this sparse appearance is an advantage or a drawback.

There are hundreds of Gopher servers. Some are planetary in scope, and others pertain just to the institution that houses the server. Many colleges, for example, maintain Gopher servers for storing files that are relevant to the curriculum and campus. Remember — Gopher is just a system of organizing files. Whether that system is applied to the entire Internet or a single office is a free choice of whoever is running the Gopher system. The upshot of this? Just browsing Gopher servers can be an adventure before you even get to the good files!

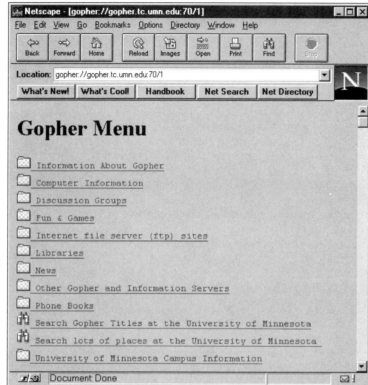

Figure 17-1:
The top
level of the
University of
Minnesota
Gopher
directory.

The best place to start is at the grandfather of all Gopher servers, which is located at the University of Minnesota. To use your Web browser to get there, enter the following URL. Notice that the *http://* prefix has been replaced by a *gopher://* prefix. This is the case with all Gopher server URLs. Type it in exactly like this:

```
gopher://gopher.tc.umn.edu:70/1
```

After you arrive at the main directory page, you can click your way around the Gopher universe.

Gopher icons

Several types of small, graphic icons help you navigate your way through Gopherspace. The most common icon is the folder icon, which indicates that at least one more directory level exists beneath that link. The folders are similar to folders in the Windows and Macintosh computer desktops: They represent a collection of files and/or more folders.

File types are flagged by their own special icons (see Figure 17-2), which makes it easy to identify text, sound, graphic, movie, and MIDI files.

Gopher keywords

Some Gopher listings have a little pair of binoculars next to them. The binoculars indicate that you can conduct a keyword search at that Gopher page. Indeed, if you click on the hypertext link next to the binoculars, you see a keyword entry form that invites you to enter one or more words for searching. In most cases, you are searching for directories, and your keywords will be matched against words in directory names — not against the body of any text files you may be searching for. Accordingly, it's best to keep your keywords general. If you're searching for medical files about vitamin supplements for heart murmurs, for example, use **nutrition** or **heart** as a keyword, rather than **heart murmur** or **palpitation**, because you're trying to match against a directory name. After you get a list of relevant Gopher directories (with folder icons), you can click your way to more specific files.

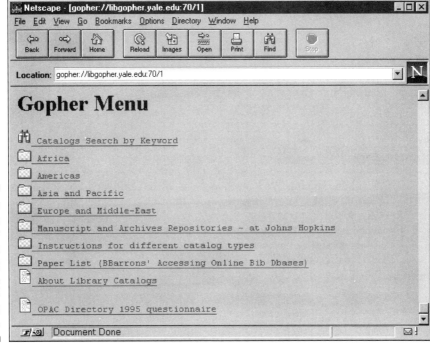

Figure 17-2: Part of a Gopher menu showing text, folder, and searching icons.

Finding Files with Keywords

Searching for files with keywords is a special challenge. Files are downloadable objects, but most keyword searches investigate topics and subjects. You can stumble across files within any topical search, but finding any specific file with keywords is hard unless you know the exact name of the file you need.

However, when you are searching for files, you can use keywords for one handy shortcut. When you want to find a certain *type* of file, you can include the file extension for that type in your keyword string. (The *file extension* is the three-letter "suffix" that follows the period in a filename.) In order for this shortcut to work, you also need to use the wild card asterisk (*) in place of the filename before the extension. Here's an example:

```
*.wav
```

As a keyword, this string matches with all files that have WAV extension, no matter what comes before the period. (The WAV extension indicates an audio file.) Of course, the results list would be immense and practically useless. To narrow it down, include other keywords in the string and tell the search engine to match *all* of them, like this:

```
*.wav AND grateful AND dead
```

This string returns a list of matches to all three words and includes sites containing audio files of the Grateful Dead.

Shareware Sites

A few commercial Web sites serve as virtual software stores that specialize in downloadable shareware. Don't let their commercial nature fool you — the sites are absolutely free to use. They have advertisements on them, but there's nothing unusual about that. Like real software stores, the Web versions divide their inventory into categories based on computer type and program type. These categories differ from one site to the next, but a few basic types of shareware are recurring.

✔ **Games:** There is a lot of replication among shareware games. You can find dozens of examples of computer versions of board games, such as chess, checkers, and backgammon, plus games that are modeled after the old arcade diversions, such as Pong and Breakout. In most cases, these files are small, and you can download them quickly, so you can test several of them to find one you really like. You also can find and acquire larger-scale adventure games for a bigger investment in download time. High-intensity graphic powerhouses are not usually downloadable, because they are so big, so don't expect to find games that rely on video footage. For those, you should shop in a CD-ROM store.

✓ **Personal:** Personal shareware includes all kinds of programs that defy easy categorization, and this type of shareware is for personal learning or entertainment, as opposed to productivity. Some examples are astrology calculators, science programs, weather forecasting software, genealogy applications, and shareware books and other electronic publications.

✓ **Computer utilities:** This category is one of the largest groups, partly because the programs tend to be small, with narrowly specific purposes, such as on-screen alarm clocks. Because there are so many little ways to enhance a computer, miniature utilities spring up everywhere and are downloaded under the shareware principle constantly. They're fun to look for, too — and finding just the right utility can really make a difference in your overall computing experience.

One common and prevalent type of shareware utility is the compression/ decompression program. Because almost all program files are compressed and must be decompressed after downloading, just about everyone who downloads files needs one of these programs. ZIP programs (for Windows) and SIT programs (for the Macintosh) are the most common.

Screen savers are one of the most popular shareware downloads. They create moving graphics on your monitor when the computer is idle and may protect your screen from "burn-in" damage while entertaining or dazzling you. You also can find desktop organizers (for the desktop of your operating system — it's up to you to keep your real desktop neat); calendars and clocks; computer diagnostic programs; and too many other types to list. It's a browser's paradise out there.

✓ **Productivity:** Shareware offers a much less expensive alternative to the big, famous, elaborate, powerful, and costly programs for writing, painting, and organizing. Word processors, graphic art packages, and database programs are three of the foundation pillars in the software world. The best, most professional, store versions of these applications can cost hundreds of dollars. Although these tools are fantastic, and worth the investment if you need to generate professional output, for many people they are a little too much bang for the buck. Furthermore, unless you read magazine reviews voraciously, you never know whether you're going to like a program until you invest in it.

Enter shareware to save the day. You can download a simple word processor, graphic viewing program, desktop publishing software, computer paint application, or database organizer without any charge. Often, the online descriptions come complete with pictures of the program's windows, helping you decide which to try. You can test programs until you find the right program level for your needs and then register and pay to keep it. Furthermore, some of the shareware files now in circulation are powerhouses in their own right. But because of the relatively inexpensive means of online distribution, they are less expensive than store-bought programs.

✔ **Internet navigation:** Everyone on the World Wide Web has one thing in common, at least to some degree: an interest in the Internet. So it stands to reason that Internet software would be a likely candidate for shareware distribution on the Web. The most obvious examples are the mainstay Web browsers. You can get Microsoft Explorer free, just by downloading it, and Netscape Navigator is sometimes available without charge from its Web site. In addition, you can find dedicated Usenet newsgroup readers, e-mail programs, other Web browsers, and many HTML-authoring applications for creating Web pages.

How do you find good shareware sites? It's easy — I've already found some of the biggest ones for you. Just type in the URLs for each of these selected Web stores, and check them out for yourself. There is no charge for visiting any of these sites, and downloading them is free too. Of course, the programs are not free in the long run. You can test them without expense and then register and pay for any programs that you decide to keep.

Jumbo

```
http://www.jumbo.com/
```

Not known for its modesty, Jumbo splashes an even mix of self-proclamations and shareware categories in your face as you enter the home page. At last count (I didn't count them), almost 60,000 programs were available for downloading from Jumbo. The main classifications are Business, Games, Home & Personal, Programming, Utilities, and Words & Graphics. An unclassified section catches new additions that haven't been integrated into the main listings. Each category is further divided according to the operating system platform (Windows 3.*x*, Windows 95, Macintosh, and so on), as is standard for a software directory.

A couple of problems besiege the Jumbo experience. For one thing, the sheer size of the program lists makes navigation through the site slow going. Some of the pages are so enormous that it takes a while for Jumbo to load into your browser. If there is a delay, or if the page stalls for some reason, you can't see the entire list. Breaking the lists into smaller pages would help. Furthermore, the promised descriptions of each program often turn up missing, which is frustrating. (Would you want to download a 1.5MB game without seeing a description?) Finally, the downloads are sometimes slow, perhaps due to the well-justified popularity of the site.

But Jumbo is well-named. It is one heck of a fun place to browse if you are a software addict or if you are looking for something in particular and can put up with the insistent circus elephant motif. (Jumbo, get it?)

Shareware.com

`http://www.shareware.com/`

You can browse, you can search with keywords, you can check out the shareware pick of the day. Shareware.com is one of the most respected download galleries on the Web. The home page includes a keyword search form that helps you find what you're looking for (though the promise of a "quick search" is a bit exaggerated). If you don't want to be that efficient, you can just browse by category. The program descriptions are as brief as can be, and the shareware is not critically reviewed at all. But you are told how big it is, and even how long it will take to download (assuming ideal conditions) with various types of modems. Unfortunately, the site is confusing without its graphics, so you need to have them activated in your Web browser, and displaying the graphics slows down the proceedings when you are moving from page to page in this enormous collection.

When it comes to downloading, Shareware.com has a good system. Rather than keeping its own cyberinventory of shareware programs, the system connects you to one of several Internet sites where the program you want is stored. The Shareware.com page remains on your screen during the download, but your browser pulls the files down from another Internet computer. Because it doesn't matter where you get the program from, Shareware.com links you to several possible transfer sites for each of its programs. These alternatives are great, because you can try one, and if the download isn't going quickly enough or is locked in a stalled mode, you can abort it and try one of the other sites. The instructions and page layout make it clear how to switch to another site — it's as easy as a few mouse clicks.

Shareware.com creates an electronic newsletter called Shareware Dispatch, which notifies subscribers of the latest additions to the library. It's free, and it is delivered to your e-mail box. Click on the Register button from the home page for subscription instructions.

Shareware Online

`http://www.bsoftware.com/sonline.htm`

Shareware Online is a dual-purpose site that serves both shareware customers and program authors. It encourages dialogue between these two groups by inviting visitors to place "Want Ads" requesting specific software program types. Programmers who have relevant programs can then get in touch with them. I can't say whether this system is of any practical value, but I can verify that Shareware Online has a good (if not overwhelming) selection of titles for downloading. You can browse by category, but you cannot search for keywords.

Screen Savers from A to Z

```
http://www.sirius.com/~ratloaf/
```

If you think that the best thing about computers is what happens to the screen when you're not using it, then you *must* visit the Screen Savers from A to Z site. Even if you're only moderately hypnotized by pictures and designs that play across your monitor when the computer is idle, you may want to enhance your collection with a few well-selected downloads from this site. And if you're currently stuck with the factory screen savers that came with your new computer, then you really must test the waters with a new saver program or two. Okay, I admit it, I'm a hopeless screen saver zombie. But you don't have to be like me to enjoy the large catalog of screen savers here. Many of them are small, quick downloads, so within minutes you too could be wasting most of your time gazing helplessly at colorful animations.

Free Stuff

```
http://www.zdnet.com/pccomp/lowband/freestuff/
```

Part of the massive Ziff-Davis Publishing Company Web domain, and maintained by *PC Computing Magazine,* Free Stuff is a well-presented collection of shareware and freeware. It's all free for the taking — though you have to pay for the shareware programs, of course, if you decide to keep them. (See the registration and payment information that comes with each shareware file for instructions.) You may want to skip directly to the "1001 Best Downloads" section, which gives you access to the complete database of files. Or choose from the categories listed on the left of the home page. This graphics-intensive site isn't the fastest in the world, but it looks nice, and the software selection is outstanding.

Chapter 18

Investigating the News

. . . .

. . . .

*T*he computer has an immediacy that satisfies news hounds who must remain up-to-the-second with world events. Even if you're not regularly a news fiend, you probably have times when an unfolding news story catches your attention and you want to get the latest developments without waiting for TV reports or — even more impatiently — the next day's newspaper.

On the other hand, computers have neither the convenience nor the ambiance of newspapers — carrying a laptop and mobile phone around isn't quite as handy as buying a newspaper — and they certainly aren't as personable as your favorite toothy TV anchorperson. What to do?

Strike a balance. Use computers for their strengths, and balance the equation with traditional news media. The World Wide Web offers a few terrific ways of not only staying informed, but being *better* informed than ever before. If you can integrate a few Web habits into your news-gathering routines, you may find yourself more deeply knowledgeable on general news items and a downright expert on issues of particular interest.

Here are some of the unique qualities that the Web brings to the news:

✔ **Continual updates:** The World Wide Web is free of broadcast schedules and printing deadlines. Different news sites handle this glorious liberation in various ways, but the general upshot is that news gets updated online mighty fast. Logging onto a Web-based source of headlines is unquestionably the quickest way to get breaking developments.

✔ **Variable depth:** News is structured on the Web in a way that gives you more control over how much you learn. Of course, you can scan headlines in a newspaper. But that simple task is made easier when the headlines are organized into lists that are linked to summaries and complete stories, as they are on the Web. By and large, after you know your way around, you can get the exact level of information you want more quickly.

✔ **Links to related information:** This feature is perhaps the best one of all for people who like to search deeply into a topic. Hyperlinks are, of course, the defining characteristic of the World Wide Web. Hyperlinks for news items can take you to sites that give background on a story, to e-mail addresses with which you can contact people involved in the story, to discussion groups for meeting other people following the story, and to various other innovations that are becoming more imaginative every month.

✔ **E-mail delivery:** A number of Web news services offer e-mail subscriptions. Some of them provide ways to tailor the news so you get an electronic newspaper that's custom-adapted to your interests. Though such deliveries don't arrive with the reassuring *thump* of a newspaper landing on the front steps (or the heartwarming *crash* of it flying through the front window), e-mail news deliveries are still very handy.

Gleaning the Headlines

One of the best ways to grab quick news on the Web, when you have only a minute to catch up, is in the megadirectories, some of which carry news headlines and stories.

The quickest of them all is Yahoo!, which offers Reuters NewMedia wire service reports as part of the Yahoo! index of Web sites. You access this feature by clicking on the Xtra! links next to some of the subjects on the Yahoo! front page (see Figure 18-1). Without many graphics to slow things down, these links deliver near-instant headlines in a few broad subject areas. Clicking on any story headline brings up the complete story, but you can get the gist with a headline-glance session that takes all of about 30 seconds. Try it for yourself at the Yahoo! home page, located at this URL:

```
http://www.yahoo.com
```

I use Yahoo! news headlines just about every day. (Try repeating "I use Yahoo! news" several times quickly.) If you surf to these headlines a few times, you may get a little impatient with the Xtra! link, convenient though it is at the beginning. The solution? Bookmark your favorite headline pages so you can go to them directly from your browser's hotlist.

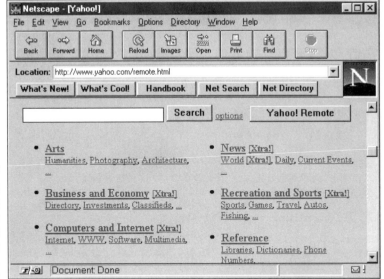

Figure 18-1:
The Xtra
links lead to
quick
headlines in
Yahoo!.

The Excite service takes a somewhat slower, but much more thorough, approach. From the Excite home page, click on the News folder at the top of the page. This link takes you to the Excite News page (see Figure 18-2), which contains headlines that are attached to one-paragraph story summaries. You can click on the headline to display the full story or be satisfied with the single paragraph. As a very useful touch, Excite provides an additional Related Web Documents link for each paragraph. This link initiates a search in the Excite engine, using words in the headline as keywords.

The Related Web Documents link is handy and fun to try. In fact, it can be downright hilarious, especially when you see the sometimes-irrelevant results of the search. The reason for the mismatched results is that the Related Web Documents search is kind of "blind," without any human refinement. The search engine simply gathers some headline words, pretends that they are keywords, and performs a search. You can't intervene with search operators or modified keywords. The results can sometimes be ludicrously unrelated to the story's subject.

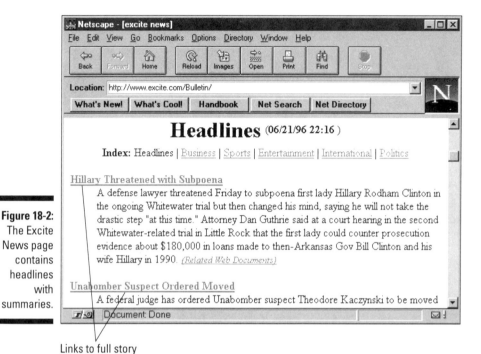

Figure 18-2:
The Excite
News page
contains
headlines
with
summaries.

Links to full story

You can jump right to the Excite News page at any time by entering this URL in your browser's bookmark list:

```
http://www.excite.com/Bulletin/
```

In the Lycos service, click the <u>Top News</u> link near the top of the home page. This link zips you over to Point, Lycos's in-house electronic publication. Here, the approach is different than with the headlines in Yahoo! or the summaries in Excite. Lycos provides headlines linked to online publications (outside of Lycos) that contain the full stories (see Figure 18-3). This arrangement is interesting because it exposes your Web browser (and you) to various newspapers and magazines, but it is much slower than providing the news within the Lycos site. You end up bouncing back and forth between Point, in Lycos, and the external sites that it links to (kind of like a Ping-Pong ball). If some of those sites are having a slow day, you might drum your fingers in impatience for a few minutes before dumping the project and getting your news elsewhere.

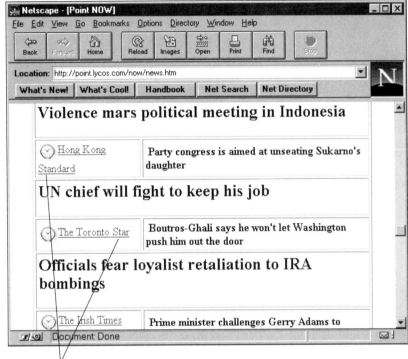

Figure 18-3:
Lycos
headlines.

Links to Web news sources

Customizing the News

If you really get in the swing of reading your news from the Web, customizing the form it takes is the next step. A few Web sites help with this process.

Crayon

```
http://crayon.net/
```

Crayon is a rough acronym for _Create Your Own Newspaper_. And that's just what you can do at this site, after a fashion. Crayon walks you through a process of creating a Web page with customized links to news sources around the World Wide Web. Crayon keeps a large database of these news locations and provides forms for you to check off what you want included in your personal news sessions.

The process could hardly be simpler. Go to the home page at Crayon's URL and click on the <u>Create Your Own Newspaper</u> link. A series of pages asks your preferences and builds your private link page, section by section. Crayon does not deliver the actual news — only the links to other news sites. After you complete the selection process, Crayon turns the whole thing into a Web page that you can store on your hard drive, using the Save <u>A</u>s selection in your browser's <u>F</u>ile menu. When you want to use the page, you just choose Open <u>F</u>ile (or Open <u>L</u>ocal File) from the File menu and select the page that you saved. It will display in your browser, ready to link to the Web news sites that you chose.

Have you ever saved a Web page to your computer's hard drive? That's what you must do to use the Crayon system, and it's not hard at all. Keep in mind that Web pages are like any other file. You can save them and retrieve them just as you would with a word processing file. Most browsers have a <u>F</u>ile menu (the usual drop-down kind, as in other programs), with <u>O</u>pen, <u>S</u>ave, and Save <u>A</u>s choices. Use Save <u>A</u>s for storing the Web page that Crayon has helped you create. Then, when you want to use it, choose <u>O</u>pen (or Open <u>L</u>ocal, or Open <u>F</u>ile, depending on the browser) to instantly see the Web page in your browser.

Don't forget to log on! (As Homer Simpson would say, "Doh!") Opening the Crayon Web page from your hard drive does *not* establish a Web connection. Just because you see the page displayed doesn't mean that you're online, and you can load the page from your hard drive whether you're online or offline. However, clicking on one of the hyperlinks will, in many cases (depending on your browser and its logon configuration) open a Web connection and take you to the link's destination.

SIFT

```
http://www.reference.com/
```

The Stanford Information Filtering Tool (get it?) provides the unique function of searching Usenet newsgroups (the Internet bulletin boards) and matching your keywords against every word posted during the preceding day. SIFT is similar to the Deja News service (described in Chapter 10) but with one important difference: You can subscribe to SIFT and have the results of your search terms e-mailed to you every day. (Or less frequently, if you decide not to be a search fanatic.)

SIFT is very easy to subscribe to:

1. **Go to the SIFT home page by using its URL.**

2. **Click on the Register link.**

3. **Enter your e-mail address and a password.**

4. **Click on the Submit button.**

Subscribing is free. Having subscribed, you can click on either the <u>Simple Search button</u> or the <u>Advanced Search</u> button. <u>Simple Search</u> lets you search and get results on the spot, using a single keyword entry form. <u>Advanced Search</u> is far more . . . well, advanced (see Figure 18-4). You can search by keyword, subject, author's name or e-mail address, organization, or newsgroup. The complicated form may seem intimidating, but every part of it contains a link to an instruction page.

Creating e-mail delivery of the search results is simply a matter of making the search an <u>Active</u> one. (Look again at Figure 18-4, at the bottom.) You can set how often the search will be run (and, therefore, how often you'll get the results delivered) and when the whole setup will expire.

Usenet postings are not News in the usual sense. But I include SIFT here because it's a great way to get information from unexpected sources — the authors of newsgroup postings, who offer expertise in almost every conceivable field.

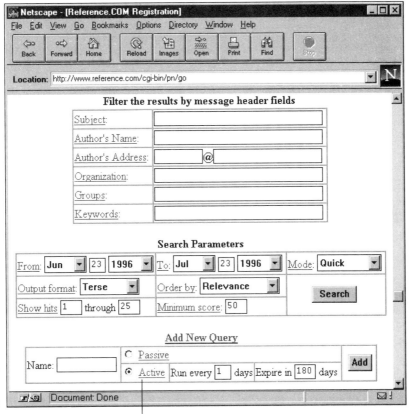

Figure 18-4: Don't be fooled by the title bar. This is the Advanced Search page of SIFT.

E-mail delivery activation

Checking the Weather

What is the news without the weather? And have you ever noticed how weather reports never seem to be broadcast when you're watching or listening? A weather report is one news item that you don't want to wait for. So — the Web comes to the rescue again. Assuming that you're near a computer and can log on quickly, that is. Well, it's not always easier than tuning in a local news radio station and waiting for the next forecast. But on the Web, you get a lot more control over whose weather is being forecast, and the online weather services are becoming more classy and intriguing all the time.

Intellicast

```
http://www.intellicast.com/
```

Intellicast, from NBC News, provides pretty good weather service at blinding speed. It doesn't cover nearly as many cities as The Weather Channel or USA Today, but the site's pages display very quickly, even when it is linking to satellite photos. World weather gets fair play here, and skiing conditions are covered (with several inches of powder).

USA Today

```
http://www.usatoday/com
```

Aside from being one of the excellent online newspapers on the Web, USA Today gives great weather. Here's how to access it:

1. **Go to the USA Today home page by using its URL.**
2. **Click on the WEATHER link.**
3. **Click on the USA Cities (by region) link.**
4. **Click on the 5-day regional forecasts link in the region of your choice.**
5. **Click on a city.**

A great deal of other weather information is linkable from the USA Today home page, including maps, statistics, records, long-range outlooks, international cities, ultraviolet forecast, extreme weather, and much more. In this department as in others, USA Today lives up to its reputation as an exhaustive information resource.

The Weather Channel

`http://www.weather.com/`

Why is it that tuning into The Weather Channel on TV is considered boring, but surfing to the same channel's Web site is cool? Because high technology has built-in status. Anyway, the Weather Channel site greets you with the same familiar logo and very quick service. It provides free five-day forecasts for cities around the country when you follow these steps:

1. **Go to the Weather Channel's home page by using its URL.**
2. **Click on Current Conditions from the home page.**
3. **Click on the state whose weather you want to know about.**
4. **Click on the city whose weather you want to know about.**

Within seconds, you'll be planning your wardrobe for the next few days.

Not satisfied with simple forecasts, the site also offers a learning experience about weather, plenty of maps, and even a history of The Weather Channel for anyone who's interested.

News Sites

News is such a significant part of the information superhighway that making suggestions about newsworthy Web sites is a predicament. It's like recommending certain gas stations to someone who's embarking on a 3,000-mile car trip. Some have clean rest rooms; others offer great prices; and still others are valued for the excellent convenience stores that are attached to them. You can fuel yourself with current events in many ways during your Web travels. What follows is a mixed selection of news sites, as well as directory pages that link to many other current events Webstops. Be sure to check Chapter 27 in the Part of Tens for a selection of great Web newspapers and magazines.

News on the Net

`http://www.reporter.org/news/`

News on the Net attempts to combine two worlds: news delivery and news linkage. The entire site is compactly contained on a single Web page, which makes navigation quick even if your graphics are turned on. At the top of the page, major headlines are featured, with an emphasis on technology news. The headlines link to outside Web news sources, not to wire service reports in the News on the Net site. Some of these links take you to C/Net, GNN, PCWeek, and other Web domains that provide great news service and are worth checking out in their own right.

A bit lower down, a directory of news sites is divided into political news, financial news, international news, computer news, and so on. Each category lists links to online newspapers, magazines, and other electronic news sources. The News on the Net directory is an excellent resource for building your own news hotlist. Of all the many and varied news sites, I gladly recommend this one as an excellent starting place for beginning and veteran searchers alike.

GNN News

```
http://reuters.gnn.com/
```

Reuters NewMedia wire service reports are found in abundance in several prominent Web locations, including Yahoo! and some of the other main directories. The Reuters news headlines and stories are especially well implemented in the GNN site, which, among other features, lists the time of posting next to each headline. Stories are archived for about a week, and you can look back to headlines of previous days. If this site has a drawback, it is the lack of breadth. Only four sections are presented: Top News; International; Politics; and Entertainment. A popular Web location, GNN News is sometimes slowed by traffic, causing pages to load only partially. This problem, of course, is common all over the Net.

The Omnivore

```
http://way.net/omnivore/
```

Speed. That's what The Omnivore is all about. Speed, and global reach. From its graphics-stripped, fast-text interface to its emphasis on headline news sources to its "QuickNews" trademark, The Omnivore aims to point you in the right direction and get you on your way in a hurry. Not that it carries any news services of its own. Instead, it links you to an impressive array of international sites, such as The New York Times, the Africa News Service, China News Digest Global News Service, Associated Press (AP) wire reports from The Boston Globe, Radio Free Europe, and others. The list isn't long, but it sure is well chosen.

The Virtual Daily News

```
http://www.infi.net/~opfer/daily.htm
```

Blending an easy-on-the-eyes, attractive home page with tons of links to news sources around the Web, The Virtual Daily News provides an alluring home base from which to discover online news publications. Set up in typical Web-directory style, with top-level categories leading to a second level of more categories and links, this site goes pretty far toward living up to its motto: "The best free news links . . . comprehensive and convenient." Adding to the convenience are keyword entry forms for Yahoo!, AltaVista, and Excite, in case you're beset by the irresistible urge to search the Web.

World Wide News Sources on the Internet

```
http://www.discover.co.uk/NET/NEWS/news.html
```

Wow! This site will slake any news shark's thirst. When they say "World Wide," they're not fooling around. Each page of this alphabetically hyperlinked directory struts listings of online news agencies and publications from around the world. Tune in your short wave radio while surfing to this site for a true global village experience. And a no-nonsense experience as well — hardly a single graphic slows down the quick display of pages here, which is generally a benefit when you are searching for news.

From the Afghanistan News Service to a newspaper from Zambia, the world is well represented *except* for the United States. No matter — you can get U.S. news anywhere. Ever wondered what the Bulgarian financial press has to say? This resource will link you right to Pari (Money), the Bulgarian Financial and Business News Daily. I won't spoil the site by giving away much more, but be sure to check out the News from Latvia while you're there.

The Electronic Newsstand

```
http://www.enews.com/
```

This directory might be more concerned with slick design than with ease of use, but if you can stand a heavy graphic load that slows down the pages, the reward is a wonderful selection of online magazines. The whole gamut is covered, from Web-created eZines to online editions of print magazines. The selection is divided into 24 categories, and you can search the database by keyword, for either a magazine name or an article. Searching for an article by keyword on a database that covers many magazines is one terrific feature and by itself should catapult this site onto many hotlists.

NewsLink

http://www.newslink.org/

Another astonishingly good launching pad for news explorations, NewsLink is particularly thorough at linking to newspapers in the U.S. and abroad. You can browse by state, country, or the level of interactivity of the newspaper site. However, NewsLink does not slight magazines, radio stations, TV stations, or other online resources. NewsLink is created by the *American Journalism Review,* and you can search the site, browse it, subscribe to the print version, and read its articles and columns. NewsLink deserves every one of its many awards.

Personal View

http://www.zdnet.com/zdi/pview/pview.cgi

Personal view is run by a large magazine publishing company, and it offers e-mail delivery of technical news items on subjects that you determine. You can track computer companies in the news, for example, or general developments in some aspect of the digital age, such as the World Wide Web. Or even World Wide Web searching. Registration is free, and members can download Password Pro, a handy utility that keeps track of all your Internet passwords. (They do add up.) A sweepstakes giveaway and an e-mail newsletter round off the package. But the main attraction is the daily e-mail news feed.

Chapter 19

Pursuing People

*W*orld Wide Web searching is mostly about finding Web pages, information, and files. Cruising around the Web to look for stuff is usually a solitary preoccupation, and you can easily forget that people are behind the sites. The Web is like a giant, planetary movie set — a global array of facades, storefronts, and fake residences erected by people who are hidden in the final result. But real people are behind the Web pages, e-mail addresses, and Usenet postings that make up the World Wide Web experience. And the Web has search tools that you can use to find them.

Finding People through Deja News

The Deja News searching service is designed to search Usenet newsgroups (the bulletin boards of the Internet) by keyword. You can use it to find any article (message) posted to any newsgroup bulletin board in the last year. Chapter 10 describes this terrific service in detail. Right now I want to let you in on a couple of tricks that enable you to search through the Deja News site for the people behind the articles. Naturally, because Deja News looks only in newsgroup postings, you can only find someone who has contributed at least one message to a public newsgroup in the past year.

Finding a person by subject

The first trick works best when you know for sure that the person you're looking for participates regularly in Usenet discussions on a certain subject.

This method is *not* the one to use when you are trying to find long-lost college buddies whom you haven't spoken to in 20 years and you have no idea what their current interests or occupations are. This method *is* good when you are searching for individuals you don't know yet but want to make contact with, such as medical experts. You also can use this method to make new e-mail pen pals if you go about it the right way.

Here are the steps to take. You may want to log onto the Web and follow along "live" with your Web browser.

1. **Go to the Deja News Query Form at this URL:**

   ```
   http://www.dejanews.com/forms/dnq.html
   ```

2. **Enter one or more keywords in the Search For box.**

   Your keywords should reflect the subject of interest or expertise within which the person you seek participates. If you're looking for medical help, type in the specific medical condition that you're investigating. If you're looking for e-mail companions with whom to discuss the TV show *Star Trek,* enter the particular *Star Trek* show that you like best. In other words, be as detailed as possible in two or three words. Your keywords will be matched against the actual texts of newsgroup messages.

3. **Adjust the Search Options.**

   I suggest, on the first run, setting the <u>Number of hits (per page)</u> option to 60 and the <u>Sort by (per page)</u> option to Date (as in Figure 19-1). Leave everything else where it is. These settings will give you results pages with the largest number of different people from which to choose. If you need explanations for the other Search Options, please refer to Chapter 10.

4. **Click on the Find button.**

5. **When the Query Results page appears, click on any article to read it.**

   This page is where you actively search for the people with whom you want to make personal contact. Read the articles until you find someone whose message grabs you. Perhaps you'll find a doctor who's talking authoritatively about exactly the condition you're researching, or maybe you'll discover a kindred *Star Trek* soul whom you'd like to know better.

6. **Click on either the Author Profile or Email Reply button at the top of the page.**

   You have a choice here. The Author Profile selection displays a list of that person's collected Usenet messages, to all newsgroups, in the database. You can get to know a person a little better by reading through them. The Reply button brings up your browser's e-mail window, where you can write a letter directly to the person's e-mail address.

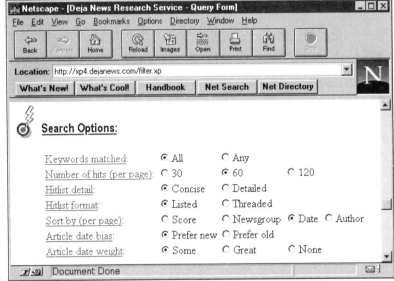

Figure 19-1:
Preferred
settings
when
searching
for a person
in Deja
News.

Remember that when you send e-mail to a stranger whom you've found through this method, you are a total unknown to this person, even though you've gotten a little bit acquainted with him or her. Take some time in your letter to introduce yourself and explain how you found them. Ask whether the person would like to correspond; don't assume it. You need to be more cautious when intruding in a person's e-mail privacy than you would need to be if you were posting a message to that person on a bulletin board. If you'd prefer to establish contact through the newsgroup in which you found the person, use the Post Article button instead of Email Reply.

Finding a person with the Query Filter

The Deja News Query Filter is one of the slickest features of the service. Don't be put off by the apparent complexity of the Query Filter page! Using it is not that hard, and this page is definitely worth learning about. I explain it completely in Chapter 10, and here I spell out how to use it to find individuals. This method works best when you are searching for people you know something about. Knowing an exact e-mail address is ideal, but rare. Knowing where the person lives or what the person's main interests are can help.

The best way to log on is to follow these steps:

1. **Go to the Query Filter page by entering this URL in your browser:**

   ```
   http://www.dejanews.com/forms/dnsetfilter.html
   ```

   Or you can link to it from the Query Form with the Create a Query Filter link.

2. **Scroll down the page until you see the Author(s) box.**

   This form is probably the only one you need to use. It's illustrated in Figure 19-2.

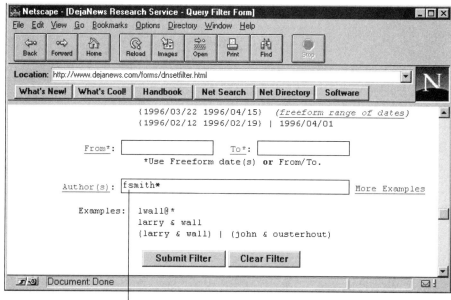

Figure 19-2:
Enter the name that you're searching for in the Author(s) box of the Deja News Query Filter page.

Entered name with wild card

3. **Type the name that you want to search for.**

   This part is the trickiest. Deja News compares your keyword name with all the e-mail addresses of people who have posted Usenet messages. People's e-mail addresses are not necessarily the same as their real names, although most people squeeze in most of their first or last name. Frederick Smith might use `fsmith` as the "name" portion of his e-mail address. Bob MacCallahan would probably shorten the last name, not the first, and end up with `bobm` or `bobmac`. Some e-mail services allow long e-mail names, so you can always try a person's whole name.

You can use the wild card asterisk (*) to help you track someone down. E-mail addresses are in this format: `name@domain.com`. In most cases, you won't know the domain name, so use the wild card instead, like this: `fsmith*`. Be careful, though! The wild card lets in every match that begins with those six letters, including names like _Smithers_. You can forestall that result by using this keyword: `fsmith@*`.

You may have to experiment several times before meeting with success.

4. Click on the Submit Filter button.

The Query Form appears, with a link to the results of your Filter (see Figure 19-3). It indicates how many documents matched your keyword.

5. Click on the link indicating the number of documents found, right next to the Filter size link.

You then see a regular Deja News Query Results page, with a list of newsgroup messages and their authors. In standard Deja News fashion, you can read any article or get a profile of any author on the list. At this point, it's worthwhile to scan down the list of authors to see whether you recognize the e-mail address for which you're searching. Don't scan down the list if you have no way of recognizing the address, of course. If that's the case, scan down the list of newsgroups, looking for an area that interests the person you are trying to find.

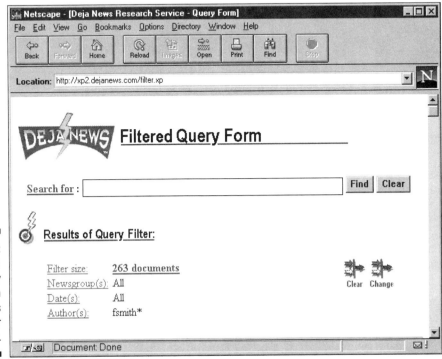

Figure 19-3:
The Deja
News Query
Form, with
the results
of your
Query Filter.

You can narrow the search in a couple of ways:

✔ On the Query Filter page, if you know the name of the newsgroup that your sought-after person participates in, enter it in the <u>Newsgroup(s)</u> box before clicking on Submit Filter.

✔ After you've received the results of your Query Filter, you can narrow them down by entering keywords in the <u>Search For</u> box. The search will be identical to a regular Deja News search, except that the search engine will compare your keywords *only* to the articles that it found from your Query Filter.

Finding People with Four11

The oddly-named Four11 search service (see Figure 19-4) specializes in finding people on the Web. A well-rounded service, Four11 offers an e-mail address finder, as well as a Web version of a white pages telephone book for the U.S.

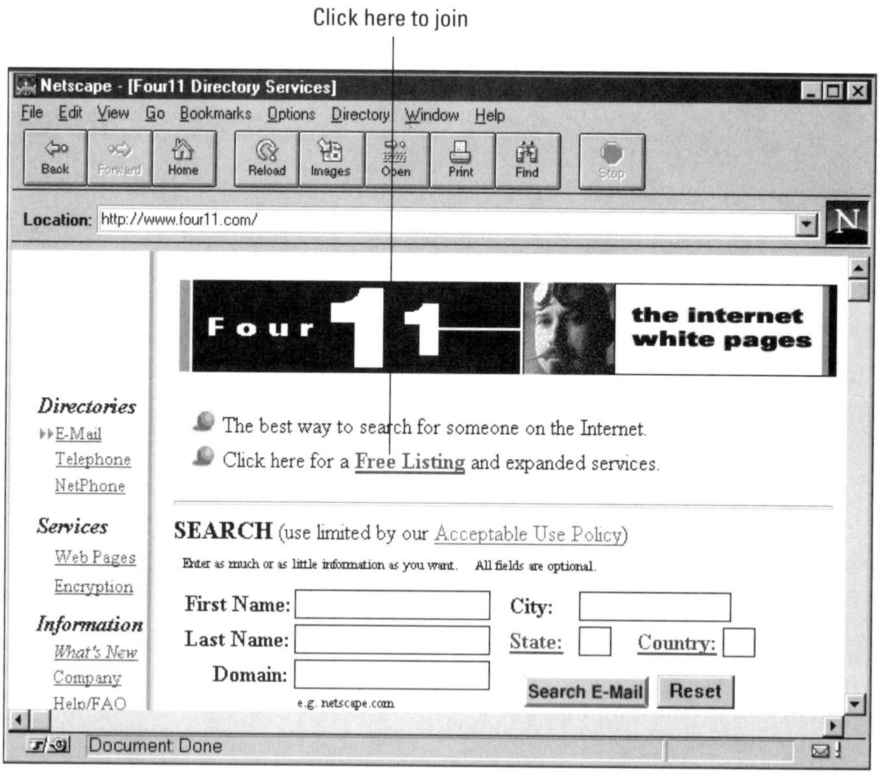

Click here to join

Figure 19-4:
The home page of Four11, as it appears before you become a (free) member.

Registering with Four11

The site is absolutely free, but it works best if you register your membership. The main benefit, actually, is that when you enter your own e-mail information, people can find *you* through the site. In addition, some features become activated only when you register. You can search Four11 whether you're a member or not, but your options are limited if you don't register. You can see the difference by comparing the two search screens in Figures 19-5 and 19-6.

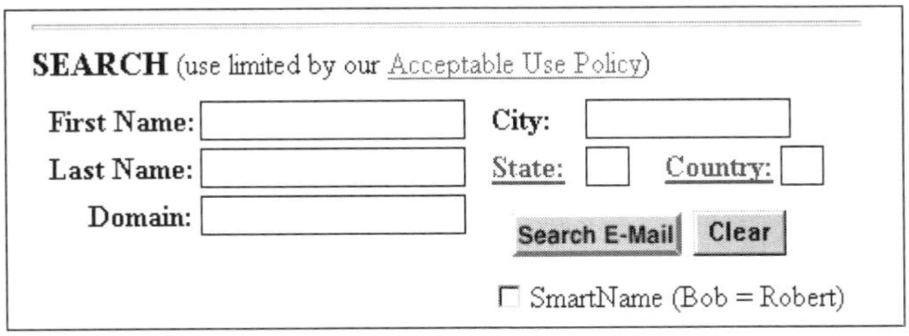

Figure 19-5: The Four11 search options if you're not a member.

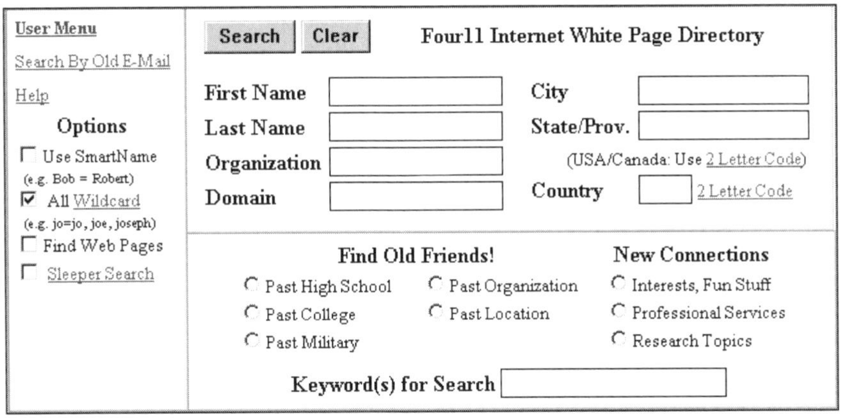

SEARCH (use limited by our Acceptable Use Policy)

First Name: _____ City: _____
Last Name: _____ State: ___ Country: ___
Domain: _____

[Search E-Mail] [Clear]

□ SmartName (Bob = Robert)

Figure 19-6: The Four11 search options for registered members.

User Menu
Search By Old E-Mail
Help

Options
□ Use SmartName
(e.g. Bob = Robert)
☑ All Wildcard
(e.g. jo=jo, joe, joseph)
□ Find Web Pages
□ Sleeper Search

[Search] [Clear]   **Four11 Internet White Page Directory**

First Name _____   City _____
Last Name _____   State/Prov. _____
Organization _____   (USA/Canada: Use 2 Letter Code)
Domain _____   Country ___ 2 Letter Code

Find Old Friends!   **New Connections**
○ Past High School ○ Past Organization   ○ Interests, Fun Stuff
○ Past College   ○ Past Location   ○ Professional Services
○ Past Military   ○ Research Topics

Keyword(s) for Search _____

Four11 gathers fairly detailed profiles about its registered members, but the purpose is not to invade your e-mail box with all kinds of junk mailings. The information that you provide is helpful to people from your past who are trying to find you. And the information from other members becomes available to you after you register.

Registering is easy; just follow these steps:

1. Go to the Four11 home page at this URL:

```
http://www.four11.com/
```

2. **Click on the Free Listing link near the top of the page.**

3. **When the Free Listing form appears, scroll down the length of it, filling in the boxes.**

4. **Click on the Submit Form button.**

You now have a free listing in the service, and you can match your personal information, as entered in the Free Listing form, with that of other members.

Searching in Four11

After you register, beginning a search is a simple matter. Follow these steps to search for an e-mail address:

1. **From the home page, click on the Search E-Mail Directory link.**

   When you enter the site in the future, you will need to use the Log In button to get to this link. That button checks your e-mail address and registered password.

2. **When the Search Screen comes up, fill in the boxes and click on the Search button.**

Searching for an individual's telephone number is simpler. You can avoid using the Log In button if you like. Just click on the Telephone link on the left of the home page, fill in the boxes, and click on the Search button.

As you can see in Figure 19-6, you have quite a few options on the e-mail search screen. The Four11 Internet White Page Directory boxes ask for the name, city, state or province, and country of the person you're looking for. Easy enough to understand. Two other boxes may require some explanation:

- ✔ **Organization:** When members fill in their registrations, they have the option of entering a "current organization." Usually, they enter the name of the company they work for. If you're searching for the e-mail address of someone and you know what company the person works for, enter the company name here. (This is different from the Past Organization that is another option to fill out when registering. I cover that option a little later in this section.)

- ✔ **Domain:** The domain is the part of an e-mail address after the "@" symbol. Most e-mail addresses have the name@domain.com format. This option offers another way to narrow down the search. You can either enter the entire domain, as in njcc.com (the domain for one of my addresses), or use the asterisk wild card if you're unsure of the whole domain portion. Here's an example: pluto.* (a domain for another of my addresses).

Looking to the left side of the screen, you see search options for all the information you've entered on the right. Here's what they do:

✔ **Use Smart Name:** Four11 has a certain intelligence when it comes to names. It knows that *Dick* can be *Richard,* that *Kathy* is sometimes confused with *Cathy,* and that a *Betty* can be an *Elizabeth.* Check this box if you're unsure which name and spelling your target person uses for e-mail.

✔ **All Wildcard:** This setting looks for extensions (not nicknames) to your entries. When it's checked, for example, Brad will also match against Bradley and Bradford.

✔ **Find Web pages:** Your target person may have a personal home page on the World Wide Web. When this option is checked, Four11 will find the URL for that Web page in addition to the person's e-mail address.

✔ **Sleeper Search:** This feature is automated. When it is checked, Four11 continually compares your search request to new member registrations and e-mails new matches to you.

The most intriguing selections are at the bottom of the search forms. These options can help you can track down long-lost acquaintances according to the personal information they have entered in their registration forms. They can be used even if you have filled in all the fields in the top portion of the form.

When Four11 is searching for someone by using personal information, such as the person's current job or old high school, it cannot locate anyone on the Internet who has not registered in the Four11 service. Nobody has to register such personal information to be on the Web or the Internet. Four11 is a private service that has a pretty big membership, and it's growing as more people find out about it. If you don't find that old college buddy right away, keep trying every now and then, or use the Sleeper Search. You never know when that friend from your past will get online and find Four11.

Using this section is easy, but you can search with only one selection at a time. In other words, you can't enter a high school name and a college name simultaneously. Try a search based on one of these options by following these steps:

1. **Select one of the "Past" options by clicking on the little circle next to it.**

   You can search for people you went to high school or college with, served in the military with, worked with (Past Organization), lived near (Past Location), and so on.

2. **Enter one or more keywords in the Keyword(s) for Search box.**

   Type in the school, military division, company name, or city. Use as many words as needed, as in **University of California at Berkeley**. The search engine will understand the phrase as long as you don't add extraneous words.

3. **Roll your mouse cursor up to the Search button and click once.**

   You see a new page that shows the search results: a list of names that are hyperlinks. When you recognize a name, click on it to see that person's entire profile (the information entered during registration).

You can follow the same process to select the New Connections options. These options enable you to search for people who have listed special interests, affiliation with professional services, and favorite research topics.

You can mix search requirements from the past and present portions of the search forms. For example, enter a name in the top, present portion (or fill in all the fields). Then enter the high school or college that person attended in the bottom, past portion. Click on the Search button, and Four11 returns all the members who match both requirements (probably not too many, unless the name is very common).

One thing you *can't* do is combine a Find Old Friends! option with a New Connections option. This makes sense when you consider that the options are meant to define the area that your keyword(s) will search. The search engine only wants to search one topic at a time, and there's no way to force it beyond that limitation.

Other Sites for Finding People

Four11 and Deja News are the most famous sites for finding people, but there are others. Search services for individuals are an up-and-coming development in Web searching. If you keep your eye on these sites, you're bound to see some innovative developments. After all, what more valuable resource is there in the Net than people?

Internet Address Finder

```
http://www.iaf.net/
```

With almost four million listings, Internet Address Finder (IAF) claims to be "the easiest and most comprehensive" white pages service for e-mail addresses on the Web. It certainly is easy. From the home page (see Figure 19-7), just type in a last name and a first name and let the search engine do its work. As the name of this service implies, its strength lies in finding Internet e-mail addresses. It doesn't work as well if you want to find an America Online (aol.com) or CompuServe (compuserve.com) address.

As with Four11, registration is encouraged and free. You can enter all your e-mail addresses, as well as personal interests, and your present work organization.

Figure 19-7:
The Internet Address Finder home page.

People Finder

http://www.stokesworld.com/peoplefinder/people.html

People Finder is a Web bulletin board. You can post messages to lost friends or lovers, and hope that they see them and respond. Of course, everyone else on the Web can see them too, so don't get too personal. The public nature of the service works to your advantage, actually, since someone else may know the whereabouts of the person you're searching for and get in touch via e-mail. If nothing else, browsing among the "lost love" stories is rather fun.

Bigfoot

http://www.bigfoot.com/

The best part of Bigfoot may be the animated footprints that walk all over the page. But if they're too cute for you, turn off your graphics and appreciate the simplicity of this e-mail directory service. The home page could hardly be easier. Type a name and country in the keyword entry forms, click on the Go Bigfoot! button, and wait for the results. Bigfoot doesn't make wild claims of being the biggest or best directory — it just delivers quick results to simple searches.

WhoWhere?

Another e-mail location service, WhoWhere takes free registrations and provides a dead-simple search engine that's impossible to get lost in. The service is
more than just e-mail tracking. You also can look up real world addresses (yes,
Virginia, the real world actually exists); telephone numbers, companies on the
Internet, and personal home pages (see Figure 19-8).

Figure 19-8:
The
WhoWhere
home page,
showing the
keyword
entry forms.

Part IV
Searching with Online Services

"You know, I liked you a whole lot more on the Internet."

In this part . . .

1 f you're a member of CompuServe or America Online —
the two giant online services — you may be wondering
how the World Wide Web relates to you. How do you get to it
from your online service? Does it overlap with the content of
your service? And what about searching within those two
behemoths — even if they are not the Web, don't they have
stuff that's worth finding?

This part answers all those questions. All you CIS and AOL
members are about to find out how to get on the Web *with*
your online service account, as well as how to search *within*
that online service.

Chapter 20

Beginning a Web Search from CompuServe

*L*ike other major services, CompuServe has jumped on the Internet bandwagon by providing its members with access to the World Wide Web, and a Web browser is built into its access program. If you're a CompuServe member, you don't need a special Internet account to log onto the Web. You can do everything in this book right from your CompuServe account, and this chapter tells you how.

Searching the Web is no different when you log on through CompuServe than it is when you log on through any other account. The Web directories and search engines described in this book are part of the World Wide Web, and that's where they stay (even for CompuServe members). You access those search sites with a Web browser whether you're going through CompuServe or not. CompuServe simply provides another way to get you on the Web, searching with a Web browser. (CompuServe is probably the most convenient logon path if you already have a CompuServe account.)

CompuServe also provides a huge network of private, non-Web destinations to visit and search through. I describe searching *within* CompuServe in Chapter 21. This chapter is to help you get on the Web *by means of* CompuServe, so you can begin your Web searching right away.

Using the Web through CompuServe

CompuServe members can log onto the system by using several different programs. In this respect, CompuServe differs from other services that can use only a single program. However, one CompuServe product is more "official" than any other: the CompuServe Information Manager (CIM), which is shown in Figure 20-1. CIM comes in three versions:

- ✔ DOSCIM (for DOS without Windows)
- ✔ WinCIM (for Windows and Windows 95)
- ✔ MacCIM (for the Apple Macintosh)

Web browser button

CompuServe Information Manager

File   Edit   Services   Mail   Special   Window   Help

Favorite Places

- ascii
Single Issue Price Hist.($)
Current Day Quotes($)
Pricing Statistics
Securities Symbols Lookup
Multi Issue Price History($)
E*TRADE Securities
Magazine Database Plus($)
Biz*File($)
AccuTrade Online
Investor's Business Daily

Go
Add
Change
Delete
Close

Figure 20-1:
The main
screen
of the
CompuServe
Information
Manager
(CIM).

Non-Windows users be aware: Most of the Web access features offered by CompuServe are currently implemented *only* in WinCIM. MacCIM will be brought up to speed later, and plans for DOSCIM are unknown. DOS and Macintosh users may now vent their frustration by screaming.

To take advantage of the CompuServe Internet gateway and mix the Web into your CIS online session, you need to be using WinCIM Version 2.0.1 or later. It's free, and you can download it (or just get information about it) from CompuServe at GO WINCIM.

You also can buy WinCIM (and MacCIM) in software stores. It's free if you download it, but you don't get a book in the deal, as you do if you purchase it. The file is large, so be prepared to settle down with a good magazine during the approximately 30 minutes that it takes to transfer to your computer with a 14.4 bps modem. That time, by the way, may detract from your free monthly hours, depending on current CompuServe pricing policy.

Time to browse

To venture onto the Web from within CompuServe, you need to open the built-in Web browser. It is a separate program called Air Mosaic that is bundled into WinCIM for easy access. You can open the Air Mosaic browser offline or online, with a simple click of the Web browser button shown in Figure 20-1. However, before you open the browser, you need to configure your dial-in settings for the Web gateway. Fear not — configuring the settings is easy.

1. **With your computer** *offline,* **pull down the Special menu and choose Session Settings.**

   The Session Settings window pops open.

2. **In the lower-right part of the window, click on the Use Winsock check box.**

3. **To check the correctness of the Winsock configuration, click on the Configure button.**

   A smaller window springs to life with an opening for Host Name. The host name should read `gateway.compuserve.com`.

4. **Click on the OK buttons of both windows to close them.**

   WinCIM is now configured to log on with the Internet gateway open.

Now that WinCIM is configured for Web browsing, you can open the Air Mosaic browser. It doesn't matter at this point whether you're online or offline. You can boot up the browser before logging on, load in a Web address, and surf straight into the Internet without stopping to smell the roses in CompuServe. Alternatively, you can be in the midst of a CompuServe forum session or collecting your e-mail and spontaneously decide to look for something on the Web. Pop open the browser at that point, and away you go. With both WinCIM and Air Mosaic open, you can navigate both environments at will.

Whether the twain shall meet

World Wide Web pages are written in a code called HTML (HyperText Markup Language). CompuServe uses an interface called HMI (Host Micro Interface). Remembering the names of the interfaces is not especially important — except for knowing that computer geeks enjoy technical words and acronyms. However, the differences between the Web and CompuServe are worth knowing about because these differences prevent the two systems from interacting with each other as smoothly as either one works by itself.

The Web operates by providing clickable hyperlinks — when you click on one with your mouse, your browser is sent to a different location, and a new screen appears. CompuServe also makes navigation easy by providing buttons and GO commands that act like hyperlinks

to other areas of CompuServe. However (and here's the bad news), you cannot hyperlink from CompuServe to the Web or back in the other direction. CompuServe does not currently feature any HTML links (the language of the Web), and the Web will never feature HMI links (the language of CompuServe). If you want to enter the Web from within CompuServe, you have to open the browser manually and enter a Web URL.

CompuServe's inability to link directly to the Web is changing. The service is planning to switch part of its internal interface to HTML in order to link more fluidly to the Web. Following the principle of two-way streets, members will soon also be able to link from the Web directly into CompuServe forums.

Using other browsers with WinCIM

Even though Air Mosaic is standard equipment in the WinCIM package, you don't need to use it when you enter the Web from CompuServe. Every browser has pros and cons, and if you are accustomed to a different program and would prefer to use it no matter how you access the Web, using your favorite browser is not a problem. In other words: Yes, you can use Netscape. Netscape Navigator and Microsoft Explorer, two popular alternatives, can operate in a WinCIM session. However, you have to boot up the browser separately as an autonomous program. This task is not difficult — just follow these steps:

1. **Make sure that the Winsock connection is checked.**

   Pull down the Special menu when you are *not* logged online. Select Session Settings. Click in the Use Winsock box at the bottom of the window (see Figure 20-2).

2. **Log onto CompuServe in the normal fashion.**

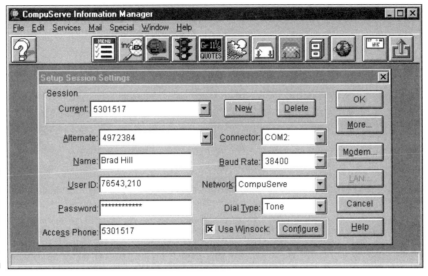

Figure 20-2:
The Session
Settings
window in
WinCIM.

3. **Run your browser of choice whenever you first want to enter the Web.**

   While you're logged onto CompuServe, use your normal method to boot up the browser program. It could be represented by an icon in the Windows Program Manager, or it could be a Start selection in Windows 95.

4. **Enter a Web address in the browser and surf to that location.**

After you're up and running on the Web and CompuServe simultaneously, using your favorite Web browser and WinCIM, you can proceed as if you were using Air Mosaic.

Using the CompuServe Internet Dialer

Before the Air Mosaic browser was integrated into WinCIM, dialing through WinCIM would not open the Internet gateway. CompuServe members needed to dial a separate online session to get on the Internet. They used a small program provided by CompuServe called CompuServe Internet Dialer (CID). This program would pop into action whenever Air Mosaic was opened and a Web address was entered into it. It would dial the computer's modem and establish an Internet gateway connection with CompuServe. Because CID shared session settings with WinCIM, it was preconfigured with the correct phone number, account number, password, and other logon information.

Figure 20-3:
The
CompuServe
Internet
Dialer —
simple, but
effective.

The CID is still available for downloading from CompuServe (see Figure 20-3) at GO PPP, and it is still a useful program to have, when all three of these conditions apply:

✔ You are logging onto the World Wide Web through Compuserve.

✔ You don't want to visit a forum or other CompuServe destination.

✔ You choose to use a browser other than Air Mosaic.

To acquire the program, GO PPP and select Information for NetLauncher. CID is included in WinCIM Version 2.0.1, but it is installed in a separate directory folder (called CID), so you can boot it up apart from WinCIM.

Using the CompuServe Internet Dialer to get on the Web from CompuServe is simple. Just follow these steps:

1. **Run the CID program.**

   After you download and install the CompuServe Internet Dialer, following the instructions provided online (GO PPP), a subdirectory is established in the Windows File Manager (or My Computer in Windows 95) under the main CSERVE directory. This subdirectory is called CID. You can double-click on the CID.EXE file listed there or use the icon in the COMPUSERVE window of the Program Manager. Windows 95 users also see CompuServe Internet Dialer listed in the Start menu under the CompuServe heading.

2. **Pull down the Settings menu and select Session Settings.**

   You see the same Session Settings window as in WinCIM. All of these access and dialing programs share session settings with each other in the common CSERVE directory. Check to make sure that the correct setting is active for your current location and account.

   You do not need to check a Use Winsock box in the CID Session Settings window because the Internet Dialer *always* establishes a Winsock Internet connection. That must be why there isn't a Use Winsock box to be found.

3. **Click on the OK button to close the Session Settings window.**

4. Click on the Dial button.

Doing so will dial your modem and create an Internet link through the CompuServe system. Remember, your session is billed according to the terms of your CompuServe account, just as if you were exploring within CompuServe.

5. When the connection is made, boot up your Web browser.

You can use the CIS-supplied Air Mosaic or any other browser, such as Netscape Navigator or Microsoft Explorer. At this point, you are connected to the Web, and entering a URL into the browser will begin your session.

The Back Door to CompuServe

The CompuServe Internet gateway is a two-way street. You can surf from within CIS onto the Web, and conversely, you can log into CompuServe from a Web session, even if you didn't use the CompuServe system to get onto the Web in the first place. This capability is useful mainly for people who have both a CompuServe account and a dedicated Internet Service Provider (ISP). Dedicated ISPs are connection companies that provide Internet access accounts. Such an account does not furnish membership in CompuServe or any other online service, but if you have that membership anyway, you can use this technique to bring CompuServe into your Web session.

When you're using an ISP connection to search on the Web, you may decide to dart into CompuServe to locate something or check your e-mail. To do so, you need Version 2.0.1 (or later) of WinCIM. Here's what you do:

1. Boot up WinCIM in the normal fashion, as if you were about to initiate a CompuServe session.

At this point, you are already logged onto the Web with your ISP account.

2. Pull down the Special menu and select Session Settings.

3. Check the Use Winsock box at the bottom of the Session Settings window.

Make sure that the listed account is the one that you want CompuServe to bill for the CompuServe portion of the session. Don't make the mistake of thinking that CompuServe is free when you're logging in through an ISP account! Your account will be on the clock just as if you were dialing in the normal way.

4. Click on the OK button to close the Session Settings window.

5. Log onto CompuServe in a normal fashion by entering a GO destination or clicking on the Mail button.

At this point, WinCIM recognizes that a phone connection is already open. Accordingly, the logon process is different — WinCIM doesn't bother trying to dial your modem, which is already connected to the Internet via your ISP account. (You won't hear any beeps, clicks, or hisses.) Instead, WinCIM enters directly into the CompuServe system through the back door of the Internet gateway. Without any fuss, you're in CompuServe! You can now check your mail, enter a forum, search a library, or engage in any other CompuServe activity as if you had made the call from WinCIM.

The CompuServe On Ramp to the Web

After you get onto the Web through CompuServe by using the Air Mosaic browser Netscape Navigator, or another Web browsing program of your choice, your Web search begins just like any other. Simply follow the instructions in this book for accessing and using a Web directory or search engine. Usually, what you need to do is type in the first URL of your session and hyperlink your way around from there.

However, you can launch your search from within CompuServe. CompuServe doesn't provide a Web searching directory or engine of its own, but you can link to Web search sites from a CompuServe destination called WebCentral (see Figure 20-4).

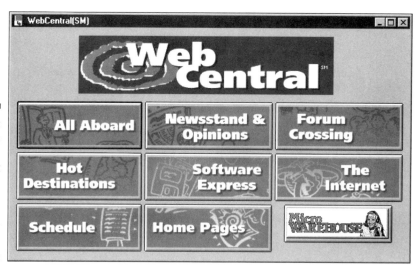

Figure 20-4: CompuServe's WebCentral. Use the Hot Destinations button to link to Yahoo! or AltaVista.

WebCentral is a CompuServe focal point for forums within CIS about the Internet, news services for information and press releases about the online world, columns and articles about the Web, and hyperlinks to the Web itself. To begin a Web search from the WebCentral page, just follow these steps:

1. **Click on the Hot Destinations button.**

2. **When the Hot Web Destinations window appears (see Figure 20-5), double-click on any item under the Internet Search Engines heading.**

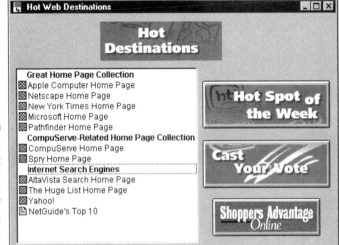

Figure 20-5: The Hot Web Destinations window of CompuServe's WebCentral.

Following those steps will pop the Air Mosaic program open and take you right out to the Web destination that you selected. Currently, Yahoo! and AltaVista are the two search engines available from Hot Destinations. The Huge List — a Web directory — is also represented. (You can read more about The Huge List in Chapter 24.)

You must be logged on with the Use Winsock box checked in your Session Settings (under the Special menu). Otherwise, Air Mosaic refuses to open (it's stubborn about having Use Winsock checked), and you are unable to cruise onto the Web.

While you're in WebCentral, check out the Software Express button. Clicking on it reveals lists of Web browsers that are available for downloading. Some are free; others are shareware programs that you need to register for if you continue to use them after a trial period. If you're not too happy with Air Mosaic as your browser or would just like to try other options, this is the place to see what those options are. One obvious omission from the list is Netscape Navigator — but it's not a problem. You can get Navigator from the Netscape Web site. Go back to the Hot Web Destinations window and double-click on the Netscape Home Page. Your current browser takes you to the Netscape Web site, from which you can download a trial version of Navigator.

Chapter 21

Searching within CompuServe

· ·

In This Chapter

▶ Finding the right CompuServe Forum to search

▶ Searching the CompuServe library stacks

▶ Getting what you need from the message boards

· ·

*T*he CompuServe Information Service (CIS) has been around for a long time — in fact, by online standards it is ancient and venerable. One of its most appreciated values is the depth that has evolved during its years as an interactive network. Part of the service is divided into *forums,* each focusing on a different subject, product, or company. CompuServe has hundreds of forums, and some of them have been active for ten or more years. They serve as gathering places for experts in many fields (not to mention thousands of regular folks who share an interest), and they encompass enormous file libraries that have been built by member contributions. Forum members can talk with each other on message boards and in real-time conference rooms (like the America Online chat rooms). The forums are self-contained, and although you do not have to pay an extra cost to join one, you cannot get the most out of a forum without joining it. (You can join as many forums as you want.) CompuServe includes other destinations besides forums, but the forums give the service its unique value as an information and community resource. And, they are fun!

While visiting a forum, you cannot access anything within another forum or talk to people outside that forum. This fragmented system, quite unlike the more open America Online design, is both a strength and a weakness. It keeps things well organized and lends a sense of cozy community to any forum you join; on the other hand, it prevents you from chatting with someone who is logged into a different forum. But that drawback doesn't matter so much when you are searching the system, and global Find menus can help you locate the forum or individual file you need.

CompuServe has a lot to offer. Searching through it can be almost as overwhelming as finding something on the Web. CompuServe has two primary types of destination:

✔ Forums

✔ Destinations such as online editions of magazines and database services (airline reservations, stockbrokers, and so on). These CompuServe services are similar to Web sites, but you can't view them in a Web browser.

Fortunately, CompuServe provides searching assistance within the individual forums as well as more global locators that operate across the entire service.

Getting Your Bearings with the Explore Directory

Just as on the Web, you can use a directory structure or a keyword-based searching system to get you going in the right direction in CompuServe. In most cases, you need to enter a specific CIS site (often a forum) and continue with more specific searching within that site.

The CompuServe directory is a graphic affair with big buttons on the top level (see Figure 21-1). Clicking on any button takes you to the next level down, where you see more specific lists of CompuServe locations. You may open the main window before logging on by clicking on the button with the CompuServe logo, called Explore (see Figure 21-2). In that case, pushing one of the directory buttons dials your modem and connects you with the service so that you can continue exploring the directory.

Figure 21-1:
The CompuServe directory, a menu-based guide to the entire system.

Explore button

Find search button

Figure 21-2:
The Index
button (for
the Find
feature) and
the Explore
button in
WinCIM.

The CompuServe search engine is called Find, and you initiate the Find
feature by clicking on the Index button in the toolbar at the top of WinCIM
(see Figure 21-2). You then see a small window in which you can enter a keyword (see Figure 21-3). In most keyword searches, you can use more than one
keyword at a time, but the CompuServe Find feature allows you to use only one
at a time. Simply type a keyword for a topic that you're interested in. It can be
as specific as **apollo** or as general as **space**. If your keyword is too specific or if
it doesn't result in any matches, the system asks for another word.

Figure 21-3:
The
keyword
entry form
for the
CompuServe
Find feature.

You can initiate this search while you are offline by clicking on the Find button
and entering your keyword. After you click on the OK button, WinCIM dials your
modem and connects to CompuServe so that the search can proceed. The
results appear on your screen.

Any keyword search is likely to return a list of several locations — sometimes dozens if you used a general keyword that could apply to many forums and other CompuServe sites. The results are gathered into the two-part Search Results window (see Figure 21-4). On the left is the search results list; on the right is the Favorite Places list. This handy arrangement enables you to copy items from the search list to the Favorite Places list. Good thing too, because the search list disappears when you double-click on one of its items! You have to perform the keyword search all over again to see the list again. In order to avoid wasting that time, just copy any locations that you want to visit into your Favorite Places list. (You can later delete any locations that prove uninteresting.)

Figure 21-4:
The Search
Results
window of a
CompuServe
Find
keyword
search.

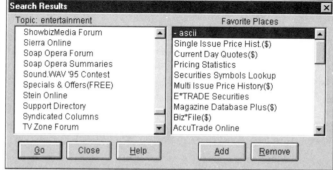

Here is the best way to deal with the keyword search results list. Remember, this stage of searching only points you toward promising CompuServe locations; you may need to do more searching when you get to these locations.

1. **Click on the Find button.**

2. **Enter a keyword and click on the OK button.**

3. **When the Search Results window appears, scroll down the search results list on the left.**

4. **When you see a site that may be worth checking out, click on it to select it.**

   Don't double-click, or you will be taken there and lose the Search Results window!

5. **Click on the Add button to add the item to the Favorite Places list.**

   Any items in the results list that are already in your Favorite Places list have a check mark next to them.

6. **Close the Search Results window.**

7. **Open the Favorite Places window by clicking on the Favorite Places button at the top of WinCIM.**

8. **Double-click on any location that you want to visit.**

    The items that you've just added to the Favorite Places list will be mixed in with previously selected locations. You can sort the list in a variety of ways. Pull down the Special menu, select Preferences, and choose General to see the options for sorting.

9. **After visiting any location that you won't need in the future, delete it from the Favorite Places list by highlighting it and using the Delete button.**

Searching CompuServe Libraries

CompuServe libraries, like Internet libraries, contain downloadable files of various kinds — texts, programs, pictures, sound recordings, and movie clips. The libraries are within CompuServe forums. One big advantage to the CompuServe forum system is that all of the forums are essentially identical. The subject matter differs, of course, but the structural features are the same. Because of this identical structure, one forum library works just like another.

Forum libraries are divided into topical sections. They are called either *library sections* or *libraries.* A forum can have up to 24 libraries or library sections. You can browse a directory of the files in these libraries or search the libraries by keyword. This is where searching gets really fun, because you can discover all kinds of unexpected files, and the Law of Instant Gratification kicks in: Every file is available immediately by downloading.

Browsing a forum library

When you are using WinCIM, browsing a forum library section-by-section is easy.

1. **Pull down the Library menu and select Browse.**

    You see a list of library sections for that forum.

2. **Double-click on any library section, or click once and use the Select button.**

    A window listing all the files in that library opens. In many cases, you see a mix of file types — texts, programs, graphics, sound bites, and movie clips. Columns of information tell you the file's title, its size (in bytes), when it was uploaded (contributed) to the library, the contributor's CompuServe ID number, and how many times it has been downloaded.

3. **Double-click on any file selection, or click once and use the Description button.**

A window pops open, giving a more descriptive rundown of the file (see Figure 21-5). The buttons at the bottom of the window give you a few choices:

Figure 21-5:
The file
description
window of a
CompuServe
forum
library.

- **Next:** Opens the Description window for the next file in the library list.

- **Mark:** Selects the file for a future download. You can mark several files and then download them all at once.

- **Retrieve:** This button starts a download of the described file. You are prompted to select a destination directory on your hard drive.

- **View:** If the file is a text or graphic image (in JPG or GIF formats), you click on this button to display the file on your screen. If it is a different file type, the View button is grayed-out, as in Figure 21-5.

- **Delete:** If you are the uploader of the file in the window, this button enables you to delete it from the library. Otherwise, it is grayed-out and inactive — you can't delete someone else's file.

- **Close:** Use this button to close the window and return to the list of files in that library section.

Searching a forum library with keywords

If you're not in a browsing mood, you can save time by using the Search for Files window. Here's how it works:

1. **Pull down the Library menu and choose Search.**

   The Search for Files window opens (see Figure 21-6). This window provides several tools that you can use to refine your search.

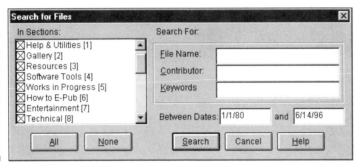

Figure 21-6: The Search for Files window of a CompuServe forum library.

2. **If you know the name of the file you want, enter it in the File Name box.**

   Knowing the file extension (the three letters after the period, such as *.TXT* in *SAMPLE.TXT*) is helpful but not necessary. Furthermore, you can use the *wild card* symbol, which is an asterisk. So, if you were looking for the popular unzipping program, PK204G.EXE, but didn't remember the exact name, you could enter PK*.EXE, and the search would work. You could even leave off the extension (PK*) successfully — of course, the less specific you are with the filename, the more results you have to sift through.

3. **If you're looking for files that were uploaded by a certain person, enter the CompuServe ID for that person in the Contributor box.**

   Names don't work here, sorry to say.

4. **If you don't know the filename or the name of the contributor, enter keywords in the Keywords box.**

   Each file in a library is assigned keywords that point to it. You may enter more than one word or only one; the system will return all exact matches.

5. **Adjust the dates to widen or narrow the time scope of your search.**

   The dates refer to the day and year that the file was uploaded to the library. If, for example, you want to download graphics of a television show that has been on the air for six months, you should narrow the search to that time period. The system moves faster when it has fewer files to check.

6. **Check the library sections that you want searched.**

CompuServe keyword tips

Keyword searching in CompuServe is a time-saving, well-implemented, basically cool feature. However, a few surprises await the unprepared. Although you can find your way through the searching process by using sheer experimentation, these tips may save you some puzzlement.

✔ CompuServe is a computer system. It is literal. It doesn't understand concepts or grammatical niceties, such as plurals. For example, if you enter the keyword **ROCKETS**, it will not match with files that have the keyword **ROCKET**. Be prepared to try variations of keywords to get the results you want.

✔ You can get around the system's unyielding literalness by using the wild card asterisk symbol. But brace yourself for a much longer results list. For example, if you're looking for files related to the television show, *The Simpsons*, you could try the keyword **SIMPSON***, thereby hedging your bet that the files won't be using a singular keyword. The results list will indeed give you all files with the plural **SIMPSONS** keyword (thanks

to the wild card), but it will also contain any files related to O. J. Simpson (if such files are relevant to the forum you're in).

✔ When you use more than one keyword per search, be aware that the CompuServe forum seeks to match *all* the keywords. Therefore, if a file matches just one of your keywords, the file will not show up on the results list. If you are getting nowhere fast with empty results, you may need to start with fewer keywords, or just one. Then you can narrow your search if need be, by adding extra keywords and re-searching.

✔ Finally, remember that keywords are an inexact science, particularly in CompuServe. Why especially there? Because they are originally assigned to the file by the uploader, who may or may not make good choices. The manager of the forum libraries may change them for the better, but this sort of library maintenance varies in quality among the forums. The upshot: Be creative, be persistent, and keep trying!

You check the library sections in the left side of the window. Use the <u>A</u>ll button to check all of the sections or the <u>N</u>one button to uncheck them all. Then click on individual check boxes to reverse the status of any single library section.

Using the CompuServe File Finder

If you're ready to magnify the scope of your search for files in CompuServe libraries, you can try the system-wide File Finder service. File Finder cuts across forum boundaries by returning matches to your keywords, no matter where the files are located. Furthermore, you don't even need to visit the forum to acquire the file; just download it on the spot.

Considering the convenience of the File Finder feature, you may wonder why anybody would do it the other way — visiting individual forums to search their libraries. File Finder cuts to the chase when you know what you're looking for.

When you're less sure of what you need, visiting a generally relevant forum can turn up some valuable surprises. For example, you may find not only a program that you want but also related text files that you wouldn't think to search for with the global File Finder. You should also keep in mind that the File Finder searches only an index of *selected* files from CompuServe forum libraries. For a full selection of any forum's files, you need to visit the forum itself.

Nevertheless, File Finder is a great time-saver, though a bit slower (understandably) than single-forum file searches. File Finder is easy to use if you have developed the hang of using keywords. File Finder is available for PC and Mac users at these locations:

✔ GO PCFF (DOS and Windows files)

✔ GO MACFF (Macintosh files)

Here are the steps for conducting a search in File Finder:

1. **Go to the PC or Mac version of File Finder and select Access File Finder from the first window.**

   You may also want to read Instructions for Searching or About File Finder. Select Access File Finder when you're ready to begin searching. The awkwardly named Select Search Criteria window opens. This window is where you select the search variables. Double-click on any of the selections that follow (which also are listed in the window on your screen) to display windows that enable you to enter different variables that will narrow your search. After you enter those variables, in each case, the Select Search Criteria window reappears with your selection placed in the brackets.

   • **Keyword:** Double-clicking on this option opens a box for entering up to three keywords. (A built-in AND search operator forces the system to try to find matches to all your keywords. Files that match only one or two keywords will not be included in the results.) As in the CompuServe forum searches, the system attempts to match your keywords exactly with the keywords assigned to files, with no latitude for spelling details.

   • **Submission Date:** Enter a date here to have File Finder return file descriptions only for items uploaded after that date.

   • **Forum Name:** You can restrict you search to a single forum, but there's no point in restricting it on your first search attempt. After all, the point is to broaden your search to multiple forums.

   • **File Type:** Double-click here to see a list of file types, such as Text, Binary, and GIF (graphic). This option is useful if, for example, you are interested only in pictures.

   • **File Extension:** This option is more specific than the file type. Enter the three-letter extension (such as .ZIP) for the file you want, if you know it.

- **File Name:** Start here, if you know the filename. This option provides the fastest way to get a specific file from CompuServe.

- **File Submitter:** Occasionally, you may know who uploaded the file that you want. Or, more commonly, you could want a list of all the uploaded programs from a certain shareware company. If you know the CompuServe ID number, enter it here.

2. **Enter your selections.**

   Each time you enter a selection, File Finder performs a search, returning the Select Search Criteria window with the number of results indicated on the top line. You can then enter a new selection, further narrowing the results. (Your previous selections remain in place and in effect during the next search.)

3. **After getting your first search result, broaden or narrow the search by adding or removing variables.**

   The top line of the Select Search Criteria window shows how many files match your search requirements. If the number is too large to cope with, you need to narrow the search by adding more keywords, a submission date, or some other information that reduces the number of files. If the number of matched files is zero, try broadening the search by eliminating keywords, making the date earlier, or removing some other information.

4. **When you are satisfied with the number of search results in the top line, double-click on Display Selected Titles.**

   A window opens that lists all the files that match your search variables. Double-click on any item in the list to see a more complete description. You can download the file directly from File Finder to your computer.

Searching the Message Boards

CompuServe message boards provide a very sophisticated way of trading notes with other members of a forum. Each forum has message boards, and they all work in the same way. The forum board is divided into topical sections (up to 24 of them), making it easier to find *discussions* of interest. Everyone is welcome to jump into any discussion by posting a message in response to any already-posted message, or to start a new discussion by posting a message on a new topic, addressed to ALL. As responses to any message pile up, and replies to those responses begin to accumulate, a complex tree of branching messages evolves. These message *threads* are fun to read and actually create a real sense of conversation and community.

CompuServe message boards are more than just community gathering places. They provide a cyberspace for sharing information, tips, experiences, insights, expertise — not to mention jokes, gossip, and small talk. The CompuServe system enables you to treat the message boards as informational databases, thanks to a thorough searching system. You can find messages by subject, time period, topic, or person. Because all the message boards are in forums and all the forums work the same way, these instructions serve you well no matter which forums you hang out in.

Browsing a CompuServe message board can be informative, and certainly fun, but in the larger forums it also can be intimidating. Even though the boards are divided into topical sections, you may want to go for quicker results. Keywords to the rescue again! And more than just keywords, too — CompuServe gives you a few different ways to hack through the tangle of message threads. To start using the Search for Messages window, take these steps:

1. **Pull down the Messages menu and select Search.**

   The Search for messages matching window opens (see Figure 21-7). Right away, you have a few choices.

Figure 21-7:
The window
from which
you search
the message
board of a
CompuServe
forum.

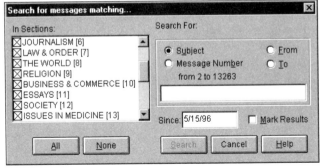

2. **Click on the Subject radio button.**

   You thereby indicate that you want to search by subject keyword.

3. **Enter a subject word (or words) in the form.**

   You should enter the subject exactly as it may appear in the message titles that you're searching for. The system is very literal. (Where is artificial intelligence when you need it?) It also will consider your entry to be *part* of larger words. Therefore, if you enter **day**, the system returns messages that have, for example, the word holiday in the title. One more thing to remember: Only the titles are searched, not the content of messages.

4. Click on the Search button to begin the search.

The search results flash on your screen in a separate window. Double-click on any of the matched items to read messages whose titles correspond (at least in part) to your keywords.

The Search for messages matching window offers a few other options for fine-tuning your search through CompuServe messages:

- ✓ **By message number:** Of course, you have to know the message number, which is unlikely in many search situations. Still, if you made a note of it during a previous session, anticipating a need to find the message again, you can pull up that message quickly. Just click on the Message Number radio button, enter the number in the box below the option and then click on the Search button.

- ✓ **By message author:** If you click on the From radio button and then enter either a name or a CompuServe ID number in the form below, the system lists all the messages on the board that were written and posted by that individual. Be aware that using the ID number will get you more precise results. People can change their name within a forum, and often do. Then that new name appears at the top of their new messages. (So entering **Mike** won't work if Mike has recently started posting under the name Michael.) Also, the system treats words as part of larger words. Therefore, **Rob** will match with Robert, **Al** with Allen, and so on. Use the name only if you don't know the ID number.

- ✓ **By message recipient:** This option is most useful for searching for messages sent to you. Click on the To radio button, enter your forum name or CompuServe ID number (or someone else's) in the form below, and click on the Search button.

- ✓ **By date:** The Since form at the bottom of the Search for Messages window contains a date. Change the date to modify whatever search you're undertaking. You can use this option with any of the search commands to have the search return only appropriate messages posted since the entered date.

- ✓ **By message section:** Likewise, any search is influenced by the sections that are checked from the list in the left side of the window. Use the All and None buttons to select and deselect the whole group of sections, and click on the boxes to affect single sections.

Chapter 22

Beginning a Web Search from America Online

*A*merica Online is the largest and most popular commercial online service, with a membership consisting almost totally of U.S. subscribers. (They don't call it America Online for nothing.) AOL has built its popularity on a philosophy that might be described as "Online for the masses," emphasizing features that appeal to a new wave of online enthusiasts:

✔ Low hourly connection costs

✔ An open, no-walls surfing environment

✔ Lots of member-to-member live chatting

✔ Fun graphics

Although CompuServe has its dignified, deeply informative forums, AOL (as everyone calls it) has a stunning array of feature locations, each designed originally, and each seemingly more slick and entertaining than the last. Like CompuServe, AOL has courted the World Wide Web as a partner, enabling subscribers to slip out of the network's confines and surf the Web during an AOL session. There have been some complaints about the AOL Web browser, and AOL hasn't made using an alternative browser easy . . . but never mind those criticisms. They have been corrected in the latest version of the America Online software.

This brings up an important point. AOL recently offered its members a free upgrade from Version 2.5 to Version 3.0 of its software for Windows. What a difference! For AOL members who want to search the Web through an AOL account, Version 3.0 is an absolute improvement. If you are still using the Web browser built into Version 2.5, I recommend that you download the updated version before setting your cyberfoot on the Web again. Downloading it takes about 20 minutes using a 14.4 Kbps modem.

All the illustrations in this chapter reflect the AOL/World Wide Web experience through Version 3.0. The new software changes the look of the system in some places, in addition to changing the appearance of the icons in the program itself. It also functions differently and better for surfing the Net. Setting yourself up to search the Web through an America Online account is easy now. Just keep reading to find out how to do it.

Using the Web through America Online

The first thing you may notice when you boot up Version 3.0 of the AOL program is that the top horizontal row of icons is different (see Figure 22-1). They're not trapped in boxes, for one thing, and one of the icons is new. The new little globe icon represents the AOL Web browser, which you can open with a single click. In Version 2.5, the browser popped into life whenever you clicked on a Web hyperlink from AOL. That setup is nice and easy, but it's like an automatic door at a supermarket: It doesn't require any effort, but you also have no control over it. Having a Web browser that you can't access separately, or leave open, is likewise inconvenient to serious Web searchers.

The Web browser icon is not *lit* — meaning that it is not active — when you're logged off. You can't use the icon until you log on and it lights up (see Figure 22-2). In other words, you can't use the browser apart from the AOL program. AOL is different from CompuServe in this respect because CompuServe installs the browser in a separate directory on your hard drive. But for people who use AOL exclusively as their World Wide Web access point, it's not a problem.

Web browser icon

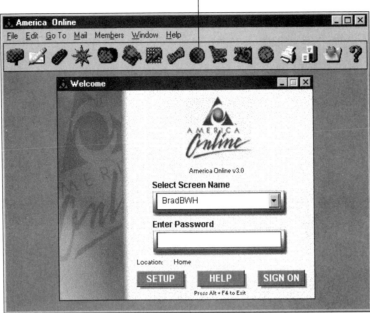

Web browser icon

Figure 22-1:
Most of
the AOL
software
icons are
inactive
before you
log on.

Figure 22-2:
Version 3.0
of the AOL
software as
it appears
when
you are
logged on.

Searching the Web from AOL

You can begin a Web searching session at any time during a visit to America Online. Whether you log on specifically to search the Web or suddenly decide to take an Internet spin while exploring AOL, the procedure is the same. Just follow these steps in Version 3.0 of the AOL software:

1. **Log on normally.**

   When you download Version 3.0, the installation program copies all the logon settings from your previous version. These settings include your access phone number, the modem type and computer port, the screen name, and your password. The logon screen has had a facelift, but you can recognize it.

2. **Roll your mouse cursor slowly over the icons near the top of your screen.**

   No, you are not doing a mouse aerobics exercise. As you move the cursor over the icons, little yellow pop-ups tell you what each icon is for. You're looking for the one that says "World Wide Web: Direct Access to the Internet!" This description is not exactly the soul of brevity, and it doesn't even mention the word *browser,* but that's what this icon is for.

3. **Click on the World Wide Web icon.**

   The AOL Web browser opens and takes you automatically to the America Online home page on the World Wide Web (see Figure 22-3). You're logged onto America Online and the Web at the same time, and you can navigate both environments at your pleasure. If you don't want to use the browser for a while, just minimize the window to get it out of the way.

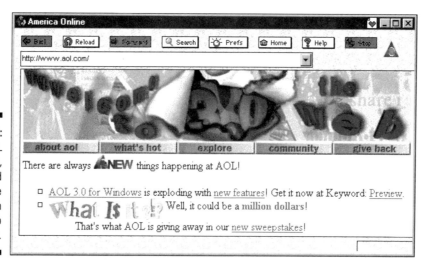

Figure 22-3:
The AOL Web page, as viewed through the built-in AOL Web browser.

The AOL browser opens within the America Online program. The browser is not an independent program. When you maximize the window, it maximizes *within* the AOL program, but it doesn't take the entire screen. If you minimize the AOL program, the browser goes down with it. As a result, you can't have the AOL program and its Web browser open side by side on your screen — but hey, life is full of tiny disappointments.

To begin searching for something on the Web, you need to go to a directory or search engine site, such as the ones described in Part II of this book. The AOL browser can be a bit confusing at this point, because it has no pull-down menus from which to make navigational selections, as are found on many other browsers. Don't puzzle over this for long. To enter a new location into the browser, just do this:

1. **Locate the Flashbar.**

   What in the world is a *Flashbar,* you may ask? Good question. It's the AOL name for the horizontal bar near the top of the browser, in which the current URL (Web address) is displayed (see Figure 22-4).

Figure 22-4:
The Web
browser
Flashbar.

2. **Click on the Flashbar.**

   The URL that is currently displayed is highlighted. If for some reason the URL remains unhighlighted, just click and drag the cursor over the address until the whole thing is highlighted.

3. **Type the URL of the Web site that you want to visit.**

   Of course, to type the URL, you have to know what it is. Many URLs are scattered throughout this book. Okay, I'll save you some work: Use this URL and let it take you to the Yahoo! World Wide Web directory:

   ```
   http://www.yahoo.com/
   ```

4. **Press Enter.**

   The browser goes to the site whose URL you typed.

You can add a Web site to your Favorite Places folder, just as if it were an AOL location. Just click on the little heart that appears in the upper-right corner of any Web page that you visit. The site will be added to your Favorite Places list, and you don't have to type the URL every time you want to visit that site. I suggest that you add each of your favorite searching services on the Web to this list — directories and search engines — so that you can launch a Web searching session by simply opening the Favorite Places list and clicking on an item.

Using other browsers with America Online

One of the major improvements of Version 3.0 of the AOL software over Version 2.5 is that you can now use other Web browsers while you are logged onto America Online. No longer are you limited to the built-in browser, improved though it is from the previous version.

The new Web browser that comes bundled with Version 3.0 of America Online displays the latest Web design elements, including frames, tables, HTML 3.0 features, and all Netscape extensions that were in effect when Version 3.0 of AOL was released. You don't need to use a different browser to see advanced Web pages as they were designed, as you did in Version 2.5. However, you may still want to use a different browser for other reasons, such as simply preferring its layout or its navigation buttons.

Using another browser with America Online could hardly be easier. Here's how it's done:

1. **Log onto America Online in the usual fashion.**

2. **Activate your browser of choice.**

3. **Enter a Web address (URL) in your browser.**

You're now free to roam about the Web while remaining logged into the AOL system. You can switch back and forth between your browser and the America Online program, with the added advantage of running two completely separate programs that you can place side by side on your screen if you like.

When you're searching the Web in a browser of your choice, you're still logged onto America Online, so you are still being billed an hourly rate (or eating up your free monthly allowance). You can easily forget that you are still on the clock, because you may not be visiting any AOL locations. But you're going through the AOL Internet gateway and still using the AOL system.

Why you shouldn't use Version 2.5 anymore

Windows users of America Online are doing themselves a disservice if they haven't yet replaced their AOL software with Version 3.0. Here's why:

✔ Version 2.5 has no browser icon. As a result, you can't open the browser manually — the program opens it for you when you click on a Web link from America Online. This setup makes it much harder to surf a site that isn't linked within AOL.

✔ Using a non-AOL browser with Version 2.5 is difficult. This inconvenience is generally considered to be obsolete design. Everybody should be able to use any browser with any Web connection, and Version 3.0 enables you to use any browser effortlessly. With Version 2.5, you must download a special utility from Winsock Central (keyword: **WINSOCK**). As long as you're going to download something, make it Version 3.0 of the AOL software instead.

The America Online program doesn't know that you're using another browser. Heck, it's a computer program; it doesn't *know* anything. It doesn't even know that you're on the Web. If you click on a Web link on an America Online page, AOL will pop open the built-in browser and use it to take you there. In other words, your other Web browser and the AOL program do not communicate with each other. Therein lies the disadvantage of using a separate browser.

The AOL Revolving Door

The new version of America Online software (Version 3.0 for Windows) opens up the Web connection for unlimited navigation in both directions. You can do any or all of the following:

✔ Slide onto the World Wide Web from America Online, using the AOL browser provided with the new program.

✔ Surf on the Web using a different Web browser, just by booting it up after logging on.

✔ Enter America Online from the Web, using an Internet service provider connection.

In other words, you can move in both directions: onto the Web from AOL and into AOL from the Web. It's a two-way street. This feature is mainly convenient for AOL members who also have a separate Internet account with an Internet service provider. If you're logged onto the World Wide Web through *another* connection (not AOL), you can get into America Online through the back door by following these steps:

1. **Boot up the America Online software.**

   Version 2.5 works as well as Version 3.0.

2. **Click on the Setup button in the Welcome window.**

   The Setup button (see Figure 22-5) opens the Network & Modem Setup window.

Figure 22-5:
The Setup button is located in the Welcome window.

3. **Click on the Edit Location button (see Figure 22-6).**

   The Network Setup window opens.

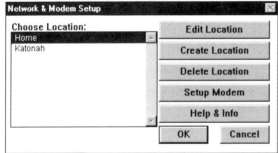

Figure 22-6:
Click on the Edit Location button.

4. **In the Network box on the left, click on the small arrow.**

   Please note that the Network Setup window has two Network boxes, one for each of your two AOL access phone numbers (see Figure 22-7). The Network box on the left corresponds to your first (main) access number.

Figure 22-7:
The
Network
Setup
window,
where you
choose the
TCP/IP
setting.

Network Setup				☒
	Location:	Home		
	Phone Type:	⊙ Touch Tone ○ Pulse		

Phone Number: 799-2266   **Phone Number:** 392-4100

Modem Speed: 14400 bps ▼   **Modem Speed:** 14400 bps ▼

Network: TCP/IP ▼   **Network:** SprintNet ▼

☐ Use the following prefix to reach an outside line: 9,

☐ Use the following command to disable call waiting: *70,

[Save]   [Swap Phone Numbers]   [Cancel]

5. **Make a note of the current selection and then choose TCP/IP from the drop-down list by clicking on it.**

6. **Click on the Save button.**

   The Network Setup window disappears, revealing the Network & Modem Setup window that was underneath it.

7. **Click on the OK button.**

   The Network & Modem Setup window disappears, revealing the Welcome window that was lurking underneath the pile of other windows.

8. **Type your password in the Enter Password box.**

9. **Click on the Sign On button.**

This procedure tell the AOL software that you have already established an Internet connection. It knows not to try dialing the phone, because you're already online. Instead, it travels through the two-way Internet connection and logs you into the America Online system with your screen name and password. Logging on is very quick; it should take only a couple of seconds after you click on the Sign On button.

The next time that you want to log onto America Online normally, without connecting to the Internet first, you must change your Network Setup setting back to what it was before you changed it. If the Network Setup setting is set to TCP/IP, simply click on the SprintNet or AOLnet setting that was originally in place. The TCP/IP selection only lets you log into AOL from a preexisting Internet connection — it doesn't dial your modem to make a new connection.

Why have two accounts?

If navigating onto the World Wide Web from America Online is so easy, why would an AOL member also pay for an Internet access account with a different company?

Because in the long run, some people actually pay less that way — especially members who use the World Wide Web (and other portions of the Internet) extensively. When you search for things on the Web through your AOL connection, you are still paying America Online for every minute that you're logged on. The Web is pretty addictive, and those minutes can add up!

Internet service providers often charge a flat monthly rate for unlimited access to the World Wide Web. A little arithmetic tells you how many

hours you'd have to spend online to make such an account pay off. (The actual numbers depend on the service provider's rate, America Online's current hourly connection rate, the number of hours you spend every month on the Web, and whatever telephone charges apply.)

Some people who have an independent Internet account always use it to log on. Then, when they want to enter the America Online system to get their e-mail or visit an AOL location, they do so by using the procedure described in this chapter. That way, they pay America Online only for the time they spend in the AOL system and not for the rest of the time they spend on the Web.

The AOL On Ramp to the Web

You can do everything in this book using the America Online gateway and browser. AOL makes an effort to get you started finding stuff on the Web by providing two helpful pages. It has more than two, actually, but in my opinion these two are the best launching pads for a Web search from America Online

Welcome to the Internet! (Thanks, AOL)

The hospitable Welcome to the Internet! page (see Figure 22-8) links you to a couple of Web search sites and lets you enter a URL for any other site. The AOL browser pops open automatically when needed by this page — you don't have to worry about booting it up manually. The keyword for Welcome to the Internet! is **Net Highlights**, and you can also get there by clicking on the Internet button from the Welcome screen. (The Welcome screen appears automatically when you first log onto America Online.)

Figure 22-8:
The AOL Welcome to the Internet! page, from which you can link to the Search the Web site.

Welcome to the Internet! offers a few options, but Web searchers can get right to the point by clicking the Search button under THE WEB. Up pops the browser, and off you go to a Web page provided by America Online, called — appropriately — Search the Web (see Figure 22-9). From this Web focal point you can initiate a search through either the Excite search engine or the WebCrawler service. (The many features of Excite are described in thrilling detail in Chapter 7; you can find a summary of how WebCrawler works in Chapter 11. Menswear is two flights up.)

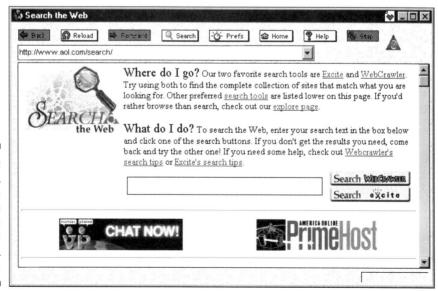

Figure 22-9:
The AOL Search the Web site, as seen through the AOL browser.

You don't have to settle for Excite or WebCrawler if you prefer another search engine. Scroll down the page for links to several other Web searching sites.

You can explore the rest of the Welcome to the Internet! page by clicking on its various buttons. Here are the main points of interest:

- **Highlights:** The Highlights button opens the browser and sends it to the AOL What's Hot? Web page, which consists of a selection of links to reviewed Web sites.

- **Best of the Web:** Click on this button to display a list of the best (in the AOL opinion) Web sites (see Figure 22-10). Double-click on any item in the list to visit the site with the AOL browser.

Figure 22-10:
The Best of the Web list in America Online.

- **Search Newsgroups:** If you want to conduct a keyword search through the Usenet newsgroups, the Search Newsgroups button connects you to the Deja News searching service on the Web. Deja News is a super-nifty (that's the technical term) search engine described profoundly in Chapter 10.

- **Search Gopher:** Gopher is a directory system that was invented before the World Wide Web. Because it was designed before the advent of the Web, it doesn't have the capability to catalog Web sites. However, you can find all kinds of files that were on the Internet before the Web came into existence — and, in fact, are still on the Internet. Clicking on the Search Gopher button brings up a keyword entry form. Type in a keyword, click on the Search button, and wait for a list of results.

✓ **Search FTP:** FTP (File Transfer Protocol) sites are the library stacks of the Internet. FTP stacks are what Gopher searches, but Gopher is not used when you click on the Search FTP button. Although the search engine is not identified, it works — which, after all, is the important thing. Just type in a keyword and click on the Search button.

Reference Internet Tools

In America Online, use the keyword **Web Tools** (okay, so it's two words) to find the AOL Reference Internet Tools page (see Figure 22-11). This page is a hub leading to sites that help you look things up. The list in the middle takes you to reference Web sites — try them out by double-clicking on the list items.

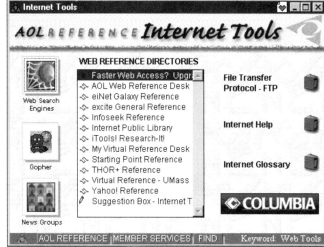

Figure 22-11:
The AOL
Reference
Internet
Tools page.

Here are the button choices in the AOL Reference Internet Tools page:

✓ The Web Search Engines button activates the AOL Web browser (when you click on the button) and takes you to the same Search the Web site shown in Figure 22-9.

✓ The Gopher button brings up a page with many options, including a search engine, a directory, and an information file about Gopher. Clicking on this button displays a slow-loading page. It's a beautiful page — some of the graphics are even animated. But if you're in a hurry, skip it.

✔ The News Groups (usually spelled *newsgroups* in other places) button leads to a selection of information about Usenet newsgroups, plus options for opening the AOL newsgroup program to select newsgroups for reading.

Click on the three book icons at the right of the AOL Reference Internet Tools page to see information about FTP and the Internet.

Chapter 23

Searching within America Online

● ●

In This Chapter

▶ Finding stuff to download from AOL

▶ Using *Find* to locate AOL destinations

▶ Browsing the service with the AOL directory

● ●

*L*ike any self-respecting commercial online service, America Online (AOL) is well organized, which makes searching easier than on the World Wide Web. The Web's big advantage is the built-in hyperlinking that ties together thousands of sites into a messy, but navigable, bundle. A commercial service, which owns all of its pages and presents them in a user-friendly, coherent manner, can establish and refine its own directory systems and search engines.

America Online uses both directories and keyword search engines to good advantage. Comparisons to CompuServe are inevitable, because they are the two major commercial networks and the two online services covered in this book.

✔ CompuServe Forums are great resources with powerful search tools. But each forum is separate, so members have to search several forums independently in order to use those search tools in different areas of the service. The global search tools, which cover the whole CompuServe system, are less powerful.

✔ America Online is a more open system, encouraging global searching of all its files. You can go into topical areas and browse its files, but true searching takes place on a system-wide level. You can use keywords to search for files located anywhere on the network. Furthermore, AOL usually assigns more keywords to each file than CompuServe does, increasing the likelihood that you can locate files with the keywords you use.

In this chapter, I describe the AOL searching experience as it is displayed in Version 3.0 of the America Online for Windows software. Most of the functions and features are the same as in the previous incarnation, Version 2.5. But some of the AOL windows look different, and the icons at the top of the screen have changed.

Finding Files on AOL

Files aren't the only thing worth finding on America Online, but they are what you use search keywords to find. AOL stores all kinds of multimedia goodies in its file libraries — texts, graphics, sounds, MIDI music files, and movies. You can browse the libraries of whatever AOL location you're visiting, or you can save time by searching the entire system-wide collection with keywords.

Beginning your file search

You can begin tracking down files from the moment you're logged on to AOL. Here's how you do it:

1. **Log onto America Online in the normal fashion.**

2. **After you log onto the system, locate the File Search icon near the top of the AOL window.**

   The File Search icon looks like a floppy disk with a magnifying glass over it (see Figure 23-1). Rest your mouse cursor on an icon until the yellow box pops open, and then roll the cursor along the icons until you find the right one.

Figure 23-1:
You can begin a search for files right from the AOL toolbar.

File search icon

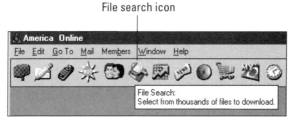

3. **Click once on the File Search icon.**

Clicking on the File Search icon opens the Software Search window (see Figure 23-2), where you have several choices to make. In this window, you set the parameters of your file search and enter any keywords that you want to use. (You don't have to use keywords.) Basically, you have three options in the Software Search window:

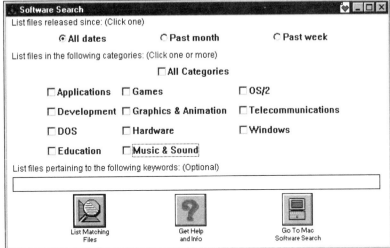

Figure 23-2:
The
Software
Search
window
opens after
you click on
the File
Search icon.

✔ **Age of the file:** You can determine how far back in the AOL archives you want to search. Files are uploaded and added to the system every day, so if you conduct searches fairly frequently, there's no point in rummaging through file descriptions that you've already looked at. You can select the All dates option to search the entire database; the Past month option to explore files released during the preceding month; or the Past week option for recently released files. Just click on the small circle next to any selection.

✔ **File category:** From these options you determine the subject area or computer operating system in which you want to search for files. The All Categories option is the broadest choice, and it will probably overwhelm you with search results unless you select the Past week option. (Even so, the list will be long.) The DOS, OS/2, and Windows selections refer to computer operating systems and will deliver files for those systems in all subjects. Applications and Graphics & Animation are likewise broad categories that will return file listings in many subject areas.

✔ **Keyword:** By using keywords, you can narrow down the search. The file categories aren't specific enough to produce lists of files in many subjects, such as entertainment. Using a keyword such as **movies** or **scifi** gets you right into a topical file list.

Using the File Search Results window

After you make your choices in the Software Search window, click on the List Matching Files button. In a couple of seconds, the results of your search are displayed in a new window called, unsurprisingly, File Search Results (see Figure 23-3). This window lists the files that match your search terms, using three columns:

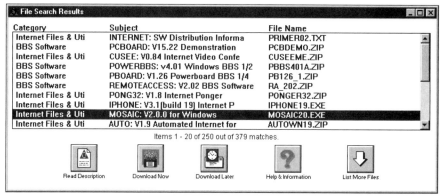

Figure 23-3:
This is
how your
keyword
matches are
listed.

✔ **Category:** The information in this column indicates which of the many AOL file categories each item falls into.

✔ **Subject:** This column indicates the purpose of each file. It usually includes the program name and a three-word or four-word description. It's not a full description of the file — that information comes later.

✔ **File Name:** Here you see the filename. Filenames are always in this format: *THISFILE.XXX*.

You can download files directly from this window by clicking on any file and then doing one of the following:

✔ Clicking on the Download Now button for an immediate download

✔ Clicking on the Download Later button to schedule a future download

Downloading directly from the File Search Results window makes sense if you see a file that you recognize and you know that you want it. In most cases, though, seeing a more complete file description is helpful. To see a more complete description, do one of the following:

✔ Click once on any file and then click on the Read Description button.

✔ Double-click on any file.

Using the file description window

The file description window (see Figure 23-4) can be quite long, and you may need to scroll down to read the whole description. Far from being inconvenient, this long-winded window provides a good way to learn about a file before investing the time (and connect charges) to download it. The description consists of a few paragraphs summarizing the features of the file you've selected. Above those paragraphs are several items of information that can help you decide whether to acquire the file.

✔ **Subj:** Here you learn the name of the file and the version number if the file is a program.

✔ **Date:** The date tells you when the file was added to America Online.

✔ **From:** This information identifies the uploader, by AOL screen name. You can try sending e-mail to this individual to get further information about the file, but remember that the uploader may not be the same person as the file's author.

✔ **File:** Here is where you find the computer filename, plus the size of the file in bytes. (One thousand bytes equal a kilobyte, and a thousand kilobytes equal a megabyte. A thousand megabytes equal a gigabyte, but if you find any files that big, you should run screaming from the room.)

✔ **DL time:** This item refers to the number of minutes required to download the file, given a modem of a certain speed. In most cases, that speed is for a 28.8K baud modem. If you have a 14.4K baud modem, double the length of the download.

✔ **Download count:** This information tells you how many people have downloaded the file before you. A high number in a short time (check the date) is a sure sign of a popular file.

✔ **Author:** The author is the name of the person or organization that created the file, which is not necessarily the same person or organization that uploaded the file.

✔ **Equipment:** Here you are told what hardware equipment might be needed for the file to work. In Figure 23-4, which is a file description for a downloadable Web browser, the needed equipment refers to a computer that can connect to an Internet server, and a live connection.

✔ **Needs:** This item tells you the requirements for the operating system and other software. If you're using a computer that is running Windows, and the file requires the Macintosh operating system, you won't be able to use this file.

✔ **Keywords:** These keywords are all the keywords associated with this file. Of course, now that you've found the file, knowing the keywords doesn't do you any good at all — except that they might give you ideas of key-words to use in future searches.

✔ **Type:** Here you find out whether the file is freeware, shareware, a commer-cial demo, or some other type of electronically distributed file.

You can download the file after reading the description or schedule the acquisi-tion for later. Just use the Download Now or Download Later buttons at the bottom of the window. The Ask The Staff button opens up a little window for writing a message to the AOL staff member who checked the file when it was uploaded. You can make a comment, point out a flaw in the file description, or ask a question. Replies to questions are sent to your AOL e-mail box.

Using AOL Find

Files aren't the only things worth searching for in America Online. The service has entertaining and informative content of all kinds, including message boards, chat rooms, and topical forums. When you're not searching specifically for downloadable files, the Find feature can help make sense of the broad and varied content of AOL.

You get to the Find tool by using the Find button. (That makes sense, right?) The Find button is located to the right of the horizontal row of icons near the top of the AOL software, Version 3.0 (see Figure 23-5). Click on it to have the AOL Find window pop open (see Figure 23-6).

Figure 23-5:
The Find button in AOL 3.0 for Windows.

Figure 23-6:
The Find
window is
where you
search
for AOL
destinations.

AOL Find works with keywords. You can dabble with the "suggested areas" in
the bottom half of the window or the buttons to the right. But when you want
to search, go straight for the keyword entry box that's to the left of the Search
button. Follow these steps to let the system search engine find a destination
for you:

1. **Position your mouse cursor over the keyword entry box and click once.**

2. **Type one or more keywords.**

3. **Click on the Search button.**

The Search Results window displays — guess what?—the results of your search
(see Figure 23-7). You see a list of destinations that match your keywords.
Simply double-click on any of them to go to that AOL location.

Figure 23-7:
The Search
Results
window
lists AOL
destinations
that match
your
keywords.

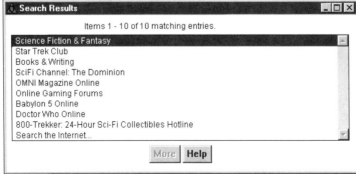

A word about AOL keywords

America Online uses keywords in three different ways:

✔ Keywords can help you narrow down a search in the File Search area.

✔ Keywords are also used in the Find feature, when locating all kinds of destinations throughout the system.

✔ Keywords are also the official *tags* that identify specific AOL locations. Like the GO words on CompuServe, they take you directly to an AOL location. This type of AOL keyword works just like a URL on the Web. Every AOL destination has a keyword associated with it. These keywords are not keywords in the same sense as you think of them when conducting a search. You use a location's keyword when you want to go directly to that location without moving through the directory system. You just click on the Keyword button at the top right of your program window and type in the destination's keyword. Of course, you need to know the keyword.

The keywords associated with any AOL location are assigned by America Online, and they don't all work as navigational keywords. AOL uses a keyword to link to each individual destination on the system, using the Keyword button near the top of the software. Each destination has just one of these navigational keywords, but several of the Find keywords. Confusing? If you want to know what the navigational keyword is for any particular location, just look at the bottom of the window to find it. And remember that the Find keyword that you use to locate a certain destination is not necessarily its navigational keyword.

Browsing the AOL Directory

Whether you're looking for destinations or files, you can go for the browsing method by using the system-wide directory.

The AOL directory works just like a Web directory (like Yahoo! or Lycos), except that it has a lot more pictures and buttons, whereas the Web directories rely more on text hyperlinks. In Version 3.0 of the AOL Windows software, the main directory page is called Channels, and it appears right after you log on (see Figure 23-8). Using this page could hardly be easier — just click on any of the subject bars to reach the second level of the directory in that topic. Each topic looks different as you proceed through the levels, and they all contain a mix of graphics, buttons, and text directory links. Just click your way through until you find destinations that you like.

Figure 23-8:
The top-
level
directory
page of
America
Online.

TIP

Don't repeat the same search twice! If you locate a destination that you really like and want to return to it without performing another search or drilling your way through the Channels directory, be sure to add that location to your Favorite Places list. To add it, drag the heart at the top right of the window to the Favorite Places icon, which also contains a heart, on the AOL toolbar.

Part V
The Part of Tens

The 5th Wave   By Rich Tennant

"WHAT CONCERNS ME ABOUT THE INFORMATION SUPERHIGHWAY IS THAT IT APPEARS TO BE ENTERING THROUGH BRENT'S BEDROOM."

In this part . . .

As anybody who has ever sneaked a peek at a friend's grocery shopping list knows, it's amazing what you can learn from a list. I considered adding my own food shopping list to this part, but decided that you are probably more interested in learning about Web searching than about me. (Good choice.)

Instead, I have collected lists of sites and tips to enhance your searching experience. The sites are unrated, except that a site has to be pretty good to make one of these lists.

Leaf through this part when you're in a mood to browse — you're bound to find a hint or a URL that's worth keeping.

Chapter 24

Ten Interesting Web Directories

*1*s there life beyond the Yahoo! directory? Sure there is, and Lycos and Excite aren't the only games in town either. Those three big directories are glorious, no doubt about it. They present monumental atlases of the Web landscape. But there are times when more local maps serve you better, and plenty of smaller, topical directories are sprinkled around the Web. They generally work the same way as the big-name services: The home page contains a top level of broad categories, and you click your way to lower-level subtopics until you eventually reach links to other Web sites. Some of the smaller directories have only one level, in which case they are basically a list of links. That's fine too. The only requirement is that a directory *direct* you somewhere, by means of Web hyperlinks.

Achoo

```
http://www.achoo.com/
```

What better name for a directory of online healthcare services? Achoo is not to be sneezed at. It provides almost 6,000 links to healthcare information resources on the Net. The main directory page is divided into four categories: Human Life, Practice of Medicine, Business of Health, and What's New. With those links you can telescope your way down to most any aspect of health, illness, treatment, and recovery and find a place on the Web to learn more. Also on the top-level directory page are a Headline News link that's devoted to healthcare news items and a Site of the Week link. Perhaps most impressive is a brand new, searchable Usenet database of healthcare newsgroups. You can ferret out articles on any subject, post a reply to any of the represented newsgroups, and even find out how to start your own newsgroup. If an apple a day keeps the doctor away, visit this site while you're eating it.

The Huge List

http://thehugelist.com/

The Huge List lives up to its name. But it certainly can't lay claim to hugeness by comparison to Yahoo!, so it has to make up the difference with unusual menu headings and links. On the top level of this interesting directory, you can find such unusual main topics as <u>Apple Macintosh</u>, <u>Disabled Persons</u>, <u>Free Webspace</u>, <u>Motorcycles</u>, <u>Museums</u>, <u>Real Estate</u>, <u>Recovery</u>, and <u>What's New</u>. The entire directory is only two levels deep, but it is balanced by breadth and careful selection. In other words, this directory is a browser's hotspot for people who like high-quality, interesting sites for topics in which they may not think to search.

The Huge List is designed slickly and with complex use of *frames,* those window divisions in your Web browser that enable you to scroll portions of a Web page independently of the rest of it. (Frames do not show up in all browsers.) In fact, the frames get in the way a bit. No problem, though. The designers have provided a <u>Hide Frames</u> link to get rid of them. (You can get the frames back later if you miss them.)

The Internet Sleuth

http://www.intbc.com/sleuth/

Wait till you see the Internet Sleuth (see Figure 24-1). If you like rummaging through the bottomless, unplumbed well of Web wisdom, you are going to adore this site. It's a combination directory and keyword search service that uses the familiar directory structure to provide hundreds of highly specific keyword search databases. Here's how it works.

Stretching down the left side of the home page is a long list of topics and subtopics. They are all hyperlinked. Click on <u>News</u> to see an example. The next level is displayed on your screen, and you suddenly have the glorious (if you're an information addict) choice of searching through the individual online databases of the *Boston Globe, CNN News,* the *Federal News Service,* the *Korea*

Herald News, The New York Times, The *San Francisco Chronicle* . . . you get the picture. Many, many more well-known and obscure publications and news agencies are here as well. You can get deliriously lost and discover information about subjects that you didn't even know existed.

When you're saturated with news, use the Back button of your browser to return to the top-level page, and select another linked topic — Sports, Science, Recreation, Health, Computers, or Education, for example. Then enjoy more keyword searching in topical databases you never dreamed of. How much time could you spend in this site? Do you believe in reincarnation?

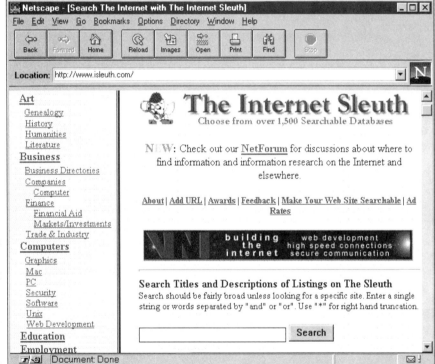

Figure 24-1:
The Internet Sleuth is one of the great, unsung Web directories.

Starting Point

```
http://www.stpt.com/
```

Working with the idea that a picture is worth a thousand — or at least a few hundred — words, Starting Point takes a graphical approach to Web navigation. Does it live up to its slightly awkward slogan, "Everything You Need to Work the Web, Every Day"? Well, it doesn't have the complexity of Yahoo!, Lycos, or the other monsters, but the coziness can be preferable, and it certainly has plenty of links.

The directory is three levels deep, with the second and third levels combined on the same page, making searching a quick experience. Nothing unusual about the directory selections, and no descriptions or reviews clutter the tastefully laid out pages. You won't give up your job to roam this site, but it is — as it says — a starting point.

WWWomen

```
http://www.wwwomen.com/
```

Women are a minority in the online world. You can show a friend what she's missing by taking her on a cruise through this specialized directory. The top-level menu includes standard topics, such as <u>Entertainment</u>, <u>Community & Government</u>, and <u>Science & Technology</u>, with a slant on women's interests, as well as more specifically focused feminist topics such as <u>Women's Resources</u>, <u>Women in the Age of Computers</u>, and <u>Women Through History</u>.

World Wide Web Pavilion

```
http://www.catalog.com/tsw/Pavilion/pavilion.htm
```

The WWW Pavilion offers one great feature that is sometimes frustratingly lacking in other directories: speed. This menu system of Web links is lightning fast. That makes up for its relatively modest size, not to mention the eye-popping yellow-on-blue design of some pages. You also may find some peculiar directory listings, such as the placement of Art Galleries under the Business heading.

Nevertheless, the WWW Pavilion is a good place to whip in and out of when you want to check out some links without pausing to make a pot of coffee while complicated pages display leisurely on your screen. The site is especially strong in education, government, and science listings.

WebWise Library

```
http://webwise.walcoff.com/library/index.html
```

WebWise Library is a virtual library that uses a standard directory system to present five main sections:

- ✔ The **Card Catalog**, which links to other directories and keyword search engines
- ✔ The **Newspaper Rack**, which provides an alphabetical list of links to online newspapers
- ✔ The **Magazine Rack**, which provides an alphabetical list of links to eZines (electronic-only periodicals that are viewed online or downloaded) and magazines
- ✔ The **A/V Counter**, which is a directory of multimedia sites, many of which are oriented toward entertainment
- ✔ The **Reference Desk**, which is a source of informational links about the Internet, such as lists of Internet Service Providers and an Internet Conference Calendar

The Web Wise Library is not huge; compare it to a small — but intelligently stocked — town library.

Yehaa!

```
http://www.yehaa.com/
```

Though the title of this directory is a playful take off on the famous Yahoo! directory, Yehaa! has the serious intent of providing links that are of interest to users in the southern United States. It is one of the best, simplest, and quickest regional directories. The top level features such typical broad categories as Entertainment, Business, and Education. A little more depth would go a long way, but for users in the southern U.S. who are looking for a regional touch, this is the place.

Culture

http://www.december.com/cmc/info/culture-people-lists.html

Don't let the small type put you off. The Culture site embodies a unique, eclectic directory of lists, people, and unusual site links that would keep anyone intrigued. Part of the intrigue, it must be said, lies in trying to decipher the method behind the menu topics. I suggest turning off your preconceptions of how a directory should be organized, in favor of the unusual categories offered here: GeoCities and Housemet, to name a couple. You won't find actual links to outside sites until the third level of this hard-to-read directory, but the wait — not to mention the ocular strain — is worth it.

Yecch!

http://www.yeeeoww.com/yecch/yecchhome.html

An uproarious lampoon of Yahoo!, produced by Yeeeoww!!! Digital Lampoon, Yecch!, surprisingly, has serious links. But the directory headings in which those links reside are another story. The main menu asks you to choose among general topics such as Night of the Living Gilligan, What Were They Drinking?, Fun With Carpaltunnel, and Huh? Unfortunately, the silliness doesn't persist down to the second level. The linked sites in this directory are chosen for their unusual content, but they are not fictitious.

A few other features for your capricious consideration are The Useless Pages, Lovely Spam Recipes, and Power Loser Bookmarks. Yecch! represents what could happen if Monty Python were let loose in a Web directory.

Chapter 25

Ten WWW Reference Sites

*U*sing the World Wide Web to look up a word definition? Isn't that taking Internet infatuation just a bit too far? Well, maybe. Certainly, picking up a book and looking up a word is easier than turning on the computer, booting up your Web browser, logging onto the Net, surfing to a reference site, typing a word, and waiting for the definition to display. Perhaps in the future Star Trek-like computer systems will be able to just answer spoken questions. In the meantime, you have your pick of Web reference pages that offer the benefits of computer database searching, which is an added value over the printed book versions. I've also included on this list some good jumping-off sites that contain lists of reference hyperlinks.

The Alternative Dictionaries

```
http://www.notam.uio.no/~hcholm/altlang/
```

The Alternative Dictionaries site is unusual in three ways. First, it is a dictionary of words not normally found in dictionaries. Second, the words are in a variety of languages (but defined in English). And third, this site is an audience-participation work-in-progress, in which you are invited to enter words from your personal lexicon, in any language. Because of the informal, unedited quality of the listings, you shouldn't relate to this site as an authoritative reference. Nor should you enter this page with tender sensibilities for obscenities or purple terms. Anything is allowed here, as long as it falls outside the standard parameters of a mainstream English dictionary.

Cyberspace Dictionary

```
http://www.edmweb.com/steve/cyberdict.html
```

If you need a good, basic, short reference of online terms for the beginner, Cyberspace Dictionary serves you well. The entire dictionary fits onto a single Web page (granted, it's a large Web page), which tells you that Cyberspace Dictionary is very basic. The beauty of it is the quickness with which the virtual book operates. In the definitions, all words that are represented as dictionary entries are hyperlinked, so you can go directly to those entries. For example, the definition of *Flame* contains the word <u>Usenet</u>, which links you to the *Usenet* definition. Cyberspace Dictionary also has links to outside Web pages scattered through it.

BABEL

```
http://www.access.digex.net/~ikind/babel96b.html
```

BABEL is an exhaustive (and maybe exhausting) glossary of computer-related abbreviations and acronyms. You can use this fantastic reference online or print it out for unwired use the next time you're trying to decipher a cryptic owner's manual. Either way, be prepared to wait a while before you can begin. BABEL is an enormous single Web page that takes some time to load into your computer or to print. You may notice a conspicuous lack of hyperlinks in the glossary, except for an alphabet at the top that you can use to jump to the beginning of any letter's entries. The best way to find an abbreviation that's puzzling you is either by browsing with the vertical scroll bar of your browser or by using the browser's "find" feature. To use the "find" feature, just enter the abbreviation in uppercase letters and check the "match case" box. Your browser will zip right to the definition of that abbreviation.

Bartlett's Familiar Quotations

```
http://www.columbia.edu/acis/bartleby/bartlett/
```

When you first arrive at this home page, a "Quotation of the Day" scrolls across the bottom of your screen. (Netscape Navigator is recommended as a Web browser; other programs may not show the scrolling feature.) So begins your venture in the Web version of the famous book of quotations that come from throughout history. You can look up quotes by author (from either a chronological or an alphabetical list) or, even better, search for quotations by using keywords to bring up a page with quotes that match your keyword. Each quote is hyperlinked, and clicking on a quote takes you to yet another page that lists all the quotes in the entire database from that author. You can get lost in this site as you browse through past decades and centuries of literature and thought. Emphasis is on the word *past,* because Bartlett's is not a classic dictionary, and it doesn't dip into contemporary writing very much. Show this site to your kids as a great homework resource.

Encyclopedia Britannica

http://www.eb.com

Yes, there is a Web version of this famous reference work. Yes, you can browse through the articles. Yes, you can gaze at cool Java graphics. Yes, you can search the entire database by keyword. But no — it's not free. You can enjoy a demo of the service, but to access the entire database, you need to subscribe. If you don't have the physical version of the *Britannica,* you may want to consider this service, especially if you plan on using the encyclopedia extensively for a certain period of time. If you're planning a lifelong encyclopedia habit, it might make more sense to just buy the books. The Web site is immense, and it includes a text-only path (look for the hyperlink at the top of the home page) to speed up navigation.

Flags of All Countries

http://www.wave.net/upg/immigration/flags.html

There's nothing fancy about Flags of All Countries, and you won't find any information that's not implied in the site's title: flags, and nothing but flags. They're all here. Just click on a country from the alphabetized list, and its flag is displayed on your screen.

GaleNet

http://galenet.gale.com/

Gale is a prominent publisher of lists of lists. Its books present directories of directories and lists of associations of various kinds. GaleNet is the Web version, bringing the exhaustive Gale databases right onto your computer screen. However, it's not a free ride. You can try out the service, but if you want to access the whole thing, you need to subscribe. This serious site is for no-frills research projects. If you need the Gale resources only occasionally, consulting the books in a public library is probably best.

Notable Citizens of Planet Earth

http://www.tiac.net/users/parallax/

You can search this biographical dictionary, but you cannot browse it. With a pretty sophisticated search engine provided through the Web page, you can enter the last name of a "notable citizen," and receive back a page of brief information about that person's life. Notable Citizens of Planet Earth provides complete instructions for accomplishing more complex searches through the 18,000-name database.

On-Line Reference Works

http://almond.srv.cs.cmu.edu/Web/references.html

An ultimate reference hotlink, the On-Line Reference Works site presents a list of links to Web reference pages. Here you can find dictionaries, atlases, encyclopedias, government references, and many other kinds of references. It's a single page, and though the selections are good, the list isn't comprehensive. (In the constantly evolving World Wide Web, no list can be.) But On-Line Reference Works is a great place to start, supplemented by the Yahoo!, Excite, and Lycos Web directories.

Popspeak

http://www.blender.com/blender1.1/digest/popspeak/popspeak1.html

Popspeak is a campy, tongue-in-cheek guide to the cultural verbal infusions of our day. Learn all about hybrid words such as *Pre-Scandal-Michael-Jackson* and *Barbie-Dream,* complete with definitions, usage examples, and even audio files of the spoken phrases in action. The site is colorful, though the multiple graphics at every stage slow down navigation, especially since viewing Popspeak in text-only mode (with the graphics turned off in your Web browser) makes no sense. Go in with your graphics turned on, and don't worry about the time spent waiting for pages to display. Popspeak isn't an educational site (although you will learn new vocabulary, if you ever dare to use it) so much as a fun one.

Chapter 26

Ten Tips for Fast Web Searching

In This Chapter

▶ Searching the Web without graphics

▶ Navigating a search with the Back button

▶ Leapfrogging backward in a search session

▶ Using your hotlist

▶ Asking directions in newsgroups

▶ Avoiding prime time

*A*lthough these pages have already inundated you with search tips, this chapter is a good place to round up some of the basics, plus some others that I haven't mentioned. The emphasis is on speed. Not that you have to rush through every Web session — being online is supposed to be a pleasure, after all. But you can reduce the tedium of long search sessions by following a few simple guidelines that are second nature to Web veterans.

Turn Your Graphics Off

One of the best parts of the World Wide Web is its colorful, picturesque nature. Many sites have evolved into impressive multimedia experiences, with complex graphics, sounds, and even animations. It's dazzling! It's cool! And . . . it can be as slow as quicksand. When you're in the middle of a search session, zipping back and forth between a results list and the sites on it, you don't want to be cooling your jets with every link, waiting for the world's most beautiful Web page to slowly display on your screen. Even with a 28.8 modem, the Web can be a sluggish environment to navigate.

The solution is to turn off the graphics of your Web browser, a feature all browsers provide. Usually, you control whether graphics will appear by making a menu selection that is sometimes called Inline Images or Auto Load Images. If that feature has a check mark next to it, remove the check mark by clicking on that menu item. From that moment, Web pages will display on your screen without their graphics. Viewing Web pages without graphics may seem dull, but most people who spend a lot of time online keep graphics turned off, and all browsers enable you to see the graphics of any particular page when you need to.

I definitely recommend using the no-graphics mode for Web searching. I use it to navigate the Web at least 90 percent of the time. You may think, "What's the point of using the colorful, graphic World Wide Web if the graphics are turned off?" The point is to avoid wasting large portions of your life waiting for those graphics. And remember — you can always get the graphics back again for any page. Read the next paragraph to find out how.

Use the Images!

Sometimes turning the graphics of your Web browser off can backfire on you. After following a hyperlink, you will sometimes be confronted with what appears to be a blank page. That's because the entire page is a single big picture and your browser has obediently refused to display it. (Most browsers indicate the hidden presence of a missing graphic with some recognizable icon.) In this situation, the page is useless to you. The missing graphic will provide embedded links, so you have no choice but to swallow your speedster pride and load the graphic. For most browsers, you simply click a tool button (in Netscape Navigator it's called Images) or enable the graphics from a menu selection and then reload the page.

After loading the image(s) of a single Web page, don't forget to disable your graphics again if you want to resume your session at optimal speed. But if you viewed the image with Netscape's Images button, you don't need to reset anything.

Use Your Back Button

Web browsers have a button, usually located in the upper horizontal toolbar, that's called Back or Backward. The button has an arrow on it that points evocatively to the left. Using the Back button during a Web session takes you step by step back through your recent series of links. It's like following a long piece of string that you unwound while searching. (Of course, your browser actually unwound it, automatically, without your needing to do anything.) This button enables you to make little trips off your main searching trail without getting lost. Imagine a dog darting away from the main path again and again during a walk in the woods. Typical search sessions proceed that same way, and the Back button can keep you on track. Here's how it works:

1. From any search results page, follow a link to an outside Web site.

2. **After exploring that site, click on the Back button.**

   You're now back at the search results page, from which you can venture on another link.

In this way, you can zigzag your way down the search results page. If you stray a few links farther away from the main path, you may have to click that Back button a few times to get back.

In certain situations, the Back button doesn't work as expected. New types of Web page design cause your browser to interpret the Back command more drastically. The new design types I'm talking about are Java programs and frames. When Java is being used, you usually see something animated on your screen, such as a figure dancing across it, swirling text, or moving graphic images. *Frames* are portions of the browser window that can be scrolled independently of the rest of the window — miniwindows, basically.

In both cases, if you have clicked your way into the site, proceeding from the home (first) page to other pages within the site, clicking the Back button will not return you to the previous page — it will shove you back to the previous site in your session! In other words, it will kick you right out of the site entirely. Rude, isn't it?

Leapfrogging

If you're the impatient type (like me), using the Back button to step back through multiple links can get on your nerves. Even though you have to wait only a second or two for each previous page to display on your screen before you can use the Back button to see the next previous page, those seconds add up.

Just about all browsers provide a Go or History feature that enables you to see a list of all your previous stops. Clicking on one of them takes you directly to that page, without having to move sequentially through all of the pages that are in between. This feature is a handy shortcut.

The History or Go list may not show all the links in your entire Web session. Probably not, in fact, if you've hit more than about 20 pages. This feature varies from browser to browser. In Netscape Navigator, the most widely used Web browsing program, the length of the Go list is tied to the size of the memory cache buffer. This setting is found in the Options menu, under Network Preferences. If you want to see larger Go lists, stretching back farther into your search sessions, just enlarge the size of the Memory Cache. This change will allot more of your computer's RAM memory to storing the sites that you visit. (Accordingly, it will reduce the amount of memory available for the other programs that you may be running.)

Make Fast Decisions

Pondering over the perfect keyword string isn't worth it. Search indexes work so quickly that you can usually know whether you're on the right track in seconds just by trying. If you see that the first page of results is off your searching track, you can just Back-button your way to the keyword page and try again. In fact, some services provide a keyword form at the top of the results page so you can make quick adjustments there without having to use the Back button.

Use Your Hotlist

In the course of searching for Web sites in a particular subject, you end up testing a lot of pages before finding the useful ones. Usually, you make a brief visit, get the gist of the site's contents, and move on to the next link. You can easily get distracted when you find a good site, or even an intriguing one that isn't exactly what you're looking for. In the long run, you'll get the most value from any search by pursuing it to the end before doing any deep exploration of individual sites. Otherwise, you may get so involved in one or two sites that you forget to keep checking others that matched your keywords. Also, a site may look great if you find it early in the search, but not so great later after you've discovered several better ones.

The solution? Use your browser's hotlist or bookmark function liberally. (Whether it's called a *hotlist* or a *bookmark,* it enables you to keep a list of Web sites for future visits. In most browsers, you can add a page to the hotlist/ bookmark by clicking a toolbar button or selecting a menu item when visiting the page you want to add.) Keep a growing list of potentially good sites, and then when your search is over, you can assess them at your leisure and narrow down the group if necessary.

Knock Twice

Delays are inevitable on the Web. I have never had a Web session without them. (Of course, my habitual eight-hour sessions might have something to do with it.) You are especially likely to experience a stalled page during prime time on the Net, when thousands of other enthusiasts are trying to surf into the same site. At such times, the page sits there, half displayed, with nothing coming in for minutes at a time. Even with your graphics turned off (as they should be), delays are not uncommon.

Don't sit there waiting for even a minute. Here's what to do:

1. **Click on the Stop button of your browser.**

2. **Click on the Reload button of your browser.**

3. **If you stall out again, click on Stop and Reload once more.**

4. **Repeat until you get a quick display of the page, or until you get fed up and move on.**

This method works on the same principle as dialing a busy phone number over and over until you get through. However, it isn't always effective. If traffic is really intense, you'd better try again at a less busy time. If you have chronic trouble getting into a site, chalk it up to an under-equipped server at the other end. In other words, the problem needs to be addressed by whoever runs the page's host computer.

Build a Searching Hotlist

This book is chock full of places from which to begin a Web search. With its help, and as you make your own Web discoveries, you should begin to develop preferences about which directories, keyword search engines, and link pages work best for you. Most people tend to return over and over to the spots that give them good results. You can make life easy for yourself by building a hotlist (or bookmark list, depending on what your Web browser calls it) of those sites. Then, whether your favorite starting point is Yahoo!, Excite, Deja News, or some other Web location, you can get to it with a single mouse click.

If your browser allows you to divide the hotlist (or bookmark list) into categories (sometimes called folders), doing so saves time. Create a folder called "Web Search Engines" and another called "Web Directories" and place the correct URLs in them, as found throughout this book. Of course, you can come up with your own, far more clever, names for these folders.

Ask Directions

For years, when I was taking auto trips in unfamiliar territory with my parents, my father and I would have the same reaction whenever we got lost. He and I would pull out maps and begin trying to find our way back on track. My mother would wonder, with justifiable exasperation, why we wouldn't just pull into a gas station and ask for directions.

That lesson took me years to learn, so I'll pass it directly to you: When you can't find what you want on the World Wide Web, you can always ask. The place to get directions is the Usenet. The newsgroup bulletin boards embody the Internet's sense of community, and users commonly ask newsgroup participants where to find the good Web pages and FAQ files. Naturally, the best place to ask for information is in a newsgroup that's related topically to what you're searching for. If you go to a political group and ask where you can find lyrics for the new Megadeath album, you are likely to get some sincere suggestions as to where you can take the question.

Avoid Prime Time

The Web has prime time, just like TV. In fact, it is more or less the same prime time, with a few differences. Lots of people log on after work, if only to collect the day's e-mail. The evening hours are prime time for surfing and downloading. Weekends are popular, too, though more in the late evening than in the daytime. Of course, you have to take time differences into consideration. Though North America is a big Internet user (in terms of sheer numbers), other continents contribute quite a bit to the traffic, too. On top of all this, more people are logging on throughout the day from work. Before long, every hour of the day will be prime time!

For now, a recognizable crowding occurs on the U.S. servers during the evenings. Sunday evenings and late Fridays are especially jammed. If you're on the Web a lot, you notice the slower response times during those periods. If possible, arrange your search sessions for the increasingly scant non-prime times.

Chapter 27

Ten Great WWW Newspapers and Magazines

- -

In This Chapter

▶ Exploring online editions of *USA Today* and *The New York Times*

▶ Being dazzled by HotWired

▶ Looking at a few great online magazines

▶ Checking out Interactive Age

- -

As the World Wide Web has grown more commercial, one of the more interesting developments has been the appearance of newspapers and magazines — online style. A big advantage is that you can't spill your morning coffee on them. A big disadvantage is that you can't tuck them under your arm. Nevertheless, they represent a highlight of the Web and are well worth checking out. Here is a selection of the best of the bunch.

USA Today

```
http://www.usatoday.com/
```

USA Today, the brightly-designed, information-rich national daily newspaper, makes a fine transition onto the World Wide Web. Accessing the site with your graphics turned on slows it down a bit but makes for a more pictorial experience that is similar to the colorful print version. Or if you prefer, do what I do: Zoom through your USA Today session with graphics turned off. I have never experienced the slightest delay with this site.

The Web version carries the same content as the print edition (It even includes the sister publication, *Baseball Weekly*) with one important exception — it's updated continuously throughout the day and night. In fact, each page of the site encourages readers to "Click reload often for latest version," and I have had the gratifying experience of checking sports scores late in the evening, clicking on Reload just before leaving the site, and seeing updates and new stories appear on my screen.

Going to the home page at the URL at the beginning of this section is one way to approach the site. But impatient speedsters (like me) may want to heed this hint: Add the index page to your hotlist instead. Here is the URL for the index:

```
http://www.usatoday.com/leadpage/indexusa.htm
```

The index is a text list of hyperlinks to the entire contents of the newspaper. From there you can check headlines, the weather, sports scores, and archives of major news topics. Although USA Today on the Web is extremely well organized and fastidiously linked within its own complex architecture, it doesn't make the best use of the Web's hyperlinked connectivity. That is to say, there aren't many links to outside sites that relate to the news story that you're reading. But no matter. This site is an enormous enterprise, and you can find plenty to read even staying within its boundaries.

The New York Times

```
http://www.nytimes.com/
```

A *New York Times* article about its own online site might carry a headline like this: Venerable Newspaper Makes Dignified Appearance on World Wide Web. The Web edition of "the *Times*" (as those of us near New York call it) is comprehensive, makes good use of hyperlinks to outside sources, and is considerate of its users' time by remaining graphically lightweight. In fact, for the truly rushed reader, a special low-graphics version is available as a hyperlink from the home page.

You can choose from several paths into the site. The URL at the beginning of this section takes you to a modified front page, Web style, with hyperlinks to various sections of that day's edition. Another option, which is my personal choice, is to skip right to the index of the day's edition. It is fully functional with graphics turned off, and I find it to be the fastest way to access the entire site. Just add this URL to your hotlist:

```
http://www.nytimes.com/info/contents/contents.html
```

Another option is to start with the front page. Actually, you can choose from three front pages:

✔ Headlines only

✔ A summary version, with links to the full articles

✔ A full-page graphic of the actual front page

The full-page graphic is nice to look at, but not very useful, since it does not link to the text of the articles.

Just about everything you expect to see in the print edition is included in the Web site, from the classified ads to the famous *Times* crossword puzzle. Past special reports are archived for later perusal, and the bottom of many stories features links to outside, related Web sites, for further background and research. Photos are sometimes included with stories. You can search the site by keyword, take part in a trivia quiz, and use an electronic clipping service. Members can even place a classified ad in the Web edition.

Registration is required, but free. Every time you enter the site, you type in your chosen name and password.

HotWired

```
http://www.hotwired.com/
```

Regardless of your age, you can join the wired generation by surfing over to this cutting-edge Web magazine. Owned, designed, and operated by the same organization that produces the print magazine *Wired, HotWired* is a completely separate publication, with little overlap of content. It has the same techno-hip attitude, though, not to mention similar dayglo design sensibilities.

HotWired must be experienced. It's one of the most advanced and aggressively updated domains on the Web. Free registration entitles you to an occasional e-mail newsletter that informs you of what's new at the site. But try visiting more frequently than that — you'll be surprised at the radical content and design changes that are presented. Up-to-the-second HTML design creates such features as a floating remote control (in Netscape Navigator) for cruising through the site's many avenues. You may want to put on sunglasses or turn down your monitor before subjecting your tender retinas to the glare of red-on-yellow text (or whatever the bold colors may be on any given day).

These are just a few of the excellent HotWired features that I make time for at least once a week:

- **Netizen:** Some people think that *Wired* and *HotWired* are magazines about computers and online networks. Indeed, they are centered around digital technology. But more than that, the charter of the *Wired* publications is to provide a voice for what is called the *wired generation,* in all its aspects. Netizen is political commentary from a digital-era, next-century point of view. It is one area of overlapping content between HotWired and *Wired,* and it's tremendously well-informed.

- **Ask Dr. Weil:** This daily medical column by — you guessed it — Dr. Weil, focuses on a different health topic every day. Readers can submit questions, but don't make them too involved. This feature covers the basics of health, with an emphasis on preventive medicine.

- **Dream Jobs:** Even people who have too much work can't resist reading these notices. Written from an insider's point of view, they promote job openings in hi-tech companies, most of which are involved in Web development and alternative publishing media. Even if you're not looking for employment, these informal accounts of what it's like to work as a designer or techhead in Silicon Valley companies are fascinating.

- **Surf Central:** This feature is basically a slickly presented selection of hot links. Where other "surf" sites proffer a plain list o' links, HotWired splashes a multiframe, searchable, scrollable contraption for finding nifty sites in a variety of categories. Not all the recommended links are exactly fresh news, surprisingly, but you can still make some wonderful finds.

HotWired is worth spending some time in, which is fortunate, because you don't have much choice. No point turning off your graphics; the server pushes the graphics into your computer anyway. (This is usually the case with tables and frames on the Web, two of the newer HTML features.) The graphic pushiness may remind you of an online service, such as America Online, which also forces graphics down your computer's throat. In fact, HotWired is a small online service unto itself.

If you're short on time and need to move on in your Web session, the HotWired remote control panel stays live on your screen until you manually close it. So you're never more than a click away from the main portions of the magazine.

U.S. News Online

```
http://www.usnews.com
```

U.S. News Online is an award-winning, graphically rich, Java-enhanced, beautifully organized Web version of the printed newsweekly. You have a choice between viewing the graphic version at this URL . . .

```
http://www.usnews.com/usnews/main.htm
```

. . . and the text version at this URL:

```
http://www.usnews.com/usnews/textmenu.htm
```

Both sites are available via links on the main home page, which is the first of the three URLs listed here. The high-graphics pathway trades speed for beauty. It's a dazzling mix of photos and varied fonts, and it takes a while to display, even with a fast modem. I usually choose the text-only path, which doesn't sacrifice any content and is very fast.

I suggest that you register your membership so that you will get e-mail delivery of an occasional *U.S. News* letter that describes what's new at the site. This magazine makes excellent use of hyperlinking to the outside Web and generally provides good coverage of mainstream national news.

San Jose Mercury News

```
http://www.sjmercury.com/
```

One of the first full-scale Web newspaper editions, the San Jose Mercury News (or the Mercury Center, as it is sometimes referred to) remains a model for other Web publishing enterprises. The project is so extensive that it commands a full directory page of its own in the Yahoo! service.

Though there is an emphasis on Silicon Valley news, the Mercury News also covers national and international items. Other good reasons to put the site on your hotlist are its good design and easy navigation. The Index feature, with its drop-down lists and Go buttons, is available from every page.

Most of the content is available free, but you need to have a low-priced monthly subscription to get full wire service reports, the comics, some columnists, and perhaps other features.

The Christian Science Monitor

http://www.csmonitor.com/

Bands of loyal, wired *Monitor* readers were no doubt thrilled when *The Christian Science Monitor* took its highly respected newspaper online. If you're unfamiliar with the *Monitor* brand of journalism, don't be misled by its religious sponsorship. It is a top-flight international news publication that also carries some inspirational material reflecting Christian Science philosophy. The Web version carries forward the *Monitor* ideals of clarity, simplicity, and great writing.

Monitor Radio, a broadcast version of the paper's journalistic resources, is included at the site, in RealAudio format. It enables you to hear Monitor Radio programming while browsing the rest of the paper, and even while moving around the rest of the Web. (You need a sound card, speakers, and RealAudio software to hear Monitor Radio.)

The site is notable for a clean design that doesn't take too long to load. Try going through with your browser graphics turned on — the experience is surprisingly undelayed. For my money, The Christian Science Monitor site is a perfect blend of attractiveness and efficiency. (The site, of course, is free.)

Other features of interest are a bulletin board forum, where you can participate in message-based conversations with other readers about current events; an interactive crossword puzzle; and continuously updated Associated Press headlines.

Interactive Age

http://techweb.cmp.com:80/techweb/ia/current/

Interactive Age is a trade publication for people who are involved in the online industry.

Despite its tagline, "The Online Newspaper for Electronic Commerce," Interactive Age covers all aspects of online news. It is published as a print magazine, and the electronic version has added a daily edition. The whole shebang is geared for the busy surfer, and the headline-driven front page gets you to the important news in a hurry. (It even has a column by Bill Gates.)

Interactive Age is not a well-known Web site outside of the industry . . . at least, until now. (Oops.) Regardless of whether you have a professional interest in the Internet, this site is a great place to find breaking news from an insider's perspective. It is famous for live reports from major computer expos.

WebZine

http://www.peli.com/

Not a translation of a print magazine, WebZine was born and thrives on the World Wide Web, and only there. Calling itself "The Internet's Premium Feature Magazine," it contains fiction, humorous essays, editorials on everything, opinion columns, cultural reviews, advice, and cartoons. Individuality, humor, and boldness are the guiding lights of its editorial policy, and although it may not aspire to the same pedestal as *The New Yorker* has (to pick a cerebral literary mainstream magazine out of a hat), it's a darn good read, packaged in an attractively simple Web page design.

Utne Online

http://www.utne.com/

The Utne Reader is familiar to many as one of the most prominent of "alternative press" magazines. In fact, it is a digest of many alternative press articles found in other magazines, plus some original writing. Because it rounds up and prints the best of hard-to-find articles, many people rely on *Utne* to keep them informed of fringe opinion and nonmainstream viewpoints. Utne Online is the Web version. From the Alternative Press Awards to the No-Jive Net Guide, Utne Online is alternative journalism at its best — even if the Web is, almost by definition, already alternative. Free registration gets you into Cafe Utne to discuss all kinds of alternative issues with kindred spirits.

The Nando Times

http://www2.nando.net/nt/nando.cgi

The Nando Times, in consideration of its many readers with varying computer capabilities, offers three levels of access: regular graphics, low graphics, and a Java version that features animation. I have experienced considerable stalling in the regular graphics pathway, probably because the popular Web newspaper handles so much traffic. As a result, I usually cruise through the faster low-graphic route, but take your chances with the pictures turned on — the graphics are worth it.

Divided into typical newspaper sections such as Sports, Politics, Business, InfoTech, Entertainment, and Classifieds, Nando is updated aggressively, making it a good site for up-to-the-nanosecond news.

Appendix

Software Searching Tools

. . . .

*Y*ou don't need very much to operate effectively on the World Wide Web. It's a travel-light kind of environment. You can boil down the essentials to just three things:

- ✔ A computer system that includes a computer (oh, really?), a modem, and a telephone line.

- ✔ An online account that permits access to the Web. The account can be through membership in America Online, CompuServe, or another commercial service that has a Web gateway; or you can use an account with a dedicated Internet Service Provider.

- ✔ A Web browser. If you have an account with an online service, you can use the browser provided by that service, or you can opt for a separate program that has features you prefer.

Equipped with these three things, you're ready to take the Web by storm. But software tools can enhance the searching experience beyond the basics. Some tools are necessary, and others are merely useful. These tools either operate as independent program utilities that you boot up and use when needed, or plug in to your Web browser and pop into action automatically when your browser calls on them.

The Web browser itself warrants some consideration. It is the program that you live in when you're on the Web. Perhaps a better analogy is to a car that you drive around the Internet. It's important to use the browser that handles best for your Web driving taste and whose features (like buttons and menus) you feel comfortable with.

A Browser by Any Other Name

Web browsers look pretty much the same. Like cars that all have four wheels, brakes, a reverse gear, and a steering wheel, all Web browsers have the same basic navigational features for tooling around the World Wide Web. You can count on any Web browser to contain the following basics:

✔ **HTML capability:** All Web browsers, by definition, can interpret HTML and display the results on your screen. HTML (HyperText Markup Language) is the native tongue of the World Wide Web, and all Web sites are coded with this language. The browser's main job is to receive the code when it arrives at a Web site and translate it into the page that displays on your screen. Understanding HTML also means understanding hyperlinks — the hot spots of any Web page that cause something to happen when you click on them. Most hyperlinks take you (and your browser) to another page that the browser displays in the same way.

✔ **Bookmarks or hotlists:** Any browser worth its name enables you to save the addresses (URLs, or Uniform Resource Locators) of Web pages that you want to visit in the future. Browsers use different methods to save the addresses. In most cases, they use some kind of folder system so you can divide up your favorite places list by topic (see Figures A-1 and A-2).

✔ **Back and Forward buttons:** These buttons are navigational aids, or shortcuts. As you surf the Web, the browser keeps track of where you've been. You can backtrack, one site at a time, by using the Back button, which simply returns you to the preceding page in your journey. After you backtrack like that, the Forward button becomes active, so you can shuttle forward again easily. Because you can use these buttons, you don't have to bother with bookmarking every site you visit during a session; nor do you have to keep track of URLs as you go along. (See Figure A-3.)

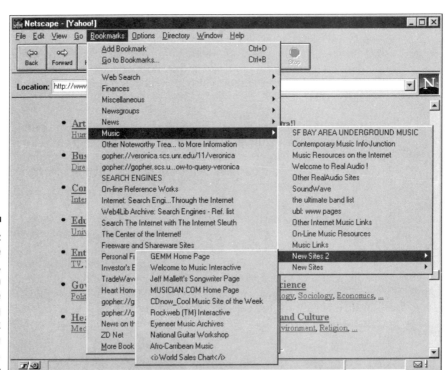

Figure A-1: In Netscape Navigator, you can organize long bookmark lists like directories.

Figure A-2:
In SPRY
Mosaic, you
organize the
Hotlist with
folders.

Figure A-3:
The
Backward,
Forward,
Stop, and
Reload
buttons in
the SPRY
Mosaic
browser.

✔ **Reload button:** Clicking Reload (see Figure A-3) displays the page again, from scratch. Most people use this button when a page display is stalled — only partially displayed and doesn't seem to be progressing. Sometimes clicking the Reload button clears the bottleneck and displays the page with no trouble. You also may want to use it in Web sites that update their pages very frequently. If you're checking sports scores, for example, clicking Reload may bring in an update that was posted after you first surfed into the site.

✔ **Stop button:** The Stop button (see Figure A-3) stops whatever is currently happening. You use it to halt the loading of a page. Why would you want to do that? If loading the page is taking too long and you decide against seeing the whole thing, you can use the Stop button to interrupt the process. In my experience, clicking the Stop button to interrupt a page load is better than using the Back button or clicking on a hyperlink. Interrupting a page load with a navigational command increases the chances that the program will crash, so stopping the load before you move on is better.

✔ **Images ON or OFF:** One of the best parts of the Web is all the pictures, but they also slow it down. Graphics take much longer to load and display than does text. Many people who spend a lot of time on the World Wide Web do so with the graphics turned off, which all browsers enable you to do. You just make sure that the selection that is usually called Auto Load Images or Inline Images isn't checked (see Figure A-4). Then, to see the pictures of any individual Web page, you check the selection and use the Reload button. (Some browsers offer an Images button that loads the images of any single page while keeping the main setting to OFF.)

✔ **Open location:** This feature is either a button or a menu selection, and it enables you to type in a URL (Web address) and go directly to that site. In addition, you can use an Open File or Open Local selection to load a Web page from your hard drive, if you've stored one there. Some people create an HTML file on their hard drive that lists their favorite sites as hyperlinks. Then they open that page into the browser and use the hyperlinks they've created to visit their favorite places.

✔ **View Document Source:** Ever wondered what HTML, the underlying code of the World Wide Web, looks like? Well, it looks pretty terrible. Nevertheless, Web browsers have a View Document Source (or just View Source) selection that enables you to view the HTML code for the page that you are currently visiting. This menu item pops open a window with the page in *raw* form — the actual HTML code that your browser has used to display the nice-looking page on your monitor. It's not a pretty sight, but if you're learning how to write HTML yourself, looking at the code is a good way to pick up tips (see Figure A-5).

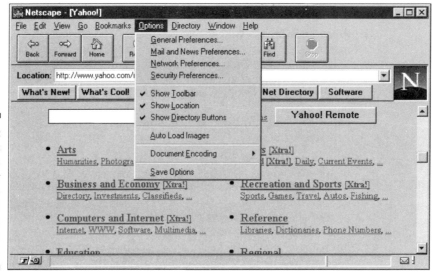

Figure A-4:
Browsing is faster in Navigator when the Auto Load Images selection is unchecked.

```
Netscape - [Source of: file:///C|/HTML/NAF/NAF1.HTM]

<HEAD>Online Studies</HEAD>

<BODY BACKGROUND="starfld.gif" TEXT="000000">
<TITLE>New Age Forum</TITLE>
<center><IMG SRC="nafcis1.gif.map.gif" ALT="WebMania!" ALIGN="middle"
<HR ALIGN="CENTER">

<A HREF="file:///c:\html\naf\naf-os.html"><center><H1>Online Studies<
<A HREF="file:///c:\html\naf\naf-se.htm"><center><H1>Special Events</
<A HREF="file:///c:\html\naf\naf-ce.htm"><center><H1>Community Events
<A HREF="file:///c:\html\naf\naf-nwe.htm"><center><H1>New World Expo<
<p>
<HR ALIGN="CENTER" SIZE=10>
<p>
<center><IMG SRC="naf-a.gif" ALT="WebMania!" ALIGN="middle" BORDER=01
<p>
<center><IMG SRC="naf-b.gif" ALT="WebMania!" ALIGN="middle" BORDER=01
<p>
<br>
</BODY>
```

Figure A-5:
Viewing the source document of a Web page makes for great reading.

> ✔ **Print:** You can print the page that is currently displayed on your screen. Remember that some pages are very long, and continue way past the boundaries of your monitor. Your printer will break up long pages into several pages.

So the question naturally arises — if all browsers are pretty much the same, what's to choose from? Why select one over another? The answer to those questions has four parts.

Buttons 'n' menus

Even though the basic features are pretty much the same from browser to browser, browsers implement the features differently. This is especially true of the Bookmark or Hotlist feature, which is an important one. But, as in any other program, you also want to be happy with how the buttons and menu selections are arranged.

When evaluating a browser, ask yourself if navigation is effortless. Are the Back and Forward buttons located in obvious and accessible places on your screen? Is it easy to figure out how to type in a URL? Does the browser give some indication — such as an animated icon or a lit-up Stop button — that a page is loading, or does it leave you guessing? Does the browser provide an easy way to load the images of a single page when you're surfing with graphics turned off? Is the bookmark feature easy to use, both in adding URLs and in accessing them from the list?

Online service members

If you're using America Online or CompuServe for your Web access, a Web browser comes with your membership (see Figure A-6). It's built right into the AOL and CompuServe programs. You may think that you have no choice in the matter, but the truth is that you can use other browsers if you don't care for the design or functionality of the house browser. (See Chapters 20 and 22 for more information about how to use other browsers.)

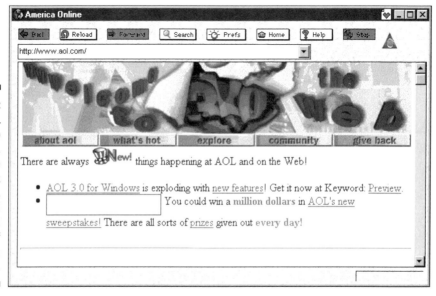

Figure A-6:
The AOL
Web
browser.
Note the
sleek
design,
small
buttons, and
lack of
pull-down
menus.

You should ask the same questions when evaluating a built-in browser that you ask when evaluating any other browser. In addition, your own computer habits and preferences come into play. Having a browser built into the online service program is convenient, and that convenience may make up for inferior features.

Internet suites

Recently, some browsers have evolved and expanded. A browser can be more than just a Web tool, just as the Internet is greater than just the World Wide Web. Internet Suites are multipart programs that contain Web browsers, Usenet newsgroup readers, and e-mail programs. Is it better to use an integrated suite of programs for all your Internet activity or to choose separate software components? The decision is similar to deciding what to purchase when you are buying a home stereo. Choosing individual components often results in better features within each component, but getting an integrated system is more convenient. If you spend most of your time on the World Wide Web — with Usenet newsgroups and e-mail as secondary activities — you should choose the best browser and accept whatever Usenet and e-mail components come with it. You can always add individual programs later if you find ones that you can't live without.

Netscape versus the world

If you've spent time on the World Wide Web, or talked with people *about* the Web, you've probably heard of Netscape. Early in the Web's surge to popularity, a company called Netscape created a program for browsing the newly exciting World Wide Web, and that program took the virtual world by storm. At one time, four out of five people used this browser — called Netscape Navigator — though those numbers may be changing even as you read this. Since, at the time, all browsers had pretty much the same features on the face of it, what was so great about Navigator?

The real value of Navigator lies under the hood. Sure, it had the same buttons, bookmarks, and generic features as the other browsers. But the Netscape developers also did something very clever and innovative: They made additions to the HTML language (the coding language that all Web pages are written in) that only Netscape Navigator could understand. The additions they made were so useful (they allowed Web page designers to lay out Web sites more attractively, using text and graphics with more flexibility) that everyone wanted to use them. The only way people like you and me could display the results of these newly designed Web sites was to use Netscape Navigator, and it quickly became the Web browser of choice.

If you go on the Web today and spend five minutes surfing around, you're very likely to encounter a page that says, "Netscape enhanced," or "This page looks best when viewed with Netscape Navigator." Any Web browser can display any Web page, but you'd be amazed at how different they can look with different browsers! Pages designed with Netscape *extensions* (the additions to HTML created by Netscape) display correctly only with a browser that understands those extensions. For a long while, Navigator was the only such browser; now other companies have caught up and added an understanding of Netscape extension to their browsers. One of them, Microsoft, has even created new extensions that can be viewed only in its Internet Explorer browser.

Search Agents

The online searching tools covered in this book — the Web directories and keyword search engines — are a powerful help in organizing and searching through the World Wide Web. Before they existed, the Web was good only for browsing, and you could only find something useful by chance. Now, with a little patience, you can go straight for what interests you. Well, a lot of patience in some cases. The Web search engines are manual tools, and making the most of their various features takes some time. It stands to reason that the next evolutionary step in Web searching is to automate the process.

This evolutionary leap has just begun. Programs are now available that enable you to input searching instructions, go to bed, and wake up to a computer full of results. In most cases, these search agent programs don't search the Web itself; they investigate Web directories and search engines just as you would if you were doing the task manually. And the results come back quickly — more like a fast lunch break than a full night's sleep.

The appeal of these programs lies not only in the fact that they do the dirty work of digging through the Web for you. (That's a big part of it, though.) They also organize the results, eliminate duplicate hits, and present their findings in coherent categories that you help determine. (Unfortunately, they don't clean up your desk.) That final step of organizing the search results is what sets the programs apart from each other.

The following list provides the names of commercial programs that are emerging into prominence in the auto-search field, along with the URLs at which you can get the programs or more information. You also can enter the program's name as a keyword in any of the search engines to find sites that mention the product. Use Deja News (described in Chapter 10) to find Usenet postings about any of these software packages. Finally, it's a good idea to keep tabs on Internet magazines (online and print) for reviews of cutting-edge software.

✔ **EchoSearch:** EchoSearch calls itself a "search accelerator" to emphasize its ability to cross-search several Web search engines simultaneously. Like the others, it also prioritizes and organizes the findings. More information and a free evaluation copy are available at the following URL:

   ```
   http://www.iconovex.com
   ```

✔ **WebCompass:** WebCompass is a search agent that utilizes the most powerful search engines on the Web to find sites and then uses advanced language processing to categorize and present the findings, ranked and summarized. As with any good search agent, you can set it to log on automatically whether you're present or not. You can get online information about WebCompass at this URL:

   ```
   http://arachnid.qdeck.com/qdeck/products/webcompass/
   ```

✔ **WebSeeker:** WebSeeker uses 20 Internet search engines in its quest for sites you need. Its main power lies in parallel searching across all those engines, plus the usual range of categorizing and organizing skills after it has the results. It can perform unattended scheduled searches, and it can distinguish updated information from previous results. Find out more at this URL:

```
http://www.ffg.com/
```

File Utilities

Unless something is very wrong, searching the Web should result in occasionally finding things that are worth downloading. When that happens, you may need programs to make sense of what you've just downloaded. The two most necessary types of file utilities for the Web are

✔ Compression utilities

✔ Graphic viewers

Both types of program run independently of your Web browser and come into play after you have downloaded a file. They have no navigational function while searching the Web.

Unpacking a file

Most program files stored on the World Wide Web are compressed to a fraction of their normal size, as if they were run through a trash compactor, and you need to decompress them before you can run them. (Nonprogram files, such as graphics and texts, don't need to be processed this way.) Programs are compressed so that you can download them faster, so the extra hassle of decompressing a download is worth the time and effort, because the download is much quicker than it would be for an uncompressed file. Besides, "unpacking" a file takes only a few seconds.

There are a few types of compression. (You knew it wasn't going to be totally simple, right?) The most common is called ZIP, and a compressed ZIP file is sometimes called a *ZIPped file.* You can identify ZIPped files by the .ZIP extension in the filename, as shown in this example:

```
program.zip
```

Several unZIP utilities on the shareware market are available for downloading. Try searching with the keywords **zip** and **compression**, or visit the Web shareware storehouses listed in Chapter 17 and browse through their utilities selections. Alternatively, you can forget about searching for the ultimate unZIPper and simply go with these recommendations:

✔ **WinZip:** This utility is probably the most well-known and popular unZIPper among Windows users (see Figure A-7). You can get information and an evaluation copy at this URL:

    http://www.winzip.com

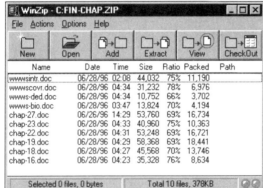

Figure A-7:
The WinZip decompression utility.

✔ **StuffIt:** For Mac users, StuffIt is a good, universal solution to all decompression needs. (A version is available for Windows too.) You can identify StuffIt files by the .SIT extension, and StuffIt traditionally has been used to decompress those files, not .ZIP compressions. But recent versions of StuffIt include a ZIP utility too, so all the bases are covered. Find out more from

    http://www.aladdinsys.com

After you have a decompression utility program, dealing with compressed program downloads is easy. Just follow these basic steps:

1. **Download the program.**

2. **Boot up (run) the decompression utility.**

3. **From within the decompressor, select the file (downloaded program) that you want to unpack.**

4. **Let the utility decompress and separate the program files.**

5. **Run the new program or its setup file.**

Unpacking the unpacker

Unpacking .ZIP files is easy if you have the right decompression utility. But because virtually every downloadable program file is compressed and unpackers are available on the Web as Shareware, the question naturally arises: How do you unpack the decompression program? It's a sort of chicken-or-the-egg problem.

The answer is called *self-extracting files.* Self-extracting files are compressed programs that have a built-in unpacker. All you need to do is run the file. They usually have an .EXE file extension, indicating that they are ready to be executed (run). You simply run them as you would run any other installed program, and the unpacker springs into action automatically. After the program files are unpacked and separated, you can then run the *real* executable file, which is either the program itself or a *setup* file that installs the program to a permanent directory on your hard drive.

And, you'll be relieved to know, all unpackers are downloaded as self-extracting files.

Viewing pictures

The other main utility type pressed into offline use is a graphic viewer that's capable of handling the several kinds of picture files that are downloadable from the Web. Why are there so many kinds of picture files, anyway? Such questions must be left to great philosophers. In the meantime, here are the main types of graphic files and how to identify them:

- ✔ **GIF:** GIF (Graphics Interchange Format) files, which CompuServe developed many years ago, are prevalent. There are a few types of GIF format, but in most cases you don't need to know or worry about that. The files have a .GIF extension, and are usually pronounced *jiff.*

- ✔ **JPEG:** Likewise very commonplace on the World Wide Web, JPEG pictures are compressed, but you don't need a separate compressor to view them. If you have a graphic utility that handles JPEG pictures, the files are decompressed as part of the viewing process. These files have the .JPG extension, and you could sprain your jaw trying to pronounce it.

- ✔ **TIFF:** TIFF (Tagged Image File Format) pictures tend to be very large files, as they contain high-resolution color graphics. They are not often found online, but when they are, you can identify them by their .TIF file extension. TIFF files are pronounced as they are spelled.

- ✔ **BMP:** BMP files are used by the Windows operating system and are also found on the Web. They carry the .BMP file extension. Pronouncing the extension just makes you sound silly, so don't try.

Ideally, your graphic viewer can load any of these formats (and other, less common ones) and display them. Graphic viewers work with files just as word processors do. Here is what you do to download and view an online picture:

1. **Download the picture file with your Web browser.**

2. **Boot up (run) your graphic viewer.**

3. **Pull down the File menu and select Open.**

4. **Select the picture file that you downloaded.**

   The viewer displays the picture in its window.

You may have to select a File Type in the lower left portion of the Open File box in order to select the file that you've downloaded. If the File Type selection defaults to GIF files, for example, and you want to display a JPG download, you need to change the File Type to JPG in order to select the file.

So many commercial, shareware, and even freeware graphic viewers are available that trying to describe all of them is pointless. Browse through the shareware centers listed in Chapter 17 for downloadable programs to try or go with this suggestion: Paint Shop and Paint Shop Pro. Paint Shop (see Figure A-8) is one of the most used shareware graphic viewers, and the Pro version is a full-bodied image editor as well. You can get online information about them at this URL:

```
http://www.jasc.com
```

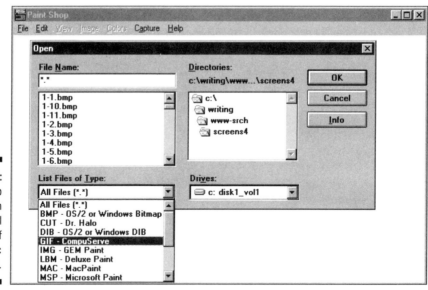

Figure A-8:
Paint Shop can open several types of graphic files.

Helpers and Plug-Ins

The evolution of the World Wide Web is proceeding so fast that hardly anyone can keep up with it — not even the companies that make Web browsers. Not a browser alive can do it all, unassisted, on the Web. As Web developers and authors continue to create a more innovative multimedia experience, new software tools are continually being created to display that experience on your screen. These small software utilities are called *helper applications* or *plug-ins*. They have a couple of things in common:

✔ Helpers and plug-ins are meant to work with the Web browser — integrated with it rather than standing alone. (In other words, they *plug in*.) They expand the capabilities of the browser.

✔ They spring into action automatically when they encounter a Web feature that they are designed to handle.

Some helper applications and plug-ins are free, but not all of them by any means. Generally, if the plug-in requires a special program on the Web site's computer in order to work, then the plug-in is free to you (because the plug-in's company makes its money selling the necessary site program, which is called *server software*). But if the plug-in offers a new way to deal with standard Web page information, you usually have to pay to enjoy the benefits.

Plug-ins are used quite a bit by Netscape Navigator, which is designed to accept and use them. They transform the Web into a multimedia playground or a business teleconferencing environment, depending on what you use. Navigator (and some other browsers) also enable you to define your existing programs as helper applications. Because of this capability, you can, for example, use Paint Shop as a helper for viewing graphic files when Navigator downloads them. Then Paint Shop will open automatically after the download and display the downloaded picture.

Here is a selection of some exciting plug-ins and helper applications that are currently on the scene and information on where to find them or find out more about them.

✔ **Crescendo Plus:** Crescendo is a plug-in that streams MIDI files the way that RealAudio streams audio files. The difference is that Crescendo will work with any MIDI file, not only with specially created ones. Now, MIDI files are relatively small, so downloading them has never been a big deal. Furthermore, MIDI files do not appear all that often on Web pages. Still, with Crescendo on the loose, you may notice an upsurge in MIDI background music on Web sites. You can find Crescendo and Crescendo Plus (guess which one is free) at this URL:

```
http://www.liveupdate.com
```

✔ **HotPage:** This handy utility, which is for use with Netscape Navigator, helps you sort your bookmarks. More importantly, it provides an entirely fresh interface for creating and organizing your favorite Web places. And even more than *that*, it grabs entire pages, not just their URLs, for offline viewing. Go to this URL for more information:

```
http://www.documagix.com
```

✔ **Internet with an Accent:** Unlike Web Translator, Internet with an Accent doesn't convert Web pages from one language to another. It does, however, make languages with foreign alphabets legible. As a complete package, it includes a multilingual browser and a plug-in for Netscape Navigator. If you search the Web with a fluency in more than one language, this utility comes in handy. Here's where to go for information about it:

```
http://www.accentsoft.com/
```

✔ **Net Toob:** This *streaming* plug-in for Netscape Navigator works with movie files. Most movie and video files on the Web are .MOV, .AVI, or .MPG files, and Net Toob handles them all. Without it, you have to download the file and then use an external viewer to play it. Since video files tend to be huge, downloading one can really tie up your Web session. Net Toob gets around the download process and plays the file in real time. You can download a temporary demo version of Net Toob from this URL:

```
http://www.duplexx.com
```

✔ **RealAudio:** The Web is striving toward a realtime multimedia experience. In order to achieve that goal, it is moving away from the download model and toward the *streaming* model. Streaming happens when a file (audio or video) is played back as soon as you select it, without your having to download the whole thing first. The development of streaming technology makes the Web a more realtime multimedia experience, uninterrupted by the finger-tapping wait for a file to download before you can enjoy it. Streaming is easier for audio files than for video files, and the most prevalent audio streaming solution is called RealAudio. With a free RealAudio helper application linked to your browser, you can listen to live radio broadcasts on the Web, prerecorded programs and interviews, and music files — all on the spur of the moment, with no downloading necessary. These realtime experiences work only with specially created RealAudio sound files, which are proliferating on the Web. You can download RealAudio from this URL:

```
http://www.realaudio.com
```

✔ **Shockwave:** Shockwave is a multimedia rendering plug-in that interacts with specially created Web pages to deliver embedded movies, sound, and certain types of graphics through Netscape Navigator (with a Microsoft Internet Explorer version in the works). The download is free, and everyone is talking about it, so surf right over to this URL if you're using Navigator:

```
http://www.macromedia.com/shockwave/
```

The site also points you toward some Web pages that use Shockwave technology, so you can try out the new plug-in.

✔ **Web Translator:** The World Wide Web is the most global, multicultural communications network on the planet. Though English is the predominant language of Web text, other tongues are certainly represented. Web Translator comes to the rescue by rendering a page in another language. (As long as that other language is French, German, Spanish, or English. Translating an Eskimo dialect to Scottish brogue is beyond its ken.) It is not, strictly speaking, a plug-in, because you need to run it separately from the browser, but it hooks into Netscape Navigator after it's up and running. You can download a small free version (with a 500-word limit) or purchase the full version from this URL:

```
http://www.globalink.com
```

The 5th Wave   By Rich Tennant

Index

• F •